Onward Catholic Soldier
Spiritual Warfare According to Scripture, the Church and the Saints

John LaBriola

Do not be afraid of the plots and attacks of the devil who might come to pillage and take over the city of your soul. No, don't be afraid, but be like knights drawn up on the battlefield, armed with the sword of divine charity. This sword is the whip that beats the devil.
Saint Catherine of Siena

Conceived on Feast of the Annunciation

Onward Catholic Soldier

Luke 1:38 Publishing
Printed in the United States of America

The photo on the cover is of the statue of Saint Michael the Archangel guarding the "Capilla del Cerrito," or "Chapel of the Little Hill" on Tepeyac Hill in Mexico City. The chapel was built on the spot where Our Lady of Guadalupe appeared to Saint Juan Diego.

Table of Contents

Dedication

We know the love of God in this way: because he laid
down his life for us. And so, we must lay down our lives
for our brothers. Whoever possesses the goods of this
world, and sees his brother to be in need, and yet closes
his heart to him: in what way does the love of God abide
in him? My little sons, let us not love in words only, but
in works and in truth
1 John 3:16-18

This book is dedicated to Father Raymond Skonezny,
S.T.L., S.S.L.

If how a man regards his mother, his spouse and his
children is any indication of his character, then Father
Raymond Skonezny qualifies as a man of exceptional character.
As a humble and holy priest he is a loving spouse of the
Church, loving son to the Blessed Mother and a loving father to
his spiritual children.

His accomplishments, during his more than 45 years of
priestly service, warrant a book of their own. The lives he has
touched, the prayers he has enjoined, the compassion he has
extended, the joy he has shared, the sacrifices he has made and
the souls he has brought to God are the fruits of a life dedicated
to serving God. He is an untiring witness to the truth, a man of
peace and a humble servant of the Lord. He is also a
courageous spiritual warrior and an inspired spiritual director.

Thank you, Father Raymond, for being a light for the
world. It is easy to see the words of Saint Clare of Assisi and

Saint John of the Cross as descriptive of you. I am a far better man, husband, father, spiritual warrior and Christian for having known you.

Love God, serve God. Everything is in that.
Saint Clare of Assisi

The soul who is in love with God is a gentle, humble and patient soul.
Saint John of the Cross

Acknowledgments

For just as, within one body, we have many parts, though all the parts do not have the same role, so also we, being many, are one body in Christ, and each one is a part, the one of the other. And we each have different gifts, according to the grace that has been given to us.
Romans 12:4-6a

The writing of this book was at once exhilarating and exhausting. It was made more exhilarating and less exhausting by the efforts of so many faithful members of the Body of Christ. I would like to thank the following people and organizations for their support:

Bridget Leonard, Carmen Ribera, Jon Roberts and Colleen Swiatek who each lent their unique talents to the forming of this book.

Megan Breen, Tim Kelly, John Neilsen and Lisa Steen, spiritual warriors all, who prayerfully offered their support and encouragement.

Mother Nadine Brown, Sam Conedera, Father Joseph Droessler, Father John Hampsch, Father Jerome Karcher, Father James Maltese, Father Darrin Merlino, Father Michael Philen and Father Raymond Skonezny who each served as a source of inspiration for the thoughts and ideas that came to form this book.

The entire Orange County chapter of the Intercessors of the Lamb prayer group who interceded mightily on behalf of this book

Lu Cortese and the volunteers at Saint Joseph Radio who provided a platform to share this information with so many people over the EWTN Radio Network.

The listeners of *Saint Joseph Radio Presents* who were effusive in their praise and strong in their support of the radio broadcasts that served as the foundation for this book.

My wife and children who sacrificed much so this book could be become a reality.

Saint Pio of Pietrelcina, Saint Teresa of Avila, Saint Maximilian Kolbe, Saint Catherine of Siena, Blessed Miguel Pro and all the holy Angels and Saints whose words and actions serve as an inspiration for us all.

Our Lady of Guadalupe, under whose watchful eye each word of this book was typed.

I thank you. I love you. I could not have done this without you. May we together walk the pathways of love that will lead us all to our Lord and Savior, Jesus Christ. May God be praised!

John LaBriola

July 11, 2008
Feast of Saint Benedict

> Whoever reads this work will carry on with me if he shares my own certainties, search with me if he shares my own doubts, come back to me if he recognizes errors of his own, and call me to account if he becomes aware of mine. And together we will set out to walk the pathways of love.
> Saint Augustine

Foreword

⊕

Amidst the mountainous profusion of movie scripts, articles, dramas and research projects dealing with the darkly fascinating subject of demonology, no Christian denomination stands out more trenchantly than Catholicism. Think of an exorcist and you almost automatically conjure up the image of a Catholic priest, ritual in hand and draped in a purple stole. Think of a tool of exorcism and you immediately visualize Catholic sacramentals like holy water or a crucifix held aloft in an objurgative blessing. When encountering a poltergeistic disturbance in one's house, the first thought (even for many non-Catholics, surprisingly) is to call a Catholic priest, just as one's first thought in an injury accident is to call 911 for paramedics. With its 20 centuries of harrowing experience in this sanguinary battlefield of spiritual warfare, the Catholic Church holds, in its doctrine and practice, the ultimate "gold standard" for confronting the underworld of demonic entities.

In this treatise on Catholic demonology, John LaBriola has gathered a remarkable sweep of occultic issues, ancient and modern, "like the master of a household who brings out of his treasure what is new and what is old" (Matthew 13:52). The antidote for each of these is set into the context of Catholic history, doctrine, tradition and practice. The result is a treasury of subjects germane to what has come to be called spiritual warfare; most of them are tagged and embroidered by quotations from popes, Church documents, saints, early Church Fathers or other august sources of the fathomless wisdom of the ages. Amazingly, the entire treatise is spangled with over

1000 such citations.

One cannot read this book without marveling at the vast armamentarium of specifically Catholic "weapons of our warfare...that have divine power to destroy strongholds" (2 Corinthians 10:4). These weapons range all the way from the rosary and Marian devotion to sacramental confession and the Sacrifice of the Mass, from blessed salt to pious ejaculations, from a Saint Benedict medal to the monstrance-exposed Blessed Sacrament on the high altar, from a blessed oil anointing to an Ash Wednesday forehead insignia, from a fervent "deliver us from evil" to the wrenching puissance of an inexorable exorcism. Each part of the "armor of God" (Ephesians 6:13) finds multiple expressions in Catholic practices.

On closing the book after the last chapter, the reader will breathe a prayer of thanksgiving for the Gift of God, Jesus himself, who working in and through his Church, has "come to destroy the works of the devil" (1 John 3:8). As we stand in the Christic glow of his serene majestic power, the forces of Hell can only recoil, cower and tremble. Secure in our Catholic armory, we can only exult in our awesome God who graciously puts in our hands such divinely protective shields and invincible weapons. Our prayer of gratitude will echo that of Paul (2 Corinthians 9:15): "Thanks be to God for his inexpressible Gift!"

Fr. John H. Hampsch, C.M.F.
Claretian Teaching Ministry
Los Angeles, California

Prayer of Protection

Be merciful to me, O God, be merciful to me. For my soul trusts in you. And I will hope in the shadow of your wings, until iniquity passes away. I will cry out to God Most High, to God who has been kind to me. He sent from heaven and freed me. He has surrendered into disgrace those who trampled me. God has sent his mercy and his truth. And he has rescued my soul from the midst of the young lions. I slept troubled. The sons of men: their teeth are weapons and arrows, and their tongue is a sharp sword. Be exalted above the heavens, O God, and your glory above all the earth.
Psalm 56:2-6

Heavenly Father, it is only by Your grace I can even begin to pray. Lord, I give You all glory and honor and praise. Help me to adore You O Lord. Help me to love and serve You in all I do. I am truly sorry for my sins and I beg for Your forgiveness. I love You and do not desire to offend You in any way. I thank You Lord for all that You have done for me, for Your gifts and graces. I now ask You Lord for Your protection over me as I read and pray through this book.

I beg You to send Your Holy Spirit upon me, to be my inspiration, my guide and my protector. Grant me the grace to be open to Your words of truth and love. Protect me from any and all evil spirits that would seek to attack, harass or annoy me because of my desire to grow closer to You through the pages of this book.

always pray this 1st.

1

Mother Mary, spouse of the Holy Spirit, I ask that you would also be with me in a special way as I read this book; wrap me in your mantle the entire time. May I find peace, comfort and safety within your Immaculate Heart. May your motherly intercession and protection extend to all my family and loved ones. May I receive through you every heavenly protection and grace.

Lord, may You send Your holy angels to form a hedge of protection around my heart, mind and body, keeping out all that is not of You. Arouse my guardian angel and call me to a greater awareness of my angel's role in protecting me from the wiles of the evil one.

I also call upon the intercession of the saints in Heaven. May their prayers afford me protection according to the will of God. I say all of this in the most holy and precious name of Jesus, our Lord, our King, our Savior. Amen.

> Our King has now conquered. Now He has destroyed sin; now He has put down death and has subjected the devil.
> Saint John Chrysostom

> In the Holy Spirit we have a great ally and protector, the great teacher of the Church, our great defender.
> Saint Cyril of Jerusalem

> When Mary supports you, you will not fail. With her as your protector you will have nothing to fear. With her as your guide you will not grow weary.
> Saint Bernard of Clairvaux

> Beside each believer stands an angel as protector and shepherd, leading him to life.
> Saint Basil the Great

> If the apostles and martyrs while still in the body can pray for others, at a time when they should still be solicitous about themselves, how much more will they do so after their crowns, victories and triumphs.
> Saint Jerome

Introduction

☩

And his disciples drew near to him, saying, "Explain to us the parable of the weeds in the field." Responding, he said to them: "He who sows the good seed is the Son of man. Now the field is the world. And the good seeds are the sons of the kingdom. But the weeds are the sons of wickedness. So the enemy who sowed them is the devil. And truly, the harvest is the consummation of the age; while the reapers are the Angels. Therefore, just as weeds are gathered up and burned with fire, so shall it be at the consummation of the age. The Son of man shall send out his Angels, and they shall gather from his kingdom all who lead astray and those who work iniquity. And he shall cast them into the furnace of fire, where there shall be weeping and gnashing of teeth. Then the just ones shall shine like the sun, in the kingdom of their Father. Whoever has ears to hear, let him hear."
Matthew 13:36b-43

During the Easter Vigil, at the renewal of baptismal promises the priest asks, "Do you reject Satan? And all his works? And all his empty promises?" "I do," is the all too reflexive response. The spiritual battle that exists behind the need for these questions and the need to answer them with conviction is often missed. War between Creator and creature was not intended to be the normal state of creation, but it is the current reality. Satan is defeated, but he is still dangerous and potentially deadly. His weeds still grow today, choking off the faith life of many.

The Scriptures are replete with implicit and explicit references to Satan and evil demons. For two millennia the Church and her saints have spoken of Satan as an actual entity, alive and well, seeking the eternal ruin of souls. Saints from every part of the world, from every economic background, from every culture, from every vocation, have continuously and passionately believed in and taught the reality of Satan.

The resistance to and the denial of this reality is a relatively recent phenomenon. To help get past the lie being told that Satan isn't real or is no longer relevant, in addition to the scriptural references cited, I've included over 1,000 quotes from Church documents and the saints. Quotes from the earliest saints to the most recent, from the East and West, from bishops, priests and deacons, from religious and lay men and women are used to support nearly every point. Those who are endlessly praising God have left clues as to the reality of Satan and how best to triumph over him. Their quotes are the historical, human expression of God's wisdom. It would be wise to recognize their relevance and heed their call.

> Oh what remorse we shall feel at the end of our lives, when we look back upon the great number of instructions and examples afforded by God and the saints for our perfection, and so carelessly received by us. If this end were to come to you today, how would you be pleased with the life you have led this year?
> Saint Francis de Sales

> How will he be able to regulate his life, cultivate virtue and flee from sin if he does not know the means by which he must seek the former and avoid the latter and does not recognize the temptations and snares of the enemy?
> Venerable Louis of Granada

The current climate notwithstanding, the evidence shows the Church has always, does now and will always teach the reality of Satan and evil. To ignore this reality serves only the liar. Let what G.K. Chesterton called the "democracy of the dead" have their say. Do not believe the vocal minority, no matter how persuasive they may seem. Instead, believe the words of Jesus in Scripture, the words of His Church as guided by the Holy Spirit and the words of the saints and martyrs. Call upon those who have gone before you on earth, and are now in Heaven, to light your path to the Lord.

> Whatever the less discerning theologians may say, the devil, as far as Christian belief is concerned, is a puzzling but real, personal and not merely symbolic presence. He is a powerful reality a baneful super-human freedom directed against God's freedom.
> Joseph Cardinal Ratzinger

> It is a departure from the picture provided by biblical Church teaching to refuse to acknowledge the devil's existence; to regard him as a self-sustaining principle who, unlike other creatures, does not owe his origin to God; or to explain the devil as a pseudo-reality, a conceptual, fanciful personification of the unknown causes of our misfortuns.
> Pope Paul VI

When I speak on spiritual warfare, the responses I get typically fall into one of five categories. The first four categories are ignorance, ambivalence, excessive zeal and fear. All four are reasons for concern. Ignorance of the reality of spiritual warfare plays right into Satan's hand. Ambivalence toward spiritual warfare is even worse, reminiscent of the "lukewarm" in Revelation (cf. Revelation 3:16). Excessive zeal for spiritual warfare, while seemingly noble, is often prideful. A response of fear serves only to obscure the truth and keep the chains of bondage secured. The fifth category, and thankfully the largest of them, is enthusiastic interest.

The ignorant see spiritual warfare through eyes of innocence. Not yet understanding the penetrating and pervasive nature of evil, they see it as an archaic metaphor, one that has outgrown its usefulness in these modern times. They view the whole notion of evil as personified by Satan and his demons with skepticism. The ignorant not only deny Satan's active presence, but also his very existence. No enemy is harder to fight than the one you think does not exist.

> Do not mock the Gospels and say there is not Satan. Evil is too real in the world to say that. Do not say the idea of Satan is dead and gone. Satan never gains so many cohorts, as when in his shrewdness he spreads the rumor that he is long since dead.
> Servant of God Fulton Sheen

> I, Sister Faustina, by the order of God, have visited the abysses of Hell so that I might tell souls about it and testify to its existence... I noticed one thing: that most of the souls there are those who disbelieved that there is a Hell.
> Saint Faustina Kowalska

> We cannot simply regard the devil as a symbol for evil; otherwise, we become sociologists, not exegetes. And those who suggest that we can no longer believe in such things have not thought very deeply about the twentieth century.
> Joseph Cardinal Ratzinger

The ambivalent see spiritual warfare through eyes of indifference. Their mistake is often equating love with acceptance, truth with tolerance. The cries of "To each his own!" and "Live and let live!" and "Judge not...!" are their common mantras. They grumble and complain that a "fair" God wouldn't permit such an evil creature to live, let alone prey on His people. They don't realize that earth is a battlefield and that Heaven is the reward. Because of their ambivalence toward the truth and their reluctance to take up arms, they are easily led astray.

> The reason why the lukewarm runs so great a risk of being lost is because tepidity conceals from the soul the immense evil which it causes.
> Saint Alphonsus Liguori

> Let us always keep before our eyes the fact that here on earth we are on a battlefield and that in paradise we

shall receive the crown of victory.
Saint Pio of Pietrelcina

The entrances to Heaven are open and death is subdued by life in the holy battle.
Saint Agnes of Montepulciano

The zealous see spiritual warfare through eyes of pride. They see it as a great battle, with shiny weapons, a large army at their side and an unworthy foe cowering at their very presence. They flex their muscles, admire their ability and marvel at their own magnificence as if their body and its deeds are their own. They love the imagery of slaying the dragon; they just don't like to have to prepare for it or get dirty doing it. They often write the victory speech before they understand the battle plan. They don't realize that if their battle plan is their own, or if they knowingly forge ahead without proper authority, they open themselves up to potential harm from Satan.

There is no human power that can be compared with his [Satan's], and thus only the divine power suffices to be able to conquer him, and the divine light alone to penetrate his wiles.
Saint John of the Cross

Only such victories as you have won without the cooperation of the body have been accomplished by your efforts, because the body is not yours, but a work of God.
Saint John Climacus

We are not asked to have shining armor to overcome Goliath, but simply to know how to choose a few stones, the right ones, with the wisdom and courage of David.
Pope John Paul II

The fearful see spiritual warfare through eyes of apprehension. They imagine that any attention given to demons will increase the likelihood of a spiritual attack. They believe that in some way spiritual warfare is a contagion that will spread if they acknowledge it as real. Others think that the domain of spiritual warfare belongs only to the clergy; in doing so, they sell themselves and their baptismal rights short. Others are afraid that they are not up to the task, so they shy away from the battle and suffer the consequences. Fear and false humility play right into Satan's hand. Your fear feeds Satan and causes him to become bolder and stronger.

[handwritten margin note: Ask for graces to combat fears]

I am really much more afraid of those people who have so great a fear of the devil, than I am of the devil himself.
Saint Teresa of Avila

Fear not, it is but an artifice of the evil one to distract you.
Saint Anthony of Padua

Do not fear the evil snares of the enemy. In the end, he will be obliged to recognize that he is powerless where a soul that is very dear to Jesus is concerned. Therefore be calm.
Saint Pio of Pietrelcina

All four categories lead away from the truth and toward the lie, either through innocence, indifference, pride or apprehension. They also, although not necessarily intentionally, do Satan's bidding for him.

The last of the categories, those who respond with enthusiasm, see spiritual warfare through eyes of faith. The word enthusiasm has an interesting etymology. It derives from two Greek words "*en* + *theos*" or in English, "*in* + *god*." Literally, enthusiasm is to be "in God." Those who are enthusiastic recognize God's victory over the evil one and their role in carrying it to its completion. They also recognize a need for liberation and protection for themselves and others. They trust in God and are open to His magnificent ways. They prepare for battle, but they don't pray for it. If it comes as part of God's will, they respond. They only seek His will, whether that places them on the frontline or the sideline. Whatever He permits they accept; whatever happens, they see the hand of God at work. Like little children, they trust in *Abba* God's promise and His power. Their strength is the Lord working through their humility.

> Be ever looking for the enemy, but do not breed a war, for this is not the attitude of a soldier but of a seditionary.
> Saint John Chrysostom

> We should never forget the two axioms: Jesus is with me and whatever happens, happens by the will of God.
> Blessed Charles de Foucauld

> Humility, humility and always humility. Satan fears and trembles before humble souls. The Lord is willing to do great things, but on condition that we are truly humble.
> Saint Pio of Pietrelcina

True spiritual warriors see spiritual warfare through the eyes of Mary, the Blessed Mother. Spiritual warfare is always accomplished by the grace of God and in accord with His permissive will. It is often hidden, quiet, and anonymous. Humility, obedience, surrender and trust are the weapons of the Lord's soldier. Next to Jesus, no greater spiritual warrior is there than the Blessed Mother. Mary's "Yes," defeats Satan's "No," every time. Scripture places Mary right in the midst of the battle. From Genesis to Revelation, Mary is the New Eve who gives birth to the New Adam (cf. Genesis 3 and Revelation 12). Mary's "*Fiat,*" was the beginning of the end for Satan. If you are called to engage in spiritual warfare, only do so under the protection of the Blessed Mother and in accordance with God's will.

> No true devotee of Mary will be damned, because she is the terrible conqueror of the devil.
> Saint Alphonsus Liguori

> Where Mary is present, the evil one is absent.
> Saint Louis de Montfort

> Listen and let it penetrate your heart, do not be troubled or weighed down with grief. Do not fear any

illness or vexation, anxiety or pain. Am I not here who am your Mother? Are you not under my shadow and protection? Am I not your fountain of life? Are you not in the folds of my mantle? In the crossing of my arms? Is there anything else you need?
Our Lady of Guadalupe to Saint Juan Diego

A word of caution is necessary when speaking of Satan. It is important to avoid ascribing too much power and influence to him. You must never fall victim to the notion that Satan is somehow equal to God in power and authority. God is Creator; Satan is creature, Both Satan's power and the ability to exercise his power are limited by God and are permitted only to the degree that they can serve God's will. God can, and does, use Satan's evil acts to bring about His glorious plan — if you let Him. Good or bad, it all falls within God's permissive will; it is all able to be redeemed by God.

> God is stronger at restoring our salvation than is Satan at continuing to imprison us.
> Saint Paulinus of Nola

> Whatever good or evil befalls you, be confident that God will convert it all to your good.
> Saint Jane Frances de Chantal

> Souls that really love God know that everything that happens in this world is either ordered or permitted by God.
> Saint Alphonsus Ligouri

Similarly, it is important to not ascribe too little power and influence to Satan. To do so is to play into his hands. You must never believe the lie that Satan does not exist; that would deny the constant teaching of the Church. Nor can you resort to the comedic phrase, "The devil made me do it." That would deny your free will and your role in your sinful acts. It would also be an obstacle to repentance and reconciliation. The truth is found, as it often is, right in the middle of these two opposing views.

The devil delights in being blamed for something. In fact he actually wants you to blame him. He is more than willing to listen to all your recriminations, as long as they keep you from making your own confession.
Saint Augustine

We do not fear the devil or his demons, because the one who fights with us is so much greater than they.
Saint Cyril of Jerusalem

With this book, I hope to shine a bold, bright light on the evil one, the light of Christ and His Church that dispels all darkness. Relying on Scripture and the saints for grounding and inspiration, the following chapters offer practical advice on how to do and how not to do battle. The realities, the cautions, the burdens and the benefits of spiritual warfare will be discussed. Satan will be spoken of, but only to the degree that it serves the kingdom of God.

It certainly gives us no pleasure to speak with you about the devil, but the doctrine which this enables me to speak of will be quite useful for you.
Saint John Chrysostom

I pass on what I have been taught and what I believe the Lord has asked me to share. Extensive use of Scripture, Magisterial documents and the wisdom of the saints back up the thoughts expressed.

Follow the saints, because those who follow them will themselves become saints.
Pope Saint Clement

These thoughts will be both offensive and defensive in nature, both preventative and curative and both moving toward virtue and away from vice.

Do this When you come to a passage from Scripture, pray it. Pray for the grace of the Holy Spirit to reveal the full meaning of the passage to you. When you come to a quote from a saint or a Church document, meditate upon its relevance. Absorb the words of Scripture and the saints; don't just scan over them.

Lastly, for the purposes of this book, when I mention Satan, please know that I am speaking of all of the fallen angels. Whether they are called evil or unclean spirits, demons, powers, principalities, the devil or the evil one, they are all united in their hatred of God the Father, God the Son and God the Holy Spirit and those who love Him.

> There is no need to be afraid to call the first agent of evil by his name: the evil one.
> Pope John Paul II

> The devil is not one person. The devil is an organized battalion of malice.
> Servant of God John Hardon

It is largely due to the collective ignorance and apathy of the people of God — and the efforts of the demons — that so many within the Church would prefer to not speak of the reality of Satan and the necessity of spiritual warfare. Ignorance and apathy lead to discomfort and fear. It is important to slay these twin dragons of ignorance and apathy and the accompanying discomfort and fear. With God's wisdom, peace, grace, truth and mercy, with proper precaution and under the protection of the Blessed Virgin Mary, it is time to speak the truth about the battle against the evil one.

> The demons do not dare to appear or exercise their deadly powers wherever the name of Mary most holy shines forth. The more frequently her name is invoked with fervent love, the more quickly do they flee and the farther off they go.
> Servant of God Thomas a' Kempis

> Mary is so powerful against the devil that he fears a single breath of hers more than all the prayers of the saints.
> Saint Louis de Montfort

> The very devils in Hell, while fearing her, [the Blessed Virgin Mary] show her respect.
> Saint Louis de Montfort

Part I
Tactics of the Enemy

✛

Then Jesus was led by the Spirit into the desert to be
tempted by the devil.
Matthew 4:1

Great!
Read

In a scriptural sense, the desert is paradoxical, it is a
metaphor for both life and death. It can be a place to grumble
at God or grow in faith, to surrender to deep despair or yield to
deep prayer. It can be seen as barren and devoid of comfort
lending itself to great temptations, or it can be seen as isolated
and devoid of distraction, lending itself to great graces. It is
either a time to detach from the world and surrender to God, or
a time to yearn for the comforts of the world and surrender to
the flesh.

Satan will attempt to lure you to the desert to weaken
you and to eventually lead you to death. God will attempt to
lure you to the desert to strengthen you and to eventually lead
you to new life. In God's plan, the desert is a time to engage in
ascetical practices. In Satan's plan, the desert is a time to focus
on scarcity. Used wisely, trusting in and aligned with God's
will, your time in the desert will be a time of preparation for
what awaits just beyond your desert experience.

As a spiritual warrior, as a soldier of Christ, desert
spirituality is important. It is important that you cultivate
attitudes and virtues that will serve you well in battle: courage,
humility, patience, charity, etc. It is also a time to grow in

13

wisdom, to learn about your mission, to gain knowledge of your enemy and his ways. It is both a training ground and a proving ground.

This first part of the book can be thought of as desert training manual, to prime and prepare you for the battle. It may serve you to sit in silence and solitude after each chapter. Allow the Holy Spirit to instruct you. Learn well, for soon He will lead you out into the world that you might accomplish the Father's will.

> Our Lord showed us an example of withdrawal from people and solitude when He would go alone up into a mountain to pray. In the wilderness too He conquered the devil, who dared to wrestle with Him. Naturally, He was not powerless to conquer him even among the multitude; but He acted thus to teach us that we can more easily overcome the enemy and reach perfection in silence and solitude.
> Saint Antony of the Desert

> We can only learn to know ourselves and do what we can: namely, surrender our will and fulfill God's will in us.
> Saint Teresa of Avila

Chapter 1
The War Begins

☦

And a great sign appeared in Heaven: a woman clothed
with the sun, and the moon was under her feet, and on
her head was a crown of twelve stars. And being with
child, she cried out while giving birth and she was
suffering in order to give birth. And another sign was
seen in Heaven. And behold, a great red dragon, having
seven heads and ten horns, and on his heads were
seven diadems. And his tail drew down a third part of
the stars of Heaven and cast them to the earth. And the
dragon stood before the woman, who was about to give
birth, so that, when she had brought forth, he might
devour her son. And she brought forth a male child,
who was soon to rule all the nations with an iron rod.
And her son was taken up to God and to his throne.
And the woman fled into solitude, where a place was
being held ready by God, so that they might pasture her
in that place for one thousand two hundred and sixty
days. And there was a great battle in Heaven. Michael
and his Angels were battling with the dragon, and the
dragon was fighting, and so were his angels. But they
did not prevail, and a place for them was no longer
found in Heaven.
Revelation 12:1-8

"Non serviam." "I will not serve." When Lucifer,

now known as Satan, uttered those words he brought evil into the created order. With those two words Lucifer ignited the mother of all battles, one that still rages today. The reality of spiritual warfare flows from Lucifer's acts of rebellious pride. It can be summed this way: God loves you and wants you to spend eternity with Him; Satan hates you and wants you to spend eternity with him. God's desire is that you join Him in the joy of His eternal love. Satan's desire is that you join him in the putrid and vile pit of Hell. God desires your eternal happiness while Satan desires your eternal separation from God. Spiritual warfare, then, refers to both the battle that took place between God and Satan and the battles that are taking place between evil spirits and human beings.

> You are united to Me; fear nothing. But know my child that Satan hates you; he hates every soul, but he burns with a particular hatred for you because you have snatched so many souls from his dominion.
> Our Lord to Saint Faustina Kowalska

Satan's initial declaration of war was a calculated decision on his part. Believing it to be beneath his dignity to serve, he freely chose to rebel against God and separate himself from God's love for eternity. Because Satan and the other fallen angels committed their sins with clear knowledge, a determined will and an absence of repentance, their sins eternally ruptured their relationship with God. Heaven is lost to them forever; they do, however, retain their natural angelic powers because sin does not change the nature of the sinner.

> Although the devil lost the dignity of his previous rank, he did not lose his knowledge which he possesses for the testing of the good and for his own confusion.
> Our Lord to Saint Bridget of Sweden

They remain eternally separated from God, miserable and malicious, yet powerful and potent. As misery loves company, Satan opened a second front in his war against God, attacking God's creatures. Satan finds twisted delight in opposing God. He relishes in snatching souls away from God. No longer capable of experiencing joy, he nonetheless experiences an evil glee in "seeking the ruin of souls." He is motivated by malice and misery to expand his crumbling empire. He'll spread partial truth intertwined with subtle deceit to try and convince you of his lies.

> The devil is allowed sometimes to speak true things, in order that his unwonted truthfulness may gain credit for his lie.
> Saint Thomas Aquinas

> Thus the evil spirit tries to transplant into man the attitude of rivalry, insubordination and opposition to God which has become, as it were, the motivation of his entire existence. This does not, however, signify the elimination of man's free will and responsibility, and even less the frustration of the saving action of Christ.
> Pope John Paul II

The reality is the moment you were conceived, you were thrust into a battle for your immortal soul. When you were born, you were born into a war zone. When you were baptized, you were fitted with combat boots. You also, in that precise moment, became a redeemed child of God and an enemy of Satan. Your baptism, which set you apart for God, set you apart from Satan. The stain of original sin, the enemy's camouflage, is wiped away. In baptism, God, the author of life, has cleansed your soul. After baptism, Satan, the hater of life, wants to stain your soul and steal your birthright.

You may be saying to yourself, "But I didn't sign up for this. I don't want to do battle, I'm not a fighter." Welcome to the Church Militant. By virtue of your baptism, you are a soldier. And you are either a soldier of and for Christ or you are a soldier against Him. "But spiritual warfare, I'm not equipped for that. Can't I just watch from the sidelines? I mean, I could get hurt!" First of all, there is a saying, "God doesn't call the equipped; He equips those whom He calls." Secondly, you can't bargain with Satan. He is a liar from the beginning. Besides, if you attempt to do less or try to ignore Satan so he won't harm you, hasn't he already won? Thirdly, as a Christian, you are a soldier, whether you think you are or not. It is your part of your baptismal legacy.

17

The Christian must be a militant; he must be vigilant and strong.
Pope Paul VI

Few souls understand what God would accomplish in them if they were to abandon themselves unreservedly to Him and if they were to allow His grace to mold them accordingly.
Saint Ignatius of Loyola

As we do battle and fight in the contest of faith, God, His Angels and Christ watch us. How exalted is the glory, how great the joy of engaging in a contest with God presiding, of receiving a crown with Christ as judge.
Saint Cyprian of Carthage

Which am I?

As a Christian, you are all called to do battle at some point, in some manner. You may be called to be a frontline soldier or you may be more on the supply side, typically supplying prayer so others may do battle. You may be called to be a leader in Christ's army or to care for the wounded. You may be called to be a stealth soldier or a highly visible one, to do battle now and to retreat later. And where the Lord calls you to serve today may not be where He calls you to serve tomorrow.

But as a baptized, confirmed believer in Christ Jesus, you are called. The truth is spiritual warfare exists whether you believe in it or not. Like gravity, you can't see it but you know it exists because you can see the effects. You can attempt to deny and defy gravity but eventually you will be subject to its pull. Spiritual warfare is much the same way. It exists even if you desire to remain ignorant of it.

Do not let willful ignorance be your downfall. The best way to pass a test is to study. The best way to make a team is to practice. When it comes to spiritual warfare a consistent, committed effort is necessary.

Time is short. Don't let the moment pass. Satan is active, perhaps now more than ever. Now is the time to recognize that the enemy wants to take you hostage and destroy your life of grace. The battle is inevitable. There is no escape, no hiding. He knows the war is lost, but that doesn't prevent him from picking off a few last stragglers. Don't be one of them. Don't fall for his traps; don't stumble into his snares. With joy in your heart and Mary's name on your lips, prepare for victory.

> O Virgin, in the hour of my death, rescue me from the hand of the demons, and the judgment, and the accusation, and the frightful testing, and the bitter toll-houses and the fierce prince, and the eternal condemnation, O Mother of God.
> Saint John Damascene

> The chief of all the enemy summons innumerable demons and scatters them. Some to one city and some to another throughout the whole world, so that no province, no place, no state of life, no individual is overlooked. He goes around to lay snares for men to seek to chain them.
> Saint Ignatius of Loyola

> My joy is by no means foolish, for in the combat there is a crown to be won, and the better the fight put up by the soul, the more numerous the palms of victory.
> Saint Pio of Pietrelcina

Despite the ugly reality of spiritual warfare, there is hope and victory in Christ Jesus. Any discussion of spiritual warfare must begin and end with these two certainties: the battle and victory belong to the Lord (cf. 1 Samuel 17:47b and Proverbs 21:31b). This is to be your focus, your strength, your peace. It is not to be an excuse for not being prepared to battle. If you truly believe and trust in these truths, then nothing the enemy can do to you will matter. If all Christians actively lived these truths, the light would overcome the darkness and Satan would whimper and whine his way back to Hell.

If that is true and the battle belongs to the Lord, then why not just sit back and watch? The answer is love. Love is at the heart of spiritual warfare. It is the love of Christ that props you up, propels you forward and provides you with the spiritual energy necessary to do battle. Love is both the means and the end for the spiritual warrior; it is to be your passion, purpose and promise. It is the love of Christ that conquers all. It is the love of Christ that will sustain you and compel you to act.

> But thanks be to God, who has given us victory through our Lord Jesus Christ.
> 1 Corinthians 15:57

> But in all these things we overcome, because of him who has loved us. For I am certain that neither death, nor life, nor Angels, nor Principalities, nor Powers, nor the present things, nor the future things, nor strength, nor the heights, nor the depths, nor any other created thing, will be able to separate us from the love of God, which is in Christ Jesus our Lord.
> Romans 8:37-39

> For the charity of Christ urges us on.
> 2 Corinthians 5:14a

Even Satan knows that the battle and victory belong to the Lord. He knows that he was defeated 2000 years ago on Calvary. He knows he is no match for the precious blood of Jesus. He also knows there are many followers of Christ who don't believe or who are lukewarm in their belief. He is counting on their collective ignorance and lack of commitment. He is counting on them not recognizing the power and authority granted them upon their baptism. He is counting on them to ignore his slow and subtle advances for he knows their lack of passionate, committed faith is what helps his cause.

> All the evils of the world are due to lukewarm Catholics.
> Pope Saint Pius V

In baptism your soul was cleansed from the stain of original sin, gained immortal life with God and became a mortal enemy to Satan. Once baptized, you become a known and noted adversary of the evil one. In fact, Satan receives a greater sense of satisfaction in capturing a soul set apart for good than he does in gaining a soul never set apart for God

20

through baptism. Satan works harder to take down souls who set themselves apart for God because they are the ones who can do the most damage to his plans. God does not, however, give Satan free reign. God always provides for His people, especially those who are under assault because of their love for Him. His grace is sufficient to overcome any assaults Satan may attempt.

> Jesus permits these assaults of the devil, because Jesus' compassion makes you dear to Him, and He wants you to resemble Himself in the torments He endured in the desert, in the garden and on the cross.
> Saint Pio of Pietrelcina

Satan stations more devils on monastery walls than in dens of iniquity for the latter offer no resistance.
Servant of God Fulton Sheen

It is characteristic of the divine goodness to protect with greater wisdom whatever the devil assaults with greater violence.
Saint Ignatius of Loyola

Spiritual warfare is suffering; it is cross-carrying; it is burden-bearing. It is heavy duty intercession, filled with intense prayer, fasting and almsgiving. Spiritual warfare is imitative of Christ's passion, death and resurrection. It is from Christ that you are to draw your strength, through Christ that you are able to endure. In obedience, through love and suffering, Christ triumphed over evil. This is to be your model, Jesus Christ crucified. By the power of His blood you have been redeemed. Through temptation and trial comes eternal glory.

Spiritual warfare really is this: is Satan going to kill you or are you willing to die to self? Are you willing to climb up on the cross of your own accord in imitation of Jesus or will you crucify yourself by your pride? To the degree that the self dies, the Lord can live and reign in you and help you overcome your temptations and trials. For it is the life of God in you that Satan wants to destroy.

The devil tempts us, not so much to do us harm, as to destroy the God in us. His aim is death, not so much

you or I; we are nothing. It is about God, a hatred of God.
Blessed Teresa of Calcutta

There are trials that God sends you as part of His perfect will; He authors them. These trials, or tribulations, should be embraced and endured in imitation of Jesus. There are also trials that God sanctions as part of His permissive will; He allows them. These trials or temptations are to be resisted and overcome. Both of these trials are designed for your edification and are a stepping stone to your eternal glory.

Tribulations and temptations can only occur according to the will of God, who can redeem evil to bring about good. So, even though you might suffer various afflictions, you are not forgotten by God. Even though you may be tempted or harassed by Satan, you are not destined to turn from God. God, in His infinite mercy, offers you bountiful graces to counteract both tribulations and temptations. From your woundedness, from Satan's temptations or harassments, can come glory — if you cooperate with God's grace.

I exhort you to confide more in divine mercy, humbling yourself before the mercy of our God, and thanking Him for all the favors He wants to grant you. By doing this you will defy and overcome all the anger of Hell.
Saint Pio of Pietrelcina

Calm yourself and be quite certain that these shadows are not a punishment proportioned to your wickedness. You are not wicked, nor are you blinded by your own malice. You are merely one of the chosen ones who are tried like gold in the furnace.
Saint Pio of Pietrelcina

Your temptations are from the devil and from Hell; but your sufferings and afflictions are from God and Heaven. The mothers are from Babylon, but the daughters are from Jerusalem. Despise temptations and embrace tribulations.
Saint Pio of Pietrelcina

22

Chapter 2
The War Rages On

☦

And answering, Jesus said to them: "Pay attention, lest someone lead you astray. For many will come in my name saying, 'I am the Christ.' And they will lead many astray. For you will hear of battles and rumors of battles. Take care not to be disturbed. For these things must be, but the end is not so soon. For nation will rise against nation, and kingdom against kingdom. And there will be pestilences, and famines, and earthquakes in places. But all these things are just the beginning of the sorrows."
Matthew 24:4-8

There seems to be a marked increase in the incidence and intensity of spiritual warfare in the world. Certainly, part of the blame can be placed on Satan's shoulders because of his ongoing disobedience and disdain for God and His followers. Pointing fingers at Satan without also taking a good, long look in the mirror, though, would be disingenuous and prideful. The first step in becoming a strong spiritual warrior is to recognize your weaknesses.

Never fight evil as if it were something that arose totally outside of yourself.
Saint Augustine

First let us purify ourselves from our sins and escape
from the bondage of Satan, and then we can talk about
God.
Saint Catherine of Siena

Nor did demons crucify Him; it is you who have
crucified Him and crucify Him still, when you delight in
your vices and sins.
Saint Francis of Assisi

In today's church, too many are reticent when it comes
to proclaiming the truth, especially regarding the reality of the
existence of Satan. This reticence only serves to further Satan's
kingdom. In many ways the relative strength of Satan can be
directly linked to the collective fear and feebleness Catholics
have of living and proclaiming their faith. For example:
Belief in the Eucharist has been diminished. Yet, in
this sacrament is the power and presence of Jesus Christ: Body,
Blood, Soul and Divinity. It is God, right here, right now; still,
many shrug. In His blood is redemption. There is infinite power
in the Body and Blood of Jesus. A soul nurtured on and
strengthened by the Eucharist is demoralizing to Satan.

The Eucharist has been one of the principal causes of
the holiness of martyrs, confessors, and virgins,
because it was the primary source of their courage and
strength in overcoming the world, the flesh, and the
devil.
Venerable Louis of Granada

Where they see the blood of the Lord, demons flee while
angels gather.
Saint John Chrysostom

Let us return from that Table like lions breathing out
fire, terrifying to the devil.
Saint John Chrysostom

Relatively few Catholics avail themselves of the
Sacrament of Penance. Yet, there exists a power in this
sacrament to strengthen the will and break the power of the

evil one that is not possible otherwise. Unrepented and unconfessed mortal sin not only leaves the door wide open for Satan, but it lights a path to your door. If you fall, get up. If your will is compromised, you can strengthen it by the grace offered to you through sacramental confession.

> The devil has only one door to enter, and in your soul that door is called will. There are no hidden doors.
> Saint Pio of Pietrelcina

> The devil never runs upon a man to seize him with his claws until he sees him on the ground, already having fallen by his own will.
> Saint Thomas More

The Liturgy has, in the hands of some, gone from the sublime to the profane. Personal agendas have led to liturgical abuses; secular has replaced sacred. The resulting confusion has led to separation, sin and scandal — all trademarks of the evil one. It is only when you worship God as the Church prescribes that you are strengthened in your faith and in battle against the evil one.

> The holiness of the sacred is despised; the majesty of divine worship is not only disapproved by evil men, but defiled and held up to ridicule. Hence sound doctrine is perverted and errors of all kinds spread boldly.
> Pope Gregory XVI

> One who offers worship to God on the Church's behalf in a way contrary to that which is laid down by the Church with God-given authority and which is customary in the Church is guilty of falsification.
> Saint Thomas Aquinas

> I am convinced that the crisis of the church which we are living through today was largely caused by the disintegration of the liturgy.
> Joseph Cardinal Ratzinger

> Today there arises the risk of a serpentine

secularization even within the Church, which can convert into a formal and empty Eucharistic worship, in celebrations lacking this participation from the heart that is expressed in veneration and respect for the liturgy.
Pope Benedict XVI

The Blessed Mother is often relegated to the status of cultural icon. Yet, it is Mary's "*Fiat,*" that counters Eve's "No." It is Mary's "*Fiat,*" that stands in contrast to Satan's "I will not serve." Satan hates and fears Mary above all creatures because of her humility. Simple, humble, holy Mary defeated Satan and his entire army with a single word. Satan's arrogance and pride far exceed his powers. He is truly a coward, especially when it comes to the Blessed Mother and her children.

He who neglects her [the Blessed Virgin Mary] will die in his sins.
Saint Bonaventure

When my soul shall be released from the bond with the flesh, intercede for me, O Sovereign Lady that I may pass unhindered through the princes of darkness in the air.
Saint John Damascene

The devils tremble if they only hear the name of Mary.
Saint Alphonsus Liguori

Traditional devotionals such as the Rosary are more likely to be worn as fashion items than to be prayed. They are even mocked as antiquated and superstitious. Yet, devotion to Mary, through the Rosary is a powerful means of protection. It is also a sure and safe passageway to Heaven, one that has been well trodden by the saints and martyrs.

It is easy to see that they have absorbed the poison of Hell and that they are inspired by the devil. Nobody can condemn devotion to the holy Rosary without condemning all that is most holy in the Catholic faith.
Saint Louis de Montfort

If you say the Rosary faithfully until death, I do assure you that, in spite of the gravity of your sins you shall receive a never-fading crown of glory.
Saint Louis de Montfort

The Rosary is my weapon.
Saint Pio of Pietrelcina

Sacramentals such as scapulars, relics, icons, medals, holy water, blessed salt, etc., seem to have lost their luster. They are relegated to the top shelf of the rarely used closet. They are seen as remnants of a bygone era. Yet, it is these very same blessed items that Satan fears. It is these same blessed items that can strengthen your will and remit venial sin.

Whosoever dies clothed in this Scapular shall not suffer eternal fire.
Our Lady to Saint Simon Stock

The episcopal blessing, the aspersion of holy water, every sacramental unction, prayer in a dedicated church, and the like, effect the remission of venial sins, implicitly or explicitly.
Saint Thomas Aquinas

These relics do you receive with a joy equivalent to the distress with which their custodians have parted with them and sent them to you. Let none dispute; let none doubt. Here you have that unconquered athlete. These bones, which shared in the conflict with the blessed soul, are known to the Lord. These bones He will crown, together with that soul, in the righteous day of His requital.
Saint Basil the Great

Those who adhere to and promote traditional Catholic moral values are ridiculed as unenlightened and old fashioned. Gospel truths are no longer tolerated and in some cases are becoming illegal. Satan's attack on the traditional biblical concept of marriage and family is so strong because he knows that if he can redefine marriage and break up the family, he can destroy society. True progress can only be achieved in accord with God's will.

> Disorder in society is the result of disorder in the family.
> Saint Angela Merici

> The collapse of morality involves the collapse of societies.
> Pope John Paul II

> Naturally, the crisis of the family presents a great challenge for the Church, as it places in question conjugal fidelity and, more in general, the values on which society is based.
> Pope Benedict XVI

Charity is preached at the expense of truth, as if you could separate one from the other. Love of neighbor has been replaced by acceptance of neighbor, as if the highest good is tolerance. Love of self is seen as dogmatic, but love of God is optional. Reverence and piety have been replaced with the informal and the ordinary. Scandal and dissent dissuade some from proclaiming what is true; yet, truth never changes. Some unwittingly follow the false path laid out for them by the enemy, when they should be heading down the path of truth.

> The soul which desires to benefit itself in the spiritual life ought always to proceed the contrary way to what the enemy proceeds.
> Saint Ignatius of Loyola

> No one in the world can alter truth. All we can do is seek it and live it.
> Saint Maximilian Kolbe

> While those who give scandal are guilty of the spiritual equivalent of murder, those who take scandal, who allow scandals to destroy faith, are guilty of spiritual suicide.
> Saint Francis de Sales

Often humility, zeal for souls, courage, fear of the Lord, etc., are seen as quaint virtues from a bygone era instead of gifts and fruits of the Holy Spirit. Yet these very virtues are essential if you are to imitate Jesus and spread His Gospel to the world. All Christians, but especially those who embrace their call as a spiritual warrior, need access to each of God's gifts and grace.

To practice humility, it is absolutely necessary for us at times to suffer wounds in this spiritual warfare.
Saint Francis de Sales

No sacrifice is more acceptable to God than zeal for souls.
Pope Saint Gregory the Great

Great courage is required in spiritual warfare.
Saint Teresa of Avila

Do not fear the devil. By fearing the Lord you will gain mastery of the devil, for there is no power in him.
The Shepherd of Hermas

Suffering and sanctity seem useless in this post-modern world of instant fixes and impatient attitudes. Lost in the shuffle is the suffering the Lord endured for the sake of humanity and the manner He endured it. His suffering opened the flood gates of grace and mercy. Your suffering in union with His allows you to drink in that grace and mercy. Embrace the cross. Hold it high as you enter into battle.

We must suffer to go to God. We forget this truth far too often.
Saint Madeleine Sophia Barat

It is suffering, more than anything else, which clears the way for the grace which transforms human souls. The Church feels the need to have recourse to the value of human sufferings for the salvation of the world.
Pope John Paul II

The highest gift and grace of the Holy Spirit that Christ concedes to His friends is to conquer one's self, and out of love of Christ, to endure willingly sufferings, injuries, insults and discomfort.
Saint Francis of Assisi

All of these reasons have left the door open for Satan. An open door is an invitation for the thief of souls. A closed door is a simple, yet effective, defense against him. A closed door allows you to remain filled with God's grace and to respond in accord with His will. A closed door will keep grace in your soul and the demons outside.

Truth, when it is acknowledged and accepted, closes the door. The simple truth is Satan is real. He wants to kill your immortal soul. There is no reason for fear, no reason to feign ignorance, no reason to deny what is true. Bring the truth to the light. The battle is won, the victory is the Lord's and you have been delivered from the power of darkness. Do not be discouraged, help is on the way. You are not alone. Many Catholics remain faithful to the Church and its sacred traditions. Many are willing to engage their baptismal obligations and to do battle against sin and evil. Now is the time. You are the soldier.

What are the Church's greatest needs at the present time? Don't be surprised at Our answer and don't write it off as simplistic or even superstitious: one of the Church's greatest needs is to be defended against the evil we call the devil.
Pope Paul VI

We are now standing in the face of the greatest historical confrontation humanity has gone through. I do not think that wide circles of American society or wide circles of the Christian community realize this fully. We are now facing the final confrontation between the Church and the Anti-Church, of the Gospel versus the anti-Gospel.
Karol Cardinal Wojtyla

Chapter 3
Temptation

☩

Watch and pray, so that you may not enter into
temptation. The spirit indeed is willing, but the flesh is
weak.
Mark 14:38

For he has rescued us from the power of darkness, and
he has transferred us into the kingdom of the Son of his
love, in whom we have redemption through his blood,
the remission of sins. He is the image of the invisible
God, the first-born of every creature. For in him was
created everything in Heaven and on earth, visible and
invisible, whether thrones, or dominations, or
principalities, or powers. All things were created
through him and in him. And he is before all, and in
him all things continue.
Colossians 1:13-17

Spiritual warfare typically takes the form of
temptation, obsession or possession. Temptation is when the
devil entices you to sin, either externally through the
excitement of the sense or internally through the corruption of
the intellect or will. Obsession is when the devil attacks the
body from the outside. Possession is when the devil takes
control of a soul. All three have as their goal the hindrance or
prevention of a spiritual good.

Temptation is the most common weapon in Satan's arsenal; all are subject to and familiar with it. Obsession can be divided into several subcategories (aggression, oppression, infestation, etc.). For the purposes of this book, these various categories will be lumped together and termed harassment. True possession, the third category, requires an exorcism. It is very rare and beyond the scope of this book.

> I do not say there are no people possessed by the devil, for I know there are, but what I say is they are few.
> Saint Anthony Mary Claret

Temptation is an enticement to sin. Sin, in the strictest sense, is not a tool of Satan. Rather, sin is the result of giving into temptation, whatever the origin of the temptation might be. Temptation is the one shared reality of all humans. It was not intended by God, but it is permitted by Him. Temptation, it must be noted, is not synonymous with sin. As long as there is not the consent of the will, temptation is not sinful.

In all temptation the mechanism is the same; there are three components. First is the suggestion of some evil. This is followed by an imagined pleasure. The conclusion of the temptation process is the decision of the will. If the decision is made to consent to the temptation, the temptation has led to sin. If the decision is made to reject the temptation, the temptation has not led to sin. It is important to keep this process in mind. There is no sin in the initial temptation. Temptation can lead to sin though, and sin leads you away from God. So at all times, be attentive, but never anxious.

> The first impulse does not belong to us, but the second does.
> Saint Bernadette Soubirous

Man is tempted in three ways, by the world, the flesh and the devil. The flesh aims for control over your body, the world aims for control over your body and spirit, the devil aims for control over your body, spirit and soul. The flesh tempts from the inside, the world from the outside and the devil from a combination of the two. The temptations of the world and the flesh are expressed in this verse from Scripture.

32

For all that is in the world is the desire of the flesh, and the desire of the eyes, and the arrogance of a life which is not of the Father, but is of the world.
1 John 2:16

The desire of the flesh, desire of the eyes and a pride of life are the main temptations of the world and the flesh. These temptations were the same three that Adam and Eve succumbed to and that Jesus triumphed over. In both cases, who was doing the tempting? It is the third source of temptation, the devil who is the prime tempter, then and now.

Peter Kreeft, in *Back to Virtue,* says, "It is said that there are three sources of evil, the world, the flesh and the devil; but the world and the flesh would be innocent were it not for the devil." This is not to pardon the flesh and the world, because both are guilty. It is to clarify that the real enemy is Satan.

Saint Thomas Aquinas states in the *Summa Theologica* that Satan is the "occasional and indirect cause of all of our sins" via his conquering of Adam, but Satan is not "the direct cause of all the sins of men." Sometimes your sin is just that, your sin. Sometimes there is more to it. A brief look at how the world and the flesh tempts is next, followed by a much more extensive look at how the devil tempts.

> Our own evil inclinations are far more dangerous than any external enemies.
> Saint Ambrose

> See, you blind ones, you who are deceived by your enemies; by the flesh, the world, and the devil; because it is sweet to the body to commit sin and it is bitter for it to serve God.
> Saint Francis of Assisi

> Not every sin is committed by the instigation of the devil, but certain sins are from our own free will and the bodily corruption.
> Saint Thomas Aquinas

Temptations of the Flesh

> For I do not do the good that I want to do. But instead, I
> do the evil that I do not want to do.
> Romans 7:19

Temptations of the flesh are fueled by concupiscence,
the propensity of human nature to sin. Concupiscence is a
lingering effect of original sin. You are, in a very real way, at
war with your own flesh. You are tempted by the flesh in two
ways; it incites you toward evil and entices you away from
good. An unholy curiosity and inordinate attachments are
formed to earthly pleasures and treasures. Selfish pursuit of
pleasure numbs your desire to seek God's love.

Disordered sexuality is a signal to Satan that he is
winning a particular battle. Indulging in the legitimate
pleasures of the flesh can keep the devil at bay. Engaging in
activities that pervert the legitimate pleasures of the flesh
opens the door to Satan's master plan regarding sexuality. He
wants to separate fertility from sexuality and sexuality from
fertility. He is bidding you to become, in effect, your own god
and is using God's gift, your human sexuality, to bring about
his plan. (Unfortunately, he has been highly successful in the
implementation of this plan. Witness the high incidence of
contraception, abortion, homosexuality, in-vitro fertilization,
cloning and infant stem cell research.)

Curiosity about the ways of the world, especially
through the eyes, tends to excite the flesh nature. Custody of
the eyes helps to maintain a chaste heart and a pure soul.
Allowing the flesh to indulge and immerse your eyes in the
stuff of the world leads to unhealthy attachments and
allegiances. The flesh tempts you to materialism, greed, excess
and self-indulgence. Doing this furthers Satan's goal of
grounding you in his kingdom as opposed to God's. Lack of
attachment allows room for God to take root in your life.

> Until a man is purged of his attachments he will not be
> equipped to possess God.
> Saint John of the Cross

The devil rules over lovers of temporal goods belonging

to this temporal world, not because he is lord of this world but because he is ruler of those covetous desires by which we long for all that passes away.
Saint Augustine

Self-love is the mirror of death. Satan is never happier than when you emulate him by engaging in his sin of pride. The flesh tempts you to power, prestige, position and self-reliance. It tempts you to use your fleshy appetite in earthly ways. This leads to gluttony, lust, envy, etc. The longer you gaze into the mirror of self-reliance and are captivated by the image you see, the less you are able to see God. The less you see God, the more you are subject to Satan's conniving ways.

You are not to stand idly by and let your flesh take over. You must resist the temptation to allow the flesh to control you. You must mortify the flesh and subjugate it to your will. You are to render the fleshy form, the sinful self, the "old man," dead. You are to die to self and live for Christ in word and deed. You need to nail the corrupt and carnal old man to the cross so that you can become a "new man" in Christ Jesus (cf. Colossians 3:9-10, 2 Corinthians 5:17, Galatians 2:20). You are to seek purity, not perversity. You need to leave your evil inclinations behind. As a spiritual warrior you live by dying. You do so by grace through faith in Christ Jesus. You must pray for this grace. Pray hard. Pray long. Pray often.

Self-love is the cause of all our miseries, and renders us unworthy to receive the favors of divine love.
Saint Ignatius of Loyola

Not the goods of the world, but God. Not riches, but God. Not honors, but God. Not distinction, but God. Not dignities, but God. Not advancement, but God. God always and in everything.
Saint Vincent Pallotti

Holy Purity, the queen of virtues, the angelic virtue, is a jewel so precious that those who possess it become like the angels of God in Heaven, even though clothed in mortal flesh.
Saint John Bosco

Temptations of the World

And the world is passing away, with its desire. But whoever does the will of God abides unto eternity.
1 John 2:17

For the wisdom of this world is foolishness with God.
1 Corinthians 3:19a

The temptation of the world is the collective and cumulative poor example of Christian living proffered by occupants of what Saint Augustine terms the "City of Man" (as opposed to the "City of God"). Satan, the leader of this city, inspires the non-believers, the ignorant, the lukewarm, the immoral, the sin promoters, etc., to export his doctrine to all corners of the world. Like a deadly virus, left unchecked and untreated, many deaths will follow.

The temptation of the world is often a temptation toward passive evil rather than a temptation toward active evil. It is more often a sin of omission rather than a sin of commission, at least at the start. The City of Man is tumbling down the slippery slope of worldly temptation one compromise, one tolerance, one look the other way at a time. Political, corporate, ecclesial, and familial leaders are leaping into dangerous and rising waters. Like lemmings, many are following them off the cliff. You must resist the urge to blindly follow, to blame others and to lose hope. Though you're temporararily a citizen in the City of Man, your permanent residence is destined to be in the City of God.

As citizens of two cities, we are to strive to discharge our earthly duties conscientiously and in response to the Gospel spirit.
Gaudium et Spes

Truly, matters in the world are in a bad state; but if you and I begin in earnest to reform ourselves, a really good beginning will have been made.
Saint Peter of Alcantara

We must never lose sight of the fact that we are either

36

saints or outcasts, that we must live for Heaven or Hell; there is no middle path in this. You either belong wholly to the world or wholly to God. If people would do for God what they do for the world, what a great number of Christians would go to Heaven.
Saint John Vianney

Book

My previous book, *Christ-Centered Selling,* details the struggle of trying to work in the world without being seduced by it. Early on it stresses that the Gospel message is not a "Sunday only" experience; its message is to be lived all day, every day. "The challenge is to not only live Christ's message on Sunday morning, but Monday morning and Tuesday morning and Wednesday evening and Thursday afternoon, and Friday and Saturday, too. You are to live in this world without being seduced by it. You are, as Christ points out, to live in the world, but not belong to it."

As a spiritual warrior you cannot lead a compartmentalized life: work here, family here, faith there and fun there. God's business should be your business. Faith is not a whim; faith is to be the foundation that undergirds all you do. Inconsistency is an open door through which Satan easily gains entrance. Inconsistency is a weakness of the will that strengthens Satan's grip.

Is it consistent to profess our beliefs in church on Sunday, and then during the week to promote business practices or medical procedures contrary to those beliefs? Is it consistent for practicing Catholics to ignore or exploit the poor and the marginalized, to promote sexual behavior contrary to Catholic moral teaching, or to adopt positions that contradict the right to life of every human being from conception to natural death?
Pope Benedict XVI

In our time more than ever before, the chief strength of the wicked lies in the cowardice and weakness of good men and all the strength of Satan's reign is due to the easy-going weakness of Catholics.
Pope Saint Pius X

37

Let us look about God's business and He will look after ours.
Saint Vincent de Paul

Living the way of the world breeds uncertainty, uncertainty breeds fear and fear breeds judgment. The world is unrelenting, it has no mercy; it offers no future, no hope. Its end is death. Those who have been seduced by the world live in fear — a fear of their own mortality. That is why the most prideful spend so much time focused on external appearances and erecting monuments to themselves.

The truth is the world hates Christians. It always has; it always will. It may not be polite, politically correct or prudent to speak so bluntly, but it is, nonetheless, true. The standards that the world proffers are in radical opposition to the truths of Christianity. Do not accept the world's standards. Carefully choose your role models. Surround yourself with those who aspire to the City of God, the city of faith, hope and love. Do not surround yourself with worldly companions, let alone evil ones. Don't be foolish when it comes to choosing your friends; be a fool for Christ. The world's wisdom and ways is foolishness to those who follow Christ.

> The world hates Christians; so why give your love to it instead of following Christ who loves you and has redeemed you?
> Saint Cyprian of Carthage

> Fly from bad companions as from the bite of a poisonous snake. If you keep good companions, I can assure you that you will one day rejoice with the blessed in Heaven; whereas if you keep with those who are bad, you will become bad yourself, and you will be in danger of losing your soul.
> Saint John Bosco

According to Sacred Scripture, and especially the New Testament, the dominion and the influence of Satan and of the other evil spirits embraces all the world. The action of Satan consists primarily in tempting men to evil, by influencing their imaginations and higher

faculties, to turn them away from the law of God.
Pope John Paul II

When the devil is called the god of this world, it is not because he made it but because we serve him with our worldliness.
Saint Thomas Aquinas

Consider seriously how quickly people change, and how little trust is to be had in them; and hold fast to God, Who does not change.
Saint Teresa of Avila

Temptations of the Devil

And when all the temptation was completed, the devil withdrew from him, until a time.
Luke 4:13

Satan is an opportunistic parasite. Once you are baptized, he can only live on in you to the degree that you allow him to do so. Outside of your consent, he has no authority to take up residence in your soul. Your will is the gate through which Satan passes, but only by your consent. Mortal sin is your consent; it is your "No," to God and your "Yes," to Satan. While Satan is permitted to tempt and harass you when you are in God's grace, he is never permitted to override your free will. He cannot capture your soul without your consent, whether implied or deliberate.

A demon spirit cannot reign by itself if it is not united with the free will of man.
Saint Pio of Pietrelcina

We have been born again in holy baptism and have been released from slavery and become free so that the enemy cannot take any action against us unless we of our own will obey him.
Saint Symeon the New Theologian

It is important to remember you can avoid many

problems by simply subjugating your mind to the mind of God, your will to God's will. When you freely say "Yes," to God, you are saying "No," to Satan. While this might increase the level of temptation or harassment, at least initially, as long as your will does not give consent to the evil spirit, you remain free of demon parasites. By the grace of God, Satan can do you no harm.

> Our minds govern both soul and body beneath the protection of sacred armor, for the mind which subjects itself to God obtains the armor of salvation.
> Saint Paulinus of Nola

Satan is sly and resourceful in his attempts to destroy you. He seeks out your weakness to tempt you exactly there. He is an expert in observational intelligence. He observes your tendencies and tempts you accordingly. He'll either incite you to do evil, encourage you to do more of a particular good — at the expense of another — or he'll manipulate you into perceiving a good where there is none. Whether tempting you to pride or vanity or passion, he is a deceiver. First he deceives, then he ensnares.

> Like a skillful general about to besiege a fortified city, he seeks out the weak points in the object of his assault and tempts a man in those things in which he sees him to be weak.
> Saint Thomas Aquinas

> Our infernal enemy observes with malignant attention what the stamp of our conscience is, whether it is delicate or relaxed. If delicate, he tries to render it more susceptible still; he endeavors to reduce it to the last degree of trouble and anguish, so as to stop our progress in the spiritual life.
> Saint Ignatius of Loyola

In his efforts at deception, Satan is exceedingly clever. He is happy to exploit the temptations of the world and the flesh to make you more susceptible to his temptations. The effect of the combination of these three temptations working together is not simply cumulative; it is exponential. Because of concupiscence the impact that the three sources of temptation have collectively is greater than their harm individually. All of this is further fueled by Satan's absolute hatred for God and all those who love God.

> It [the temptation of the devil] is stronger than those of the world and the flesh, because the devils reinforce themselves with these other two enemies, the world and the flesh, in order to wage a rugged war.
> Saint John of the Cross

> No one hates God more than the devil, so he puts hatred for God in action by destroying us, by making us commit sin.
> Blessed Teresa of Calcutta

For example, imagine a person who is allergic to bee stings. This predisposition is not, nor was it meant to be, the natural state of his humanity. It is, perhaps, a genetic weakness that has been transmitted from one generation to the next. Think of this inherited weakness as similar to the idea of concupiscence. *(sinning)*

The allergic reaction caused by one or two bee stings would be cause for medication and monitoring of the situation. Properly and promptly treated this would not usually be a life-threatening situation. Yet, even though treatment has been successfully applied, a residue remains. This residue can cause future bee stings to have a cumulative and, therefore, a more serious reaction. Of course, left untreated, even a singular bee might be deadly.

> The actual sins we have committed, whether mortal or venial, even though forgiven have intensified our base desire, our weakness, our inconsistency and our evil tendencies and have left a sediment of evil in our soul.
> Saint Louis de Montfort

Satan doesn't sting like a regular bee; he stings as killer bees would, in a relentless and swarming pattern. He doesn't just throw darts; he throws fiery darts. He also likes to set traps. These traps, seemingly harmless at first, lure you ever deeper into darkness. Like a gentle rolling hillside that leads to a cliff, Satan's traps are deceiving. What feels like a good may actually be a trap, one that Satan has set. He sets his traps with the bait of temptation to be bad, bored, busy or boastful. Don't take his bait and you'll avoid his traps.

> The devil can bark, but he cannot bite, unless a person lets himself be bitten.
> Saint Augustine

> The devil only tempts souls that wish to abandon sin and those in a state of grace. The others belong to him: he has no need to tempt them.
> Saint John Vianney

> The devil's snare does not catch you unless you are first caught by the devil's bait.
> Saint Ambrose

Bad

> Most beloved, do not choose to sojourn in the passion which is a temptation to you, as if something new might happen to you. But instead, commune in the Passion of Christ, and be glad that, when his glory will be revealed, you too may rejoice with exultation.
> 1 Peter 4:12-13

Satan's first temptation tactic is to try and make you bad. He is not overt. Rather, he is usually sly and subtle. He deviously suggests to you those sins to which you already have an inclination toward or a desire for (he's been watching and taking notes). He starts with the lesser sins, perhaps even with something that isn't even sinful. He is patient. As you respond favorably to his promptings, at least from his perspective, he will increase the pleasure associated with the temptation. After he has progressed from a toehold into a foothold, he will increase the pressure of the temptation, hoping to take it from an occasional act to an ongoing one. Bad is deadly for you as a spiritual warrior. It compromises your life and the lives of those

Responding to temptations

around you.

Instead of tempting you to an adulterous affair, he'll initially tempt you with a seemingly harmless flirtation. Instead of tempting you to embezzle money, he'll initially tempt you to cheat on your income taxes. Instead of tempting you to abuse your position of authority, he'll initially tempt you to bend the rules just a little bit.

After your initial misstep, he'll return later to further induce you to greater missteps. A doubt is raised where none had been before, a truth is shaded or a lie is defended. Perhaps it is an act of omission, a virtue is not protected, a word of truth is not spoken or a good deed is left undone. Slowly, but surely, you're on your way to being bad. Once you start to justify, excuse and rationalize your behavior, you are well on your way to separating yourself from a life of grace. Don't let him bait you into being bad, not even a little. Remember, your free will lives between the temptation and the sin. Focus your mind on Christ.

Occupy your mind with good thoughts or the enemy will fill them with bad ones. Unoccupied, they cannot be.
Saint Thomas More

Only the free will is capable of good or evil. But when the will sighs under the trial of the tempter and does not will what is presented to it, there is not only no fault but there is virtue.
Saint Pio of Pietrelcina

The soul possesses freedom; and though the devil can make suggestions, he doesn't have the power to compel you against your will.
Saint Cyril of Jerusalem

Bored

For we have heard that there are some among you who act disruptively, not working at all, but eagerly meddling.
2 Thessalonians 3:11

But what if he can't make you bad? Well, then he'll gladly make you bored. Boredom is disordered. Whether it falls under the heading of apathy, sloth, indifference, idleness, dreariness or lethargy the end result is a dulling of the senses and a loss of interest in the seeking of truth. This dulling of the senses often leads to sin by way of boredom. Boredom, an act of the will, comes from the inside. It is caused by a lack of action on the inside, not the outside. It is like a drug; it sets an ever increasing stimulus threshold. Boredom is deadly for a spiritual warrior because it kills the prayer life, the warrior's source of strength.

Walker Percy, a twentieth century Catholic novelist, once noted that there is no word for boredom in any pre-modern language. It was an invention of necessity, born of the postmodern search for a meaningful, happy life apart from God. The truth is that there can be no meaningful, happy life apart from God. Jesus is infinitely fulfilling; He is the answer to every fruitless search for meaning and purpose. When you give in to boredom, you move away from God. When you give in to boredom, you give Satan a foundation upon which to begin building his evil empire.

> Everyone is ready to run after the latest novelty. But as for Jesus Christ in the Blessed Sacrament, He is deserted and forsaken.
> Saint John Vianney

How often does boredom lead to sin in your life? The maxim, "Idle hands are the devil's workshop" is true because when you are idle the will is not directed or focused. If you don't direct your will, someone else will do it for you. As boredom is not a natural state, your body seeks to rid itself of it, almost at any cost. Through the abuse of drugs, alcohol, sex, sports, shopping, work, etc., endless amounts of time and money are spent trying to fill the God-shaped hole inside with anything and everything but God. Stop seeking temporal solutions to an eternal equation. Do not let boredom be a contributor toward evil; let it be a catalyst toward good. Allow the restlessness you feel to motivate you toward seeking God's will.

Be ever engaged, so that whenever the devil calls he

may find you occupied.
Saint Jerome

Idleness is Hell's fishhook for catching souls.
Saint Ignatius of Loyola

The principal trap the devil sets for the young people is idleness. This is the fatal source of all evil.
Saint John Bosco

Busy

Now Martha was continually busying herself with serving. And she stood still and said: "Lord, is it not a concern to you that my sister has left me to serve alone? Therefore, speak to her, so that she may help me." And the Lord responded by saying to her: "Martha, Martha, you are anxious and troubled over many things. And yet only one thing is necessary. Mary has chosen the best portion, and it shall not be taken away from her."
Luke 10:40-42

But suppose he can't make you bad or bored? He'll then try and make you busy. Did you ever wonder why, with all the modern time saving devices available, there seems to be less time, not more? Schedules are more complicated, commitments more numerous and time more precious. And too often it is God who is omitted from the calendar. Busyness is deadly for you as a spiritual warrior because it distracts you from what is most important, God and His will for you. You come to know Him in the stillness, not in the craziness.

Have you ever had the experience of doing a great work for God? After you were done, did you ever wonder how you accomplished so much in such a short amount of time? It's like the story of the loaves and fishes; God multiplies your efforts and seemingly time itself when you serve Him. When you are in His will your every act is a prayer and somehow prayer seems to multiply time. Conversely, it seems that a lack of prayer creates a lack of time. Feelings of being rushed, always trying to meet deadlines and a sense of constant anxiety can often be traced back to a weak or infrequent prayer life.

If you have too much to do, with God's help you will find time to do it all.
Saint Peter Canisius

The great thing about this temptation, again, from Satan's perspective, is this is the easiest way to tempt good people. Many instances of doing more can be for a good end, but if the focus on God is lost in the busyness, Satan has a grip. If God's will for you is lost in the busyness, then the good that is done is tainted. And busy doesn't always imply physical activity. If Satan can keep your mind filled with a constant barrage of thoughts and ideas and noise he can prevent you from hearing God's voice. If your soul feels disturbed because you are not doing something, if you are anxious when you're not busy, if you are more focused on doing and not being, then Satan has helped you to choose the lesser portion. If Satan gets you to set aside charity in the name of expediency and efficiency, what have you really accomplished?

> Be very careful of your health. The devil employs a trick to deceive good souls. He incites them to do more than they are able in order that they may no longer be able to do anything.
> Saint Vincent de Paul

> While I am busy with little things, I am not required to do greater things.
> Saint Francis de Sales

> We can do no great things; only small things with great love.
> Blessed Teresa of Calcutta

Boastful

> But now you exult in your arrogance. All such exultation is wicked.
> James 4:16

Satan is not particular about what method he uses to tempt you or ensnare you; he takes what he can get, any way he can get it. He is flexible and patient in his approach, always keeping focused on his goal, separation of your soul from God's grace. If bad, bored or busy doesn't work, then he'll try to make you boastful, perhaps even about your ability to resist him. He'll leverage your goodness, attempting to turn it into pride, bringing you from grace into sin.

As pride is Satan's sin, he knows his way around flattery. As intelligent and watchful as Satan is, he knows how best to strike at you with the poisonous venom of pride. He doesn't come at you directly and forcefully; he comes at you indirectly and almost imperceptibly. Stroking your ego, he gets you to pay homage to your sinful self. Stoking the flames of self-importance, he diverts your attention from God's will. Satan attempts to use your strengths against you, puffing you up, enticing you to go it alone. One step at a time, he encourages you down the path of conceit. *Stay Strong!*

God, who is Creator to Satan who is creature, is infinitely wiser than Satan. God uses your weaknesses (of which there are many) to bring about His plan for you; He knows that you tend toward your weaknesses (cf. 2 Corinthians 12·9). God, because He is God, is able to use your faults and weakness for your good and His glory. It is in your weakness, your littleness, that you place your total trust in Him. He, in turn, will shield you from the deceit of the evil one. Trust in God, not in yourself. *Reflect on this often teach this in PSR.*

He who trusts in himself is lost. He who trusts in God can do all things.
Saint Alphonsus Liguori

Pride is denial of God and an invention of the devil.
Saint John Climacus

God will not permit him [the evil one] to deceive a soul which has no trust whatever in itself, and is strengthened in faith.
Saint Teresa of Avila

Satan's temptations are real, powerful and compelling. Yet, God's grace is more real, more powerful, more compelling. Never take Satan's temptations lightly and never use Satan's temptation as a pretext to do evil. Jesus' death and resurrection has brought you out of the darkness and into the light. Seek the Father's will in all things and you'll never give in to the temptation to be bad, bored, busy, boastful or any other strategy Satan may employ.

The devil comes and tempts all the servants of God. Those who are strong in the faith resist him and he goes away from them, because he cannot find entrance. So then he goes to the empty and, finding an entrance, he goes into them. In this way he does in them whatever he pleases and makes them his slaves.
The Shepherd of Hermas

Water that does not flow and comes to a halt in holes becomes stagnant and filled with impurities. In the same way, the body that is worn down by prolonged idleness produces and fuels the fire of covetousness and illicit pleasure.
Saint Bernard of Clairvaux

In all the efforts by which we try to please God, the demons dig three pits. First they try to obstruct our good undertaking, second they try to make our work not according to God. If that doesn't work, they then steal noiselessly to the soul and flatter us.
Saint John Climacus

First they [the demons] are to tempt them to covet riches, as Satan himself is accustomed to do in most cases, that they more easily obtain the empty honors of this world and then come to overweening pride. The first step then, will be riches, the second; honor, the third; pride, from these three steps the one leads to all other vices.
Saint Ignatius of Loyola

You must ask God to give you power to fight against the sin of pride which is your greatest enemy — the root of all that is evil, and the failure of all that is good.
Saint Vincent de Paul

Chapter 4
Harassment

☩

And lest the greatness of the revelations should extol
me, there was given to me a prodding in my flesh: an
Angel of Satan, who struck me repeatedly.
2 Corinthians 12:7

One of the sufferings a faithful follower of Christ will
undergo is harassment. Though Satan would rather tempt you
to be bad, bored, busy or boastful, he will alternately harass,
distract and annoy you. (Temptation and harassment are not
mutually exclusive. He may at times tempt and harass you
simultaneously.) Did you ever wake up grouchy, with no peace
in your soul? Did you ever pick a fight with your spouse for
seemingly no reason? Did you ever pester or annoy or
aggravate someone else just to do it? Ever been sitting minding
your own business when suddenly an evil thought pops into
your head? Perhaps for no reason you begin to doubt the
goodness of others. Or maybe you're suddenly overwhelmed by
a sense of depression? Did you ever react to someone totally out
of character? Perhaps you ridiculed them or picked on them.
Later on, when you reflected about some of these incidents, you
probably felt terrible. Did you ever wonder why you did what
you did?

Certainly, there could be legitimate physiological and
physical reasons for all the above. Some can even be freely
chosen. But there can also be hidden spiritual influences at

work. The evil one revels in sneak attacks and in not playing by the rules. He'll gladly kick you when you're down. He'll exploit whatever weakness or predisposition to sin he recognizes in you, especially when you are seeking to do what is right and holy and true, for he find such things repugnant.

> It is characteristic of the evil spirit to harass with anxiety, afflict with sadness and raise obstacles backed by fallacious reasoning to disturb the soul. The enemy of human nature, roaming about, looks in turn at all our virtues, theological, cardinal and moral; and where he finds us weakest and most in need for our eternal salvation, there he attacks us and aims at taking us.
> Saint Ignatius of Loyola

> Everything honorable, everything holy, they [the demons] find repugnant.
> Pope Saint Leo the Great

Satan's harassments typically take the form of intimidation or retaliation. Intimidation is an attack that occurs just before you are about to serve the Lord in some capacity. The timing of these attacks is designed to instill in you a sense of fear or anxiety or to distract you with a sensual pleasure so as to prevent you from proceeding as planned. Retaliation is an attack that occurs just after you serve the Lord in some capacity. The timing of the attack is designed to discourage you from the continuance of your good work.

Often I am asked, "If I do this spiritual warfare stuff, won't it make Satan mad? Won't it open me up to further attacks?" Satan would certainly appreciate you thinking that; fear of him makes his job that much easier. Like any bully, Satan's means of maintaining his image is through intimidation. Your response of fear gives him the power and permission to continue.

Do you trust more in God's love or Satan's fear? If you trust more in Satan's fear, you trust more in Satan. Fear of Satan is faith in Satan. Trust in God instead. If God permits an increase of temptations and harassments, then who are you to say no? Satan is already causing as much harm as is permitted. More than that, every harm of Satan directed toward you can be used for the glory of God and the salvation of souls. In that light, Satan's temptations can be seen as an extension of God's mercy and His omnipotence. Even evil is used to bring about God's will if you cooperate with Him. Fear not; God is in control.

> If the devil could do everything he wanted, there would not remain a single living human being on the earth.
> Saint Augustine

> If this Lord is powerful as I see that He is and I know that He is and if the devils are His slaves, what evil can they do to me since I am a servant of this Lord and King? Why shouldn't I have the fortitude to engage in combat with all of Hell?
> Saint Teresa of Avila

> You must turn to God when you are assaulted by the enemy; you must hope in Him and expect everything that is good from Him. Don't voluntarily dwell on what the enemy presents to you.
> Saint Pio of Pietrelcina

As a spiritual warrior, expect to be subject to both intimidation and retaliation. Expect it, but don't fear it. Just before (intimidation) or just after (retaliation) you do a work for the Lord, you might notice an increase in the intensity and frequency of temptations. Satan is hoping to ensnare you in sin.

Much like your Guardian Angel can have a positive influence upon you, the fallen angels can have a negative influence. Whether these harassments are mental, emotional, physical, social or spiritual, they are equally real and equally able to get underneath your spiritual armor if you provide an opening.

Mentally

The evil one attempts to afflict you with the spirits of past sins, especially those of the flesh. Suddenly, you'll be assaulted with unpleasant memories, words or images from the past in an attempt to prove your present unworthiness. Spirits of games, mockery, confusion, guilt, shame and doubt are active here. He may even inspire those who "knew you when" to remind of your past sin and make claims of hypocrisy against you.

Equally, he'll try and cause an internal dissonance regarding your prior bad acts and your present desire to serve the Lord, convincing you that somehow they are incompatible. He'll try to make you doubt the reality of God's mercy and the forgiveness of your sins, especially as you, by God's grace, increase in sanctity.

> Have courage, then, and conquer by your generosity the shame that the devil magnifies so much in your mind.
> Saint Alphonsus Liguori

> Calm the tormenting anxieties of your heart, and banish from your imagination all those distressing thoughts and sentiments which are all suggested by Satan in order to make you act badly.
> Saint Pio of Pietrelcina

> As soon as worldly people see that you wish to follow a devout life they aim a thousand darts of mockery and even detraction at you. The most malicious of them will slander your conversion as hypocrisy, bigotry, and trickery. They will say that the world has turned against you and being rebuffed by it you have turned to God. Your friends will raise a host of objections which they consider very prudent and charitable. They will tell you that you will become depressed, lose your reputation in the world, be unbearable, and grow old before your time, and that your affairs at home will suffer. You must live in the world like one in the world. They will say that you can save your soul without going to such extremes, and a thousand similar trivialities.
> Saint Francis de Sales

Emotionally

The evil spirit might attempt to afflict you with spirits of agitation or aggravation. He will either try to excite, exaggerate or deaden your emotions. All at once you find yourself irritable and angry for seemingly no reason. Or you may find yourself flat and devoid of feeling. Spirits of pride, false humility, anger, envy and overwhelm are active here.

Spirits of hypercriticism or hypersensitivity may attack you negatively impacting your relationships with others. He'll play with your emotions and push your buttons to the point of distress and distraction, agitation or apathy. He'll use either end of the spectrum to try and lure you into the sins of despair or presumption. Mired in either, he can lay a trap for your soul.

> Sometimes the devil inspires souls with an inordinate zeal for a certain virtue or some special pious exercise, so that they will be motivated by their passion to practice it more and more. This temptation is more to pride rather than virtue. Sometimes, on the other hand, the devil coaches souls to do less than they can really do. This temptation is more to false humility. In both cases, the devil's goal is to make the soul discouraged when the virtue is found to be unattainable; and to be wearied and disgusted if his efforts are below his abilities. The soul ends up neglecting everything. It is necessary to overcome the one snare as the other.
> Saint Catherine of Bologna

> Jesus' yoke is easy and His burden light, so we should not allow the enemy to creep into our hearts and rob us of this peace. The devil who is well aware of this makes every effort to have us lose our peace. We should be on the alert for every slightest sign of agitation.
> Saint Pio of Pietrelcina

Physically

You may notice an unusual sense of weariness or lethargy. This may be the result of a draining spirit or a spirit of fatigue attacking you. You may also notice other manifestations such as nausea, headaches and other unexplained aches and pains. Here the spirits of mockery, infirmity, depression, fatigue, overwhelm and pain are active.

Evil spirits can mimic symptoms of disease and cause actual pain. They can even imitate symptoms of a disease or disorder that has been cured in an attempt to bring you to question and doubt your faith and hope in the Lord. The pain may be fleeting or long lasting, intense or dull, internal or external. Rarely, but it can happen, you may even feel an actual physical presence oppressing you. Whether it is experienced as heaviness on the chest or throat, the smell of smoke, an overwhelming stench or some other manifestation, evil spirits can cause physical sensations.

> Let us be clear about this; the fiend must be taken into account. Anyone beginning this work of contemplation is liable to feel, smell, taste or hear some surprising effects concocted by this enemy in one or another of his senses. So do not be surprised if it happens.
> Anonymous, *The Cloud of Unknowing*

> It is possible that in certain cases the evil spirit goes so far as to exercise his influence not only on material things, but even on man's body.
> Pope John Paul II

Socially
The evil spirits might inspire others to petty attacks against your name, your work or your ministry. The evil spirits will even use those closest to you to do their bidding, so as to add salt to the wound. Spirits of division, retaliation, jealousy, suspicion, mockery, lies and judgment are active here. He revels in dividing marriages, destroying friendships and disrupting work environments.

Anything or anybody that he can use to disturb your peace, he will use. Often, those used did not consent to be Satan's mouthpiece, nor were they necessarily aware of the implications of the words or actions. They unwittingly became Satan's cohorts. Even knowing this, the sting is no less painful. Let humility be your response to any and all provocations and the sting of the words spoken will be minimal.

> The demons either tempt us themselves or incite against us people who have no fear of God. They tempt us themselves when we go into seclusion from men, as the Lord was tempted in the wilderness. They tempt through people when we have dealings with them, again as they tempted the Lord through the Pharisees.

But if we keep our eyes fixed on our example, that is, the Lord, we shall repulse them alike in each case.
Saint Maximus the Confessor

Has someone vilified you? Do not hate him; hate the vilification and the demon which induced him to utter it. If you hate the vilifier, you have hated a man and so broken the commandment. What he has done in word you do in action. To keep the commandment, show the qualities of love and help him in any way you can, so that you may deliver him from evil.
Saint Maximus the Confessor

Let all act as they like; you are to act as I want you to. If someone causes you trouble, think what good you can do for the person who caused you to suffer. Do not pour out your feelings. Be silent when you are rebuked.
Our Lord to Saint Faustina Kowalska

Spiritually

A decreased desire to pray often goes hand-in-hand with an increase in mental fatigue, emotional anguish or physical lethargy. In such a state confusion or arrogance about spiritual truths can easily lead to doubt and despair. This is tied to spirits of disobedience, pride and false religion. These spirits, three of Satan's favorites, are strong in their desire to undermine your very foundation of faith. If they can interrupt your desire to pray, they can interrupt your life of grace. This is Satan's goal, to cause you to commit spiritual suicide. As prayer is vital to a healthy relationship with God and is the antidote to the poisonous attacks of the evil one, any attack on your desire to pray is a definite cause for concern. Soldiering on in the name of the Lord is the best advice.

Empty out all poisons from your hearts by calling on the name of the savior.
Saint Augustine

If you encounter different kinds of struggles in your prayer, or if you experience confusing darkness of mind (this is the devil making the soul feel that her prayer is

not pleasing to God) you ought, nevertheless, never give up on account of struggles and darkness, but rather to stand firm with courage and perseverance, remembering that the devil does this to draw you away from your mother, prayer.
Saint Catherine of Siena

The more you are tempted the more you must persevere in prayer.
Blessed Angela of Foligno

The fiend selects for his most furious attacks the time when we feel most unable to pray.
Saint Nilus Sorsky

These are just a small sampling of spirits that are out there seeking to cause you harm. Despite that, there is nothing to fear. Trust in the Lord and His mercy. Give Him praise even in these circumstances of temptation and harassment. Be humble. Beg God's grace upon the situation. Pray for your enemies. Resolve to let nothing disturb your peace. When you feel like Satan is pushing you to the limit trust in Jesus with all of your heart, mind and strength.

If God is for us, who is against us?
Romans 8:31b

You say you are anxious about the future, but don't you know that the Lord is with you always and that our enemy has no power over one who has resolved to belong entirely to Jesus?
Saint Pio of Pietrelcina

Do not worry about me; I am in God's hands. I want to assure you that I feel His help at every step. Despite the present situation, I am happy and completely at peace. At every step I feel the power of God. Wherever I am, whatever happens to me I am in the hands of Divine Providence which watches over nations and over every individual.
Blessed Joseph Kowalski

As Satan is a coward, his acts of retaliation are often cowardly. He attacks you, or rather the image of God in you, because he knows he cannot directly hurt God. He attacks the image of God in you because of your desire to know, love and serve God. Even more cowardly, rather than retaliate against you directly, he'll often retaliate against those whom you love and are, perhaps, more vulnerable. Whether his acts of revenge target a spouse, a child, the family pet, an elderly parent, an unsuspecting friend, etc., his goal is the same, to prevent you from continuing in God's work and His grace. Be not afraid; be not surprised. Expect the evil one to do what he does, but do not fear it.

> Expected darts wound us less severely.
> Saint Thomas Aquinas

> Show us, then, O our good master, some way in which we may live through this most dangerous warfare without frequent surprise.
> Saint Teresa of Avila

In many ways, harassment (and temptation) from the evil one are a badge of honor, a back-handed compliment. The more temptation and harassment you face from him, the more you know you are doing God's will. Satan doesn't need to bother with those who are lukewarm; he already has them under his sway. The presence of temptation and harassment in your life is a sign of closeness to God and the means by which He can mold you to fit His most perfect will. Keep in mind, there is nothing Satan can do that God cannot use for His own glory. Temptation and harassments can even serve to bring about humility, the hallmark of every saint. By God's grace (and Satan's consternation) God doesn't allow Satan to act upon you without the seed of a greater good also present. Cooperate with God's grace and Satan's efforts will draw you closer to God.

> The devil, in spite of himself, becomes, as it were, an instrument and coefficient of holiness.
> Saint John Chrysostom

Bear in mind that the more the enemy assaults you, the

closer God is to your soul. Think about, and penetrate this great and comforting truth.
Saint Pio of Pietrelcina

We always find that those who walked closest to Christ were those who had to bear the greatest trials.
Saint Teresa of Avila

God did not inspire your enemy with the will to harm you, but He gave him the power to do so.
Saint Claude de la Colombiere

If God causes you to suffer much, it is a sign that He has great designs for you, and that He certainly intends to make you a saint. And if you wish to become a great saint, entreat Him yourself to give you much opportunity for suffering; for there is no wood better to kindle the fire of holy love than the wood of the cross.
Saint Ignatius of Loyola

Chapter 5
DID IT

✚

...so that we would not be circumvented by Satan. For
we are not ignorant of his intentions.
2 Corinthians 2:11

To repeat, spiritual warfare really is this: is Satan
going to kill you or are you willing to die to self? Will you
surrender your life to the will of the Father or will you die
clinging to the will of the evil one. Will you, with intention and
purpose, die for the Lord or apart from Him?

Christ was crucified between two men, one who died
with the name of Jesus on his lips and one who didn't. One
"stole Heaven" because he acknowledged Jesus as God; one
refused. Though both were brought to the cross because of their
sins only one gave up his life for the Lord. One reached for
truth and life, the other clung to sin and death.

The Lord wants you to be an intentional soldier for His
Kingdom. To the degree that the self dies, the Lord can live and
reign in you. To the degree that you surrender your will, the
Lord can render it pure in its intention and purpose. Thus your
battle becomes His battle.

Do everything for the love of God and His glory without
looking at the outcome of the undertaking. Work is
judged, not by its result, but by its intention.
Saint Pio of Pietrelcina

Satan's intentions, diametrically opposed to God's, are clear and simple. He wants to extinguish your life in God. Through temptation and harassment he seeks to destroy your life of grace by any means necessary. Though evil, he is efficient. He has a plan in place to best serve his evil plot. A spiritual warrior should know Satan's plan so as to best defend against it.

In terms of harassment, the acronym DID IT can help you understand what tools Satan uses to get at you. Each letter of the words DID IT stands for a series of words related to how Satan likes to harass. Often Satan will employ a few different attributes from a few different categories to maximize his malicious intent

DID IT **Division, Dissension and Discord**

The most common, and typically the first of Satan's attempts, is to create division, dissension and discord. Understated, not obnoxious, is Satan's manner here. He plays to the ego, hoping it will turn a spark into a flame. He is like an opportunistic arsonist. When the fields are overgrown and dry, he strikes. He likes to start a couple of different fires at once to compound the effect.

Division is the devil's calling card and often his initial tactic. "Divide and conquer" is a phrase on the lips of every demon. Satan attempts to create division inside yourself, between you and others and between you and God. If he can create even a tiny division, he can later rip it open with one of his many crowbars, like guilt, shame or humiliation. Division is different than a separation or cleaving or pruning done by God for your own good. Division in this sense seeks to divide what is good and holy and true: the Church, marriages, families, friendships, etc.

Dissension is one of Satan's favorite games because it flows from his sin, pride. Dissension's goal is to weaken and destroy proper order. By fanning the flames of dissent, Satan can topple the strongest organizations and families quickly. Appealing to people's baser instincts, he whispers words of rebellion, false logic and inflammatory lies about others in your ears. Just enough truth is contained in the whispers to make them sound plausible. He is a master at utilizing fears, worries and anxieties as leverage.

Discord is lack of harmony, a sense of being off-balance with oneself and others. More subtle than division or dissension, it often shows itself as an uncomfortable or uncertain feeling about a spiritual good or a spiritually good relationship, for seemingly no reason. You may feel a certain agitation or anxiety, especially toward someone or something good, which disturbs your soul. When there is no legitimate basis for feeling negative toward someone or something good, don't deny that Satan might just be involved. In fact, if discord occurs without any obvious factors, especially while you are in a state of grace, it is likely from the evil one.

> How unhappy we are, my children, thus to be the sport of demons? They do whatever they please with us; they suggest to us evil-speaking, calumny, hatred, vengeance: they even drive us so far as to put our neighbor to death.
> Saint John Vianney

> In the face of such strong attacks by the enemies of the Church of God, are we to remain inactive? Is that all we can do — complain and cry? No! Every one of us has a holy obligation to build a trench and personally hurl back the assaults of the enemy.
> Saint Maximilian Kolbe

DID IT Instigate, Inflame and Intoxicate

Another level of Satan's attacks is to instigate, inflame and intoxicate. Here Satan adds fuel to the fire, the stoking of your emotions, to ensure that the fire has abundant fuel to burn well.

Instigation is a critical tool in Satan's arsenal. Satan is the accuser; he is a liar and a murderer. He loves to whisper in people's ears. It is what he did in his first encounter with humans, Adam and Eve in the Garden of Eden. He loves to shade the truth in such a way as to start trouble where previously there was none. You can almost see him slithering from one person to the next, egging them on to increased levels of anger, hatred and violence. His forked tongue flickers with delight as his half-truths gain traction among the people of God.

Inflammation of your emotions is Satan's next step. Once he instigates he tries to arouse you to evil action. Feelings of pride, anger, envy and lust are easily manipulated by his seductive words and his subtle lies. Thoughts of rage and revenge pollute the soul. This is a dangerous time as you're heading close to the point of no return, the point at which the decision making process is hijacked by your emotions. Once the emotions take control of the will, the rational part of the soul yields to the animal part and inflamed emotion takes the lead. Though still culpable for your actions, there is little chance for resistance. That is why it is essential to deny Satan even the smallest of entry points.

Intoxication of the will leaves you with little or no restraint. If he can arouse you to the point of intoxication, most of his work is done. It may be a continuation of the inflaming process where the emotions take full control of the will or it may be a separate process altogether. Much like consuming too much alcohol in too short of a time leads to inebriation and a loss of control, emotional intoxication works the same way. Your emotions take over, courtesy of Satan's wiles and you're no longer in control of your ability to assent or decline. Highly inflamed passions do not make prudent decisions.

Do you really know the living Jesus, not from books but from being with Him in your heart? Have you heard the loving words He speaks to you? The devil may try to use the hurts of life, and sometimes our own mistakes to make you feel it is impossible that Jesus really loves you, is really cleaving to you. This is a danger for all of us. And so sad, because it is completely the opposite of what Jesus is really wanting, waiting to tell you. Not only that He loves you, but even more, He longs for you.
Blessed Teresa of Calcutta

Close your ears to the whisperings of Hell and bravely oppose its onslaughts.
Saint Clare of Assisi

DID IT Doubt, Discouragement and Despair
The next level of Satan's plan is to ratchet up the level of doubt, discouragement and despair. He started the fire, but

he wants you to take the blame for it. He started the fire, which at this point is still containable, yet he wants you to think that any effort to control and extinguish it would be futile.

Doubt whispered in your ear is one of Satan's favorite means of attack. It is a simple, yet effective means of achieving his goal of drawing souls away from God and into his web of suspicion and uncertainty. Questions run through your mind, your imagination takes off and suddenly you ascribe guilt to the innocent and fault to the blameless. Doubt is insidious in that it is not an overt attack; it is subtle toxin. Its poison is low acting, but still deadly. Doubt is an attack on the virtue of faith; it is what gripped the apostle Thomas.

Discouragement is another weapon in Satan's arsenal. Etymologically, it is a "lack of" or "away" from the "heart." Essentially, it is a lack of faith and hope. It usually involves judgment and the shifting of blame to others. Sins of vanity or pride can easily appear alongside discouragement, as can feelings of unworthiness and futility. A lack of progress in the spiritual life is common. Discouragement is an attack on the virtues of faith and hope; it is what gripped the apostle Peter.

Despair is giving in and giving up. It is Satan distorting and manipulating your reality toward achieving his goal. It is the rope with the noose on the end of it that Satan throws to those in need. Despair is a sin against the Holy Spirit, not trusting in God's infinite supply of mercy. It is a dangerous place to be; it's like being high up on a cliff with a strong wind and a weak stomach. Unchecked, despair can lead to depression and death. Despair is an attack on the virtues of faith, hope and love; it is what gripped the apostle Judas.

> Do not listen or pay any attention to what the enemy suggests to you, telling you that God has rejected you, or that because of some hidden failure, God is punishing you and wants to chastise you until you eliminate those things from your soul. This is by no means true.
> Saint Pio of Pietrelcina

> Just as the Lord is concerned about our salvation, so does the devil, the slayer of men, concern himself about bringing the soul of man to despair. Judas the betrayer

was faint-hearted and inexperienced in struggle, which is why the devil, seeing him in a state of despair, attacked and persuaded him to hang himself. Peter, the formidable rock, falling into great sin and experienced in struggle, did not despair and did not lose the presence of the spirit, rather he shed bitter tears from a warm heart and, seeing that, the devil fled from him as though burned by fire.
Saint Seraphim of Sarov

DID IT Ignorance, Indifference, Isolation

To maximize his efforts, Satan tries to inspire feelings of ignorance, indifference and isolation. He continues his assault against the senses, trying his best to dull them into submission, and you, into death. He wants you to do nothing while the flames are burning all around you.

Ignorance is one of Satan's preferred weapons for two reasons. In order for it to be effective, he doesn't have to get you to do anything, just have you remain as you are. Secondly, a lack of knowledge of God can keep you away from doing His work in your life, which is one of the primary goals of Satan's attacks. By your ignorance, you are doing Satan's work for him. If he can simply get you to grow no more in wisdom, understanding and knowledge of your faith he has claimed a small but important victory. The good side to this weapon is that it is easily repelled through the growing in knowledge and use of the gifts of the Holy Spirit received at baptism.

(The Church teaches of invincible ignorance which is distinct from the ignorance spoken of here. Invincible ignorance is when you aren't even aware that you don't know something. True invincible ignorance is not culpable, nor is it a tool of the devil.)

Indifference is related to ignorance in that it tends toward apathy, not action. It is different in that very often those who are indifferent are not ignorant about their faith, they are apathetic. Indifference kills inspiration; it stifles spiritual growth and it poisons potential. The argument could be made that if you truly knew your faith you couldn't help but be inspired and grow to God's full potential for you. That is why indifference is so deadly. When you allow indifference to reign in your life, intentionally or otherwise, Satan is enthroned as king, at least temporarily.

Isolation is another leverage point of Satan. If he was unable to ensnare you previously, he will do his best to isolate you from community, either physically, emotionally or spiritually. As humanity is made for community, isolation is an abnormal condition. Solitude, a necessary pillar of the spiritual life, is good for the soul. Isolation, Satan's mockery of solitude, weakens the faculties of the soul. By isolating you and then surrounding you with evil, he hopes you begin to doubt your sanity and your faith. If he can get you to think you're alone in your efforts to resist him, he can often get you to give up on or at least compromise your commitment to God and His church.

> These three giants of the evil one, who seem to be strong, are ignorance, forgetfulness and indifference.
> Saint Mark the Ascetic

> The evil spirits, because of their pride, anger and envy will attempt to turn your gaze away from God through either temptations or harassment. They seek to surround you with their temptations and harassments so that every thought and action you engage in might be in opposition to what the Lord desires for you.
> Saint Pio of Pietrelcina

DID IT Turmoil, Terror, Torment

The least frequent, and typically the last resort of Satan's attempt at harassment, is to create turmoil, terror and torment, to set you aflame. All three represent a new level of active animosity on Satan's part, but equally they typically represent a new level of intimacy with God, hence the attacks. If God permits you the burden, He will provide you the grace to overcome or endure it.

Turmoil can be internal or external. It can manifest as illness ranging from headaches, backaches, breathing problems, etc. It can also manifest as feelings of anxiety, stress, overwhelm, etc. Externally, Satan can create turmoil at home, at work or at play. Satan will often enlist others to help him carry out his plan. Some do so willingly. More often than not, people are deceived into doing Satan's dirty work for him. He often uses those closest to you, family, friends, spouses and children to maximize the impact of his poisonous barbs. Perhaps he "inspires" a spouse to speak a mean spirited word or a colleague at work to share a private, unflattering comment you made about the boss. Be on guard, especially when you are preparing to do a mighty work for Him. And don't ever take it personally. Remain humble, trust in God, forgive those who were used.

Terror is an attempt to incite you to fear and panic. It is also a sign of Satan's frustration and futility. The terror does temporarily frighten, but it is fleeting and easily overcome. Whether it occurs in the form of a nightmare or a night terror or aural harassments, such as noises in the dark, understand it is Satan's pathetic attempt to scare you away from God. (Imagine the humiliation Satan must feel in such an advanced creature having to resort to such infantile scare tactics.) A quick way to end the fear is to bring the Blessed Mother to mind through prayer. Satan is cowardly around Mary and those who are devoted to her. He fears her.

Torment is the final category. It is the rarest form of harassment. Only a privileged few ever get to experience the pain and suffering that Satan is permitted to inflict. It is permitted by God for the purposes of His glory and the salvation of souls. It may be physical, mental or emotional, direct or indirect, temporary or ongoing. It may even seem like defeat is imminent or inevitable. The truth is that Satan is nearer defeat the more he attacks. In carrying out these torments, he has become, in effect, a spiritual bully. Much like an earthly bully, his need to resort to such measures speaks far more to his frustration and fear than to any position or power. The saints knew this and responded accordingly.

> If you are harassed and afflicted with every kind of privation, temptation, and trials by the devil and his followers, raise your eyes on high, redouble your courage. The Lord is with you and there is no reason to fear.
> Saint Pio of Pietrelcina

> Now the will of God manifests itself by the events He ordains or permits; let us adore His designs and submit to them with love, persuaded that all will be for our

greater good.
Saint Therese Couderc

Saint Catherine of Siena was both terrified and tormented. As a holy one of God, her humility was a source of frustration for the demons. Her humble submission to God caused the demons more suffering than they caused her.

> And then after a little the terror of the demons began so that I seemed to be stupefied. They were mad with rage, as though I, a worm, had been the cause of their having had the Holy Church which they were holding so long, snatched from their hands. And so great were both the terror and the physical pain that I wanted to fly from the study into the chapel.
> Saint Catherine of Siena

Saint John Vianney had numerous encounters with Satan, or "Grappin," as he nicknamed him. Satan was permitted to physically beat and torture the Cure of Ars. Saint John Vianney gladly endured the attacks for he knew that the next day's "catch," the souls who would show up at confession, would be great.

> At first I used to be afraid, I did not know what it was all about, but now I am happy. It is a good sign, the next day the catch is always good.
> Saint John Vianney

Saint Teresa of Avila experienced visions of Satan designed to terrify her. God did not permit Satan to physically harm her, but he permitted Satan to attack her spiritually. By God's grace, and through prayer, the great saint of Avila was able to remain at peace despite the devil's best efforts.

> I feared them so little, that the terrors, which until now oppressed me, quitted me altogether; and though I saw them occasionally, I shall speak of this by and by, I was never again afraid of them. On the contrary, they seemed to be afraid of me. I found myself endowed with a certain authority over them, given me by the Lord of

all, so that I cared no more for them than for flies.
Saint Teresa of Avila

Satan possessed a particularly personal and intense animus toward Saint Faustina Kowalska because of her love for Jesus and her zeal for souls. As Jesus' "Secretary of Mercy" she infuriated Satan with every soul she reclaimed for His kingdom by her works of prayer, fasting and almsgiving.

> At about eleven o'clock Satan shook my bed. I awoke instantly, and I started to pray peacefully to my guardian angel.
> Saint Faustina Kowalska

Saint Pio of Pietrelcina was violently assaulted by the evil one. Often, he would be beaten bloody from evening to early morn, being able to sleep for just a few minutes before he was to awake. By God's grace, he was beaten and bloodied, but never defeated.

> That wicked thing beat me continuously from about ten o'clock, when I went to bed, until five o'clock in the morning. I thought it was going to be the last night of my life.
> Saint Pio of Pietrelcina

Saint Gemma Galgani was assaulted by Satan physically and aurally. Through it all she kept her faith, never giving in to fear or despair. Her sense of "holy indifference" in the face of the demon's assaults bears witness to her love of God.

> Once more I have passed a bad night. The demon came before me as a giant of great height and kept saying to me "For you there is no more hope of salvation. You are in my hands!" I replied that God is merciful and therefore I fear nothing. Then, giving me a hard blow on the head in a rage he said "accursed be you!" He began again to strike me with a knotted rope, and wanted me to listen to him while he suggested wickedness. I said no, and he struck me even harder,

knocking my head violently against the ground.
Saint Gemma Galgani

Though terrifying, these encounters are rare and permitted by God for His greater good. So, do not fear.

There is an immense number of ways that Satan can harass you. These are some of the more common ones; the list is far from exhaustive. Know that anything that God permits, He can redeem. The very acts of harassment that seem to weaken you, God can use to strengthen you - if you unite your soul with His. Any act of harassment that God permits Satan to engage in can be used to bring about God's plan in your life and the lives of others.

God suffers the demon to rage against you that you may learn by trial the force of your strength
Saint John Chrysostom

The soul that is united with God is feared by the devil as the one who is where God Himself is.
Saint John of the Cross

They seem to me such cowards, as soon as they see that anyone despises them they have no strength left. They are enemies who can make a direct attack only upon those whom they see as giving in to them, or on servants of God whom, for their greater good God allows them to be tormented.
Saint Teresa of Avila

The more doors and windows you leave open the more access Satan has to tempt and harass you. The more fear, pain, wounds, frustration, envy, shame and anger you cling to, the more vulnerable you become. The more time you absent yourself of God's grace, the more of a claim Satan has on you. The more time you spend away from prayer and the sacraments, the harder it becomes to remain strong. The more you run to Jesus and cling to Him, the more you will be covered in His grace.

At each new occasion of combat, when my enemies provoke me, I conduct myself bravely. I turn my back on my adversaries without once looking them in the face and I run to my Jesus.
Saint Therese of Lisieux

Now, if by the grace of God Satan can't tempt you or harass you into his snare, he usually will back down and not bother you for awhile. When he returns, and rest assured he will, maintain your faith and focus on God; for God's grace, which abounds in the presence of evil, is sufficient. Pray and have confidence in God who is greater than any demon.

After you have made a decision that is pleasing to God, the devil may try to make you have second thoughts. Intensify your prayer time, meditation, and good deeds. For if Satan's temptations merely cause you to increase your efforts to grow in holiness, he'll have an incentive to leave you alone.
Saint Ignatius of Loyola

There is no tribulation or temptation whose limits God has not appointed as to serve not for our destruction but for our salvation.
Saint Pio of Pietrelcina

Believers know that the presence of evil is always accompanied by the presence of good, by grace. Where evil grows, there the hope for good also grows. In the love that pours forth from the heart of Christ, we find hope for the future of the world.
Pope John Paul II

In my opinion there is hardly anything else that the enemy of our soul dreads more than confidence, humble confidence in God. Confidence in God is the very soul of prayer.
Servant of God Solanus Casey

My weapons are prayer and sacrifice.
Saint Bernadette Soubirous

Chapter 6
Woundedness & Suffering

Be sober and vigilant. For your adversary, the devil, is like a roaring lion, traveling around and seeking those whom he might devour. Resist him by being strong in faith, being aware that the same passions afflict those who are your brothers in the world. But the God of all grace, who has called us to his eternal glory in Christ Jesus, will himself perfect, confirm, and establish us, after a brief time of suffering.
1 Peter 5:8-10

"To suffer and to endure," as Pope Leo XIII said in his encyclical, *Rerum Novarum*, "is the lot of humanity." Suffering is here to stay, and you as a spiritual warrior are not exempted. Be assured if you are a visible, vital Christian, you will suffer while on earth. Satan can cause you earthly suffering; but he cannot cause you eternal harm. God's grace is sufficient for you to endure and triumph over any suffering that He chooses to allow. As a spiritual warrior, you are God's soldier. As part of God's permissive will, Satan will test for weakness in your resolve by sneak attacks and quick strikes.

Satan will exploit whatever weaknesses he perceives, especially any woundedness and suffering. Though these attacks on woundedness and suffering can be classified as either a temptation or harassment, they warrant their own chapter. Woundedness and suffering is the most common entry point for Satan. In many cases, Satan has no need to tempt you directly to be bad, bored, busy or boastful if he can manipulate your woundedness or suffering to do the job for him. He desires to open your wounds and cause a severe bodily infection so that you'll plunge head first toward a life of despair or decadence.

> The strategy of our adversary can be compared to the tactics of a commander intent upon seizing and plundering a position he desires. The leader of an army will encamp, explore the fortifications and defenses of the fortress, and attack at the weakest point.
> Saint Ignatius of Loyola

The despair or decadence that Satan prompts you to engage in, through the exploitation of your woundedness and suffering, has its roots in the sin of Adam and Eve. Original sin creates an opening for your woundedness and suffering to be used against you.

> 405. Baptism, by imparting the life of Christ's grace, erases original sin and turns a man back towards God, but the consequences for nature, weakened and inclined to evil, persist in man and summon him to spiritual battle.
> *Catechism of the Catholic Church*

> 407. By our first parents' sin, the devil has acquired a certain domination over man, even though man remains free. Original sin entails "captivity under the power of him who thenceforth had the power of death, that is, the devil." Ignorance of the fact that man has a wounded nature inclined to evil gives rise to serious errors in the areas of education, politics, social action and morals.
> *Catechism of the Catholic Church*

Woundedness

> He heals the contrite of heart, and he binds up their sorrows.
> Psalm 147:3

For I will close up your scar, and I will heal you of your wounds, says the Lord.
Jeremiah 30:17a

Each of us is wounded in one way or another; the reality of original sin exacts a toll. Whether as a result of personal sin, trauma, divorce, death or abandonment, "walking wounded" is an apt description of humanity. Whether it is expressed as a fear, or an ongoing struggle, or an addiction, or a virtue taken to extremes, we are all subject to woundedness. As a spiritual warrior you are sometimes more vulnerable to its effects because of your vocation. The need for healing of self is so important if you wish to be able to minister to others.

Woundedness arises from either one of two sources, a lack of love or a perceived lack of love. And in most cases, the source is a perceived lack of love. Think about that for a moment. The fears, anxieties and frustrations, the compulsions, obsessions and addictions you experience almost always originate in a perceived lack of love. That is, you perceive that you are not loved, either by God, by your parents, your spouse, your friends, etc., regardless of whether or not you are actually loved. You blot out or ignore or distort the expressions of love you actually did receive and cling to the distorted notion that you are not loved. In this case, your perception becomes your reality.

As God is love (cf. 1 John 4:16), when you experience a lack of love, you experience a lack of God. This lack of God you experience is perceived, not actual. If there were an actual lack of God in your life, that is, if God did not exert His life-force upon you, you would cease to exist. There would be no experiencing a true absence of God, for it is His love that sustains you. (The "dark night" of the soul experienced by some saints is not in any way a lack of God. It is in fact an invitation to and a preparation for a higher union with God.)

Even the demons in Hell exist only because of God's life-force dwelling within them. This life-force is God's love. Though those in Hell, by their own volition, are eternally incapable of returning God's love, God still loves them.

This is the trick of the evil one, to make you think that you are lacking in love and that the solution to your woundedness can be found apart from God. The truth is in the moment you experience the Beatific Vision, all woundedness ceases to exist. It ceases because then you will "know" in a way you could never know now that God is love and that you always were, always are and always will be loved by God.

In this perceived experience of a lack of God, you attempt to create a god so you can once again perceive love. Though the god you create is false, and the love you perceive is phony, you will attempt to promote and defend this god. G.K. Chesterton put it this way, "Every man who knocks on the door of a brothel is looking for God." (It is important to note that your attempt to fill the void by creating a different god does not in fact create one. It does, however, open the door to Satan to exploit you in your pain and to cause you further separation from the one, true God.) The world and the flesh, aided and abetted by Satan, deceive you into "creating" a false and finite god to worship. The god that is worshipped is often money, sex and power — all in a vain attempt to fill the emptiness felt inside. Satan wants to offer his "Counsels of Perdition" to counter Christ's "Counsels of Perfection."

Satan will provide plenty of evidence that the pursuit of money, sex and power is a way for you to experience the love you crave. He'll lure you to the bait, reward you and encourage you to redouble your efforts at creating a false sense of love. Like a drug pusher who offers free samples to get a person hooked, once Satan has you in his camp, he'll keep you dazed and confused so that you can't escape. Do not be fooled, the pleasure is fleshy, fleeting and, ultimately, false. No amount of finite can ever satisfy that which was created for the infinite.

> Nothing created has ever been able to fill the heart of man. God alone can fill it infinitely.
> Saint Thomas Aquinas

> Do not let the false delights of a deceptive world deceive you.
> Saint Clare of Assisi

> He [Satan] does not at once suggest to man something that has an appearance of evil, but something that has a semblance of good.
> Saint Thomas Aquinas

Counsels of Perdition

Money

For some, it is money-making that becomes the (perceived and mistaken) source of their redemption and salvation. "Look at me, I'm successful," or "I'm rich; therefore, I'm somebody," are expressions of this attitude that takes hold. The busyness and incessant need to control outcomes are a cover-up to the woundedness inside. Money, not grace, becomes the currency of record for their life. Money, not grace, becomes the measure of their vitality and worthiness. Yet, it is grace, not money, whose reward is eternal. Unlike money, you can take grace with you. As a spiritual warrior, money should not be your master. Wealth passes, life in Christ is eternal.

Spirits of arrogance, pride, anger, fear and insecurity are common here.

> But these things were not spoken indifferently or at random. For no one when asked whether he loves the devil, answers that he loves him, but rather that he hates him; but all generally proclaim that they love God. Therefore either he will hate the one, and love the other; or will hold to the one, and will despise the other.
> Saint Augustine

> Riches are foreign to us, because they are something beyond nature, they are not born with us, and they do not pass away with us. But Christ is ours, because He is the life of man.
> Saint Ambrose

Sex

Sins of a sexual nature are often an attempt to achieve love via the flesh. Immodesty and extremes in attire are another attention-getter. Sins of the flesh shout, "I need love," as assuredly as they shout, "Look at me." Control, especially for woman, and domination, especially for men, are the outward expressions of an inner woundedness as they are expressed through sexuality. Purity is sacrificed in the relentless, yet futile, pursuit of infinite love from a finite flesh. Satan's (and the world's and the flesh's) pull is especially strong here. Satan takes double delight in sins of the flesh, because of the personal sin and the corporal desecration that takes place. As a spiritual warrior, you need to ensure that your sexuality retains its purity and its sacred character, whatever your vocation may be. Do not lose your purity; do not lose your peace.

Spirits of control, domination, deception, lust, fear and insecurity are common here.

> Be extremely prompt in turning away from all that leads and lures to impurity, for this evil works insensibly and by small beginnings progresses to great mischief.
> Saint Francis de Sales

> As soon as you willfully allow a dialogue with temptation to begin, the soul is robbed of peace, just as consent to impurity destroys grace.
> Saint Josemaria Escriva

Power

"I'm special." "I'm powerful." "I'm in control." These are expressions of those who use power to cover-up their woundedness. A fixation on power and control shouts woundedness more clearly than it expresses any true authority. Virtues that tend toward excessive, habits that become compulsive and strengths that are exaggerated are often woundedness seeking love. As a spiritual warrior, especially if you are in the position of leadership, it is important to remain humble. Recognize that your power resides fully and only in Jesus Christ.

Spirits of control, domination, deception, fear and insecurity are common here.

> For the human mind is prone to pride even when not supported by power; how much more, then, does it exalt when it has that support.
> Pope Saint Gregory the Great

> Satan sees the strength and firmness of will of those who pay attention to spiritual life, and strives to conquer their minds by means of such curiosity, in

order to gain possession of their mind and will. For this purpose, he is wont to suggest to them thoughts that are lofty, subtle and wondrous, especially to those who are sharp-witted and quick to make lofty speculations. Attracted by the pleasure of possessing and examining such lofty thoughts, they forget to watch over their purity of heart and to pay attention to a humble opinion of themselves and to true self-mortification; and so they are enmeshed in the bonds of pride and conceit; they make an idol of their own mind and thus, little by little, without realizing it, they fall into the thought that they no longer need any advice or admonition from others, since they are accustomed in all cases to hasten to the idol of their own understanding and judgment.
Saint Nicodemos of the Holy Mountain

Temptations of money, sex and power are Satan's big three when it comes to exploiting woundedness. He offers to trade pleasure for pain in what initially seems like a good deal. The pleasure he offers is as injurious as it is immediate and intoxicating. This short-term pleasure offers short-term relief from reality, from the pain and heartache. It is these short-term pleasures that keep you coming back for more and turn temptations into strongholds. The initial seeking of love becomes a curiosity, then a habit, then an addiction.

The enemy had a grip on my will and so made a chain for me to hold me a prisoner. The consequence of a distorted will is passion. By servitude to passion, habit is formed, and habit to which there is no resistance becomes necessity.
Saint Augustine

Just as in addictions, the level of satisfaction derived from the short-term pleasures diminishes over time unless the dosage or frequency increases. As with addictions, the short-term pleasures lend themselves to other types of addictions such as alcohol, drugs and gambling. The desire to avoid pain is so strong that you seek extreme measures to avoid living in it and with it. Even suicide is an attempt to be rid of the pain of this life. Your woundedness is an easy target for the evil one's manipulation. He'll tempt you toward earthly security and satisfaction which, ultimately, is false and illusionary, a foundation of sand and not solid rock.

> He who builds only on visible and tangible things like success, career and money builds the house of his life on sand.
> Pope Benedict XVI

An antidote to the exploitation of your woundedness can be found by knowing what it is that Satan seeks to mock with his promotion of the big three temptations of money, sex and power. Satan, as he often does, takes what is holy and true and perverts it for his own end. The temptations of money, sex and power are a mockery and a perversion of the virtues of poverty, chastity and obedience. The Church has consistently spoken of poverty, chastity and obedience as an antidote to the vacant and vacuous temptations of the world, the flesh and the devil.

Poverty, chastity and obedience were practiced and preached by Jesus. They are proffered by the Church as means of pursuing and attaining Christian perfection. For all Christians, and especially those actively engaged in battle, they are an excellent source of spiritual strength and protection against Satan. They are not the empty honors or earthly trophies of money, sex and power. They are the tools God has given you to aid you on your journey toward your eternal reward.

> The best way to prepare for death is to spend every day of life as though it were the last. Think of the end of worldly honor, wealth and pleasure and ask yourself: And then? And then?
> Saint Philip Neri

The Counsels of Perdition is Satan's attempt to get you to replace God, the uncreated Creator, with a god of your own creation; money, sex or power, to trade the rewards and pleasure of Heaven for the pleasures of the world, the flesh and the devil, to trade life for death. The Counsels of Perdition will lead you straight to Hell.

Counsels of Perfection

Poverty

Actual material poverty is not, in and of itself, a moral good. It is only good to the degree it aids spiritual growth. For example, poverty can lead to detachment and trust in God's providence. The voluntary renouncing of temporal goods for the sake of God's Kingdom is virtuous and provides Satan little opportunity to use money or possessions as an inducement to evil. It is not necessary for you to rid yourself of every possession to be a faithful soldier of Christ, though as He said in the Gospels, it is the way of perfection to do so. It is only required that you rid yourself of the superfluous, not the essential.

When you give all you have to God, when you place all that you possess at God's service, then, and only then, will your possessions not weigh you down. This is true spiritual poverty, laying it all down, all you are and all you have, before the Lord.

> Every earthly possession is but a sort of garment for the body, and therefore he who hastens to contend with the devil should throw aside these garments lest he be borne down.
> Pope Saint Gregory the Great

Chastity

Chastity is a virtue that moderates sexual desire in both action and thought. It does so according to the dictates of faith and right reason and in accordance with one's state in life. Thus all soldiers of Christ, single, married or celibate are called to chastity, albeit with different understandings and expressions. Chastity for singles requires them to refrain from sexual relations until and unless they enter a sacramental marriage. Chastity for married couples requires that their sexual relations be holy, be exclusive to one another and open to life. Chastity for those who are ordained or those who are professed religious is normally concomitant with a call to celibacy.

The goal, regardless of vocation, is the same, to prevent the flesh from defiling or despoiling the soul. Fornication, adultery, contraception, homosexuality, masturbation, et al., are contrary to chastity. Lustful, licentiousness or lewd thoughts are also contrary to chastity and provide Satan with the cover necessary to ensnare you.

> Amongst other pious considerations, remember that our soul is the temple of God and, as such, we must keep it pure and spotless before God and his angels. Let us blush for having given access to the devil and his snares many times, with his enticements to the world, his pomp, his calling to the flesh, by not being able to keep our hearts pure and our bodies chaste; for having allowed our enemies to insinuate themselves into our hearts, thus desecrating the temple of God which we became through holy Baptism.
> Saint Pio of Pietrelcina

Obedience
The etymology of the word obedience connotes a twofold action, first to hear, then to respond. True obedience involves the submission of self, the subduing of pride, the leaving behind of attachments to this world, the willing suspension of ego. It implies an authority worthy of being obeyed and a subject humble enough to do so. Jesus Christ and His one, true Church properly and perfectly possess this authority. Faith in God and His Church is manifested and deepens through obedience.

Perfect obedience requires the submission of body, will and intellect to proper authority. All true soldiers of Christ are called to acknowledge and to humbly submit to this authority. Obedience is the anti-Satan.

> The devil knows well that on obedience the salvation of souls depends. That is why he tries so hard to prevent it.
> Saint Teresa of Avila

> Obedience is your greatest possible sacrifice.
> Saint John Bosco

> Submit to the yoke of holy, true obedience.
> Saint Catherine of Siena

There are two options to pursue in filling that God-shaped hole inside of you; Satan's options or God's options. Money, sex and power are the options the devil offers; poverty, chastity and obedience are the options God offers. While poverty, chastity and obedience will not necessarily heal the woundedness inside of you, they will give meaning and purpose to it. They will allow your woundedness to cry out to God, to give glory to Him and, by His grace, to help save souls. Money, sex and power, as a remedy to woundedness, are devoid of meaning and purpose and can only mask and, therefore, exacerbate the woundedness. Your heart will be restless until the God-shaped hole inside of you is filled with God, for God is love.

> You have made us for yourself, O Lord, and our hearts are restless until they rest in You.
> Saint Augustine

> Who except God can give you peace? Has the world ever been able to satisfy the heart?
> Saint Gerard Majella

> Our heart finds rest solely in God.
> Saint Francis de Sales

Suffering

> Since Christ has suffered in the flesh, you also should be armed with the same intention. For he who suffers in the flesh desists from sin, so that now he may live, for the remainder of his time in the flesh, not by the desires of men, but by the will of God.
> 1 Peter 4:1-2

When most people think of suffering, they tend to focus on the bodily aspect of suffering. From headaches to heart attacks, colds to cancer, eczema to emphysema, bodily suffering comes in many forms. Equally distressing are mental and emotional sufferings which can also take their toll on the body.

There is another suffering that goes deeper than bodily suffering, suffering of the soul. When you are misunderstood, rejected, ignored, isolated, persecuted, humiliated, forgotten, slandered, betrayed, denied or doubted, it wounds and pains the soul. It may also pain the body, but it is the soul that bears the brunt of the suffering. Suffering of the soul often remains undiagnosed or, at best, misdiagnosed.

> Loneliness and the feeling of being unwanted is the
> most terrible poverty.
> Blessed Teresa of Calcutta

Each type of suffering can be painful in its own way and each can be sanctifying. Suffering, as it is allowed by God, is a powerful opportunity to grow in sanctification. Ultimately, every action permitted by God is ordained for your sanctification. As a spiritual warrior, you must be attentive to all kinds of suffering and their effects on you. You must be ready and able to sanctify whatever suffering God permits you to experience.

All suffering has at least its remote origins in the sin of Adam. Suffering's more proximate causes are your own actions, placing yourself outside of God's mantle of protection or the actions of others who, perhaps, seek to impose their free will upon you. Suffering can also be the work of demons or God's pulling back of His mantle of protection. God may permit these suffering for obvious reasons such as punishment, discipline, or testing. Some not so obvious reasons why God may permit suffering include atonement for sins, appeasement of divine justice and for correction, purification or penance. Suffering, whatever its cause, should never be wasted; it should always be offered up.

> For evil remains bound to sin and death. Suffering
> cannot be divorced from the sin of the beginnings, from
> what Saint John calls "the sin of the world." At the
> basis of human suffering, there is a complex
> involvement with sin.
> Pope John Paul II

Satan will attempt to use your suffering as a means of leverage. He will attempt to use it to weaken your resolve, to turn you away from God and His grace and to turn you toward despair and death. You can overcome Satan's attempts by offering up and sanctify your woundedness and suffering. When you do so, you give Satan no chance to use it against you and you give God the chance to use it for His glory and your salvation. Though you may not understand God's reasons for allowing a particular suffering, you must trust that with His grace you can endure.

> Let me suffer or let me die.
> Saint Teresa of Avila

> Moreover, if the Christian know and keep fast under what condition and what law he has believed, he will be aware that he must suffer more than others in the world, since he must struggle more with the attacks of the devil.
> Saint Cyprian of Carthage

> You say that you are a sinner, then do not be amazed that you sin! How can one being sick not show signs of his illness! I would add how can your brother in Christ who is also sick not show signs of his illness. This is where the Church tells us "bear one another's burdens for the sake of Christ." It tells us this in order that we would not be perplexed at the fiery trial that comes upon us.
> Saint Cyril of Alexandria

At the bottom of every reason for woundedness and suffering, even beyond sin, is love. Love is the only answer to the question of woundedness and suffering. Divine love, which is often inscrutable but always perfect, comes to you through brokenness and suffering. The crucifixion is sufficient proof of that.

As God is love, you can come to know the truth of God through your woundedness and suffering. You don't come to know this truth hypothetically; you come to it by participating in the redemptive work of Christ Jesus. It is in carrying and embracing your cross and forgiving those who have hurt you that you come to know about woundedness and suffering and, therefore, love. It is in carrying and embracing your cross and forgiving those who have hurt you that you can overcome Satan's temptations and harassments. Love your God; love your neighbor. If you do so perfectly you will be able to suffer well, in imitation of Jesus on the cross.

> Love is the first ingredient in relief of suffering.
> Saint Pio of Pietrelcina

> The words of that prayer of Christ in Gethsemane prove the truth of love through the truth of suffering.
> Pope John Paul II

Woundedness and suffering not offered up are potential open doors for Satan. Don't allow him any source of leverage. Frequently avail yourself of the sacraments, especially the Sacrament of Penance. Give over all of your pain and suffering, all of your hurt and woundedness, all your anxieties and fears, all of your temptations and harassment to God. Surrender your will totally to God. Your fulfillment and happiness is in Him alone. Allow Satan's temptations and harassments to work for God's kingdom, for God's glory. Now is the time for the sanctification of your woundedness and suffering. Suffer well by suffering for Him, with Him and through Him.

> We can only go to Heaven through suffering, but it is not all that suffer who find salvation. It is only those who suffer readily for the love of Jesus Christ, who first suffered for us.
> Saint Vincent de Paul

> Christ does not force our will; He only takes what we give Him. But He does not give himself entirely until He sees that we yield ourselves entirely to Him.
> Saint Teresa of Avila

> No one is really happy because he has what he wants, but only if he has things he ought to want.
> Saint Augustine

Chapter 7
Body & Soul

✚

Abstain from every kind of evil. And may the God of peace himself sanctify you through all things, so that your whole spirit and soul and body may be preserved without blame unto the return of our Lord Jesus Christ.
1 Thessalonians 5:22-23

Concerning the rest, brothers, whatever is true, whatever is chaste, whatever is just, whatever is holy, whatever is worthy to be loved, whatever is of good repute, if there is any virtue, if there is any praiseworthy discipline: meditate on these.
Philippians 4:8

Therefore, let not sin reign in your mortal body, such that you would obey its desires. Nor should you offer the parts of your body as instruments of iniquity for sin. Instead, offer yourselves to God, as if you were living after death, and offer the parts of your body as instruments of justice for God.
Romans 6:12-13

Spiritual warfare involves the whole being, body and soul. The body, with its senses and passions, was made to work in harmony with the soul and its faculties of intellect, memory and will. The lingering effects of original sin, and the ongoing consequences of personal sin, create an unnatural state of disharmony between body and soul.

Satan will attempt to take advantage of this disorder and coerce you into giving up your free will. He will attempt to incline your senses, inflame your passions, ignite your imagination and incite your thoughts toward evil. Your will is the last line of defense. Your will, by God's grace, can remain inviolate. Resist the cunningness of the devil by training your will to recognize his handiwork and fortify it in the light of faith and prayer.

> Avoid the craftiness of the devil.
> Pope Saint Leo the Great

> "By the darts of the evil one," he means, both temptations, and vile desires; and "fiery," he says, for such is the character of these desires. Yet if faith can command the evil spirits, much more can it also the passions of the soul.
> Saint John Chrysostom

> For the devil, the light of faith is worse than darkness.
> Saint John of the Cross

Man is created by God, in His image and likeness. God created man as a rational creature with a free will. In doing so God conferred upon man dignity and freedom and has given to man the possibility to choose between good and evil. It is this God-given freedom that Satan tries to exploit.

> 13. Although he was made by God in a state of holiness, from the very onset of his history man abused his liberty, at the urging of the evil one.
> *Gaudium et Spes*

This abuse of liberty takes place through the misuse and exploitation of the senses, passions, intellect and will. Your senses are the means through which you interact and experience the world; the senses sense. Your passions react to what the senses sense. Your intellect processes what the senses sense and what the passions experience. Your will, with access

86

to all this input, chooses to act or to not act, accordingly. Each step of this process is subject to influence, either direct or indirect, by the evil one.

> On account of human nature, composed as it is by soul and body, the mind knows things naturally by grasping them through the five senses. It is the sense which feels and senses all manner of qualities. Truth then cannot be known by the senses, they only know what can be sensed; and the mind cannot know pleasures, it can only know what is true or false. The will knows good and evil by desiring it; but it is the intellect which knows it properly speaking by understanding it. Hence the senses do not know what is true or false, good or evil; they feel only what is painful or pleasurable.
> Saint Hilary of Poitiers

Senses

Your senses are the means by which you experience the world. The external senses react to stimuli on the outside; the internal senses react to stimuli on the inside. The senses are effectively morally neutral in their action. That does not mean that your senses are free to roam where they will. Satan will gladly place attractive sights and sounds within the range of your senses hoping he can coax the first domino to fall. Guard against those stimuli that could be called a near occasion of sin.

> The devil often purveys objects to the senses, affording to the sense of sight, images of saints and most beautiful lights, to the sense of smell, fragrant odors; and he puts sweetness in one's mouth, and delight in the sense of touch. He does all of this so by enticing persons through these sensory objects he may induce them into evils.
> Saint Teresa of Avila

> We must also struggle to protect our senses.
> Saint Nicodemos of the Holy Mountain

> Control your senses, guard your mouth, bridle your tongue, subjugate your heart, bear all provocations

with charity, and you shall perfectly fulfill the will of God.
Blessed Henry Suso

Passions

Your passions or emotions are often the expression of what is being sensed or your feelings. Your passions were made to be governed by your reason, not the other way around.

If not properly protected, your passions are subject to exploitation by Satan. With your consent, and only with your consent, do your emotions and feelings turn from virtue to vice. Without consent, the trial of the evil one can strengthen your virtue. You are not to slavishly serve your passions or else your passions will end up serving you over as a slave to the evil one.

> Remember it is not feeling which constitutes guilt but the consent to such feelings. Only the free will is capable of good or evil. But when the will sighs under the trial of the tempter and does not will what is presented to it, there is not only no fault but there is virtue.
> Saint Pio of Pietrelcina

> Alas, my dear brethren, the man who lives according to the direction of his passions and abandons the service of God is both unhappy and capable of so little.
> Saint John Vianney

> Save me, Lord, from my sins; free me from my evil inclinations and snatch me from the power of tyrants. Do not let me follow the bestial impulses of my passions, but defend the dignity and glory of my soul.
> Venerable Louis of Granada

Intellect

The intellect is comprised of what might be commonly called thought, reason and imagination. It relies upon and operates from the input of the senses and the passions. Ideally, the intellect works in concert with the will to arrive at morally correct decisions and actions.

The intellect cannot be directly penetrated by Satan. It

is subject, however, to indirect attacks. Satan will offer you sinister suggestions disguised as pleasurable propositions. He will attempt to stir up your imagination, pollute your thoughts and suborn your reason in an attempt to corrode your intellectual faculty. He will gladly play your emotions off of your intellect in order to bring about an illogical and falsely pleasurable conclusion.

> An evil thought defiles the soul when it is deliberate and consented to. Our Lord placed evil thoughts at the head of all crimes, because they are their principle and source.
> Saint John Baptist de la Salle

> The action of Satan consists primarily in tempting men to evil, by influencing their imaginations and higher faculties, to turn them away from the law of God.
> Pope John Paul II

> Turn your thoughts to some good, commendable activity. When such thoughts enter and find place in your heart they will drive away temptation and evil thoughts.
> Saint Francis de Sales

Memory

Your memory is a prime target for the evil one. It is the storage unit for the passions and intellect. To the degree that it is pure, the evil one is powerless to use your memories against you. To the degree that your memory is impure, Satan is able to use that as leverage. Whether it is an impure act stored in your memory, an unconfessed sin, a harboring of resentment, a hanging on to a hurt or a lack of forgiveness, Satan can make use of all of these to set in motion his plan.

If you find yourself feeling disturbed and you don't know why, check your thoughts. If you are feeling attached to old wounds or memories, especially sinful ones, check to see who is playing with your memory and imagination. If you frequently find yourself criticizing, complaining and judging, check to see who is goading you on. If you feel a darkness overshadow you from the inside out, check to see who is attempting to dim your interior lights. If you find your mind awash in a cacophony of sound, check and see who is cranking up the volume. Do not beat yourself up over past sins. Purge yourself of points of leverage through sacramental confession.

> If the memory is annihilated, the devil is powerless, and it liberates us from a lot of sorrow, affliction and sadness.
> Saint John of the Cross

> Must you continue to be your own cross? No matter which way God leads you, you change everything into bitterness by constantly brooding over everything. For the love of God, replace all this self-scrutiny with a pure and simple glance at God's goodness.
> Saint Jeanne de Chantal

> Do not scrutinize so closely whether you are doing much or little, ill or well, so long as what you do is not sinful, and that you are heartily seeking to do everything for God. Try as far as you can to do everything well, but when it is done, do not think about it; try rather to think of what is to be done next. Go on simply in the Lord's way, and do not torment yourself.
> Saint Francis de Sales

Will

The purpose of the will is to select the proper object of attention at any given moment. A pure will, one that has not been compromised, is inclined to act according to what is good, holy and true as opposed to what is bad, unholy and false. Properly speaking, the will can never choose what is "bad;" it can only choose what is "good." The problem is your perception and judgment of what is "good" and what is "bad" can differ according to the strength and vitality of your will.

Your will is strengthened by the avoidance of vice and progress in virtue. Your will is weakened by just the opposite. A weak-willed soldier is a compromised soldier, one who is apt to be wounded or captured by the enemy. You are to train your will to stay aligned with God's will.

A compromised or corrupted will ignores its God-given

inclination toward good and aligns itself with the pleasures of the world, the flesh and the devil. Satan cannot force the will, but he can attempt to incline the will by flaring up of the passions and the imagination. He will attempt to penetrate and corrupt your will any way he can. Since original sin still affects all of humanity, Satan is able to make considerable inroads here. He attempts to create a minefield of your mind, by sowing seeds of negativity, doubt, despair, isolation, etc.

> Disordered lust springs from a perverted will; when lust is pandered to, a habit is formed; when habit is not checked, it hardens into compulsion.
> Saint Augustine

> The prince of this world is determined to lay hold of me and to undermine my will which is intent on God.
> Saint Ignatius of Antioch

> If it were given to a man to see virtue's reward in the next world, he would occupy his intellect, memory and will in nothing but good works, careless of danger or fatigue.
> Saint Catherine of Genoa

Satan knows well the landscape of the body and soul. He also knows of concupiscence and its effect on the soul. He engages every level of the decision making process to try and pepper the landscape with destructive mines. He figures if he can lay enough mines he can paralyze your prayer life, cripple your conscience or destroy the life of grace in your soul.

Satan leverages concupiscence to exploit your senses to seek out whatever might be a precursor to sin. He then seeks to have your flesh and passions enflamed by what near occasion of sin your senses perceive. He'll next attempt to have your weakened flesh and your disordered passions coerce the intellect. His final blow is to have your intellect ignore right reason, override the will and consent to sin. It is then that the landscape of your body and soul has become a minefield.

> The first is sensual desire; the second, consent; the third, the action; the fourth, habit; the fifth, contempt.

Take care then to resist with all your strength the first movements of sensual desire lest they lure you to consent, and then the whole fabric of wickedness will vanish.
Saint Bernard of Clairvaux

"If only...," is one of Satan's favorite mines that he lays. If he can get you to trigger a couple of his "if only" mines, pretty soon the terrain of your mind is severely damaged. If only I were rich, if only I were pretty, if only I were thin, if only I were tall, if only I were... If only my husband was, if only my wife was, if only my parents were, if only my kids were, if only my friends were, if only God was, if only, if only, if only. With these two little words, Satan sows negative seeds which can blossom into flowers of destruction. The spirits of pride, envy, greed and despair are strong here. Satan also lays mines of anger, revenge, jealousy and lust. Mines of loneliness, isolation and unworthiness are favorites as well. Give no credence to these involuntary images; pay no heed to the whispers of the evil one.

Lord, may I think what you want me to think. May I desire what you want me to desire.
Saint Pedro Castroverde

Give not ear to what the devil whispers to you.
Saint Catherine of Siena

Know that none of this is from God. It is from the coward of cowards, the evil one. Tune him out and tune God in. Do not dwell on the negative. Do not listen to the lies. Do not be discouraged. Discipline your thoughts, your imagination and your will. Think of Him who created you. Think of Him who redeemed you. Think of Him who has desired your salvation from the beginning of time.

When you are exposed to any trial, be it physical or moral, bodily or spiritual, the best remedy is the thought of Him who is our life, and not to think of the one without joining to it the thought of the other.
Saint Pio of Pietrelcina

We may be sure that if our spirit is agitated, the devil's assaults will be more frequent and direct. As soon as we become discouraged, we must revive our faith and abandon ourselves in the arms of the Divine Father.
Saint Pio of Pietrelcina

In order to ward off Satan's attempts at polluting or capturing your soul, it is necessary to safeguard your senses, restrain your passions, guard your intellect and train your will. To do otherwise is to permit Satan to make use of your senses, passions, intellect and will to take control of you. Much like God has no hands but yours, neither do the demons. You must not risk becoming Satan's hands. You must not risk becoming a debtor to the world, the flesh or the devil. You must not risk becoming a trap to others. Become God's hands and proclaim His glorious victory.

Spiritual virtues require bodily virtues.
Saint Peter of Damaskos

When a soul has been taken, she becomes a snare to deceive others.
Saint Ephrem of Syria

In order that His victory might be more glorious, He willed to fight Satan in our weak flesh. It is as if an unarmed man, right hand bound, were to fight with his left hand alone against a powerful army; if he emerged victorious, his victory would be regarded as all the more glorious. So, Christ conquered Satan with the right hand of His divinity bound and using against him only the left hand of His weak humanity.
Saint Lawrence of Brindisi

Demons are not visible bodies, but we become their bodies when our souls accept dark thoughts from them. For, having accepted these thoughts, we accept the demons themselves and make them bodily manifest.
Saint Antony of the Desert

Hence carnal men cannot but abhor and detest the

truth made known by Christ and His apostles, passed down in the Catholic Church, since it is this very truth which dethrones the world, the flesh and the devil; and which restores sense to intellect, intellect to will, and will to God by virtue, faith and charity.
Saint Hilary of Poitiers

The first step to be taken by one who wishes to follow Christ is, according to Our Lord's own words, that of renouncing himself - that is, his own senses, his own passions, his own will, his own judgment, and all the movements of nature, making to God a sacrifice of all these things, and of all their acts, which are surely sacrifices very acceptable to the Lord. And we must never grow weary of this; for if anyone having, so to speak, one foot already in Heaven, should abandon this exercise, when the time should come for him to put the other there, he would run much risk of being lost.
Saint Vincent de Paul

There is no danger of a true child of Mary being led astray by the devil and falling into heresy. Where Mary leads, Satan with his deceptions and heretics with their subtleties are not encountered.
Saint Louis de Montfort

Chapter 8
Mouth, Eyes, & Ears

☦

Nor any indecent, or foolish, or abusive talk, for this is
without purpose; but instead, give thanks.
Ephesians 5:4

For whoever wants to love life and to see good days
should restrain his tongue from evil, and his lips, so
that they utter no deceit. Let him turn away from evil,
and do good. Let him seek peace, and pursue it. For the
eyes of the Lord are upon the just, and his ears are with
their prayers, but the countenance of the Lord is upon
those who do evil.
1 Peter 3:10-12

So also the tongue certainly is a small part, but it
moves great things. Consider that a small fire can set
ablaze a great forest. And so the tongue is like a fire,
comprising all iniquity. The tongue, stationed in the
midst of our body, can defile the entire body and
inflame the wheel of our nativity, setting a fire from
Hell. For the nature of all beasts and birds and
serpents and others is ruled over, and has been ruled
over, by human nature. But no man is able to rule over
the tongue, a restless evil, full of deadly poison. By it
we bless God the Father, and by it we speak evil of
men, who have been made in the likeness of God. From

the same mouth proceeds blessing and cursing. My brothers, these things ought not to be so!
James 3:5-10

The hearing ear and the seeing eye: the Lord has made them both.
Proverbs 20:12

O Timothy, guard what has been deposited with you, avoiding the voice of profane novelties and of opposing ideas, which are falsely called knowledge.
1 Timothy 6:20

So much damage is wrought in the Body of Christ through sins which gain traction through the eyes, ears and mouth. These sins denigrate your senses and open you up to the advances of Satan. Satan loves to poke and prod you into saying something you might not normally say. By taking his bait, you provide him with perfect cover. He also enjoys inundating the senses, from the outside and the inside, with sounds and images that excite the eyes, ears and mouth.

You need to gain control of what you say and gain custody of what you see and hear so that you don't unwittingly aid and abet the efforts of the evil one. You don't want to let your senses wander close to potential sin. By God's grace, you need to seal off your house and deny every attempt by the evil one to gain entrance.

Every sense that wanders with ease sins.
Saint Gregory Nazianzus

Even when we do not want it, the thieves will enter through the senses. For how is it possible for a house not to be darkened by the smoke entering from outside through the doors and windows that have been left opened?
Saint Syngletike

Each of these three areas, the mouth, the eyes and the ears, through which you speak, see and hear are open to exploitation. They are capable of contributing to a life of sin or a life of virtue. They were, obviously, made for good not evil. They were meant to be used as tools to advance God's Kingdom of Heaven, not Satan's kingdom of the damned.

Sins of the Mouth

Language is a powerful force. God spoke and creation was brought into existence. Language has the capacity to incite or inspire. Language is the landscape of the mind. It speaks to who you are and what is important to you. It forms the basis for much of your social interaction. The mouth can be an instrument of war or peace. Sins of the mouth cut deep, deeper than any sword. These sins may not be able to pierce the skin, but they can pierce the heart and do damage to the soul.

When you blaspheme you endanger your immortal soul. When you slander, gossip or calumniate you do damage to yourself and others. When you speak vulgarity or issue curses you do the devil's work. When you tell off-color, racist or inappropriate jokes you put out a welcome mat for the evil one.

Satan will take your ill-spoken words and give them a life of their own, with the ultimate goal of using them to separate you and others from eternal life with God. He'll keep those words echoing in your personal woundedness to the point where you believe and propagate them. He'll keep them reverberating in your pride to the point where you begin to defend sin, deny your responsibility and even justify your actions. Satan will twist your heart and mind to the point where you become his instrument against Christ and the Church.

Jesus is the Word. His every utterance gave glory and honor to God. When you speak in truth and love you give glory and honor to God. You should always speak in a manner that honors the second commandment.

> The evil speaker eats the flesh of his brother and bites the body of his neighbor.
> Saint John Chrysostom

> Speak ill of no one and avoid the company of those who talk badly about their neighbors.
> Blessed Jacinta Marto

Alas! Such is our weakness, that we often more readily believe and speak of another that which is evil than that which is good.
Servant of God Thomas a' Kempis

There are many different sins of the mouth that provide an opening for Satan. Once spoken, words cannot be taken back. Be careful how you use your words.

Gossip

Gossip is idle talk, especially about others. It can be the revealing of secrets, the spreading of rumors or simply worthless conversation. The relative truth of what is being gossiped about is irrelevant to culpability; not all of what is true is permitted to be shared. Gossip can also be a sin of sloth; the time and energy wasted gossiping could have been put to better use. Satan uses gossip to spread his lies, to open doors and to weaken your resolve.

Let listening to worldly news be bitter food for you, and let the words of saintly men be as combs filled with honey.
Saint Basil the Great

Detraction

Detraction is the spreading of a truth that will cause harm to someone's reputation, either through the spoken or written word. The mere fact that you know something about someone else does not give you the right to disclose it. More harmful than gossip, which may or may not have an evil intent, detraction's intent is to cause harm. Detraction is more clearly a work of the evil one. It is often the second wave of gossip.

Would we wish that our own hidden sins should be divulged? We ought, then, to be silent regarding those of others.
Saint John Baptist de la Salle

Slander

Slander is verbally defaming someone's character with the truth. It differs from detraction only in its method of delivery; it is spoken aloud. The intent is the same, to malign someone's good name. While the written word is typically longer lasting, the spoken word is often more immediate and more painful. Satan will goad you into gossiping and then inflame your passions so that you combine the two in an act of slander.

> The one who slanders and the one who listens to a slanderer have the devil in their company. One man has Satan on his tongue and the other in his ear.
> Saint Bernard of Clairvaux

Calumny

Calumny is the malicious uttering of a falsehood causing injury to someone's good name. The sin of calumny is compounded in that it involves a lie and an attack on someone's reputation. With gossip and detraction, what is being spread may be true. With calumny, it is a lie from the start. Much as Satan was a liar from the beginning, engaging in calumny places you deep inside the enemy's camp.

> To deprive a man of his reputation and honor, one word is sufficient. By finding out the most sensitive part of his honor, you may tarnish his reputation by telling it to all who know him, and easily take away his character for honor and integrity. To do this, however, no time is required, for scarcely have you complacently cherished the wish to calumniate him, than the sin is effected.
> Saint John Chrysostom

Vulgarity

Vulgarity is a misuse of the gift of language. Crude, coarse and obscene language is fertile soil for Satan's poisonous seeds. When combined with the taking of the Lord's name in vain, it becomes doubly serious. It grates on the ears as it dims the light of the soul. Vulgarity's greatest harm is not necessarily the words themselves; rather it is the doorway that is propped open by the use of vile language. Many other sins feel at home where vulgarity is spoken.

Filthy talk makes us feel comfortable with filthy action. But the one who knows how to control the tongue is prepared to resist the attacks of lust.
Saint Clement of Alexandria

Curses

Curses, the calling down of evil upon a person, are a grave evil and a misuse of the gift of speech. They are not harmless and they are not imaginary. Curses are real, they are malevolent and they are a mortal sin. Mortal sin blocks the path to God and opens the door to Satan. Curses should never be uttered by you, but don't be surprised if they are uttered against you by those who are under Satan's influence. If they are uttered against you, an ongoing, fervent prayer life and a grace-filled soul is your best protection.

The evil words of which we are speaking now are those whereby evil is uttered against someone by way of command or desire. Now to wish evil to another man, or to conduce to that evil by commanding it, is, of its very nature, contrary to charity whereby we love our neighbor by desiring his good. Consequently it is a mortal sin.
Saint Thomas Aquinas

Blasphemy

Blasphemy is expressing contempt, dishonor or irreverence toward God, either directly or indirectly. It may be a thought, word or action; though, its most frequent manifestation is spoken. Whether it is spoken as a false oath, a swear word attached to God's name or the use of God's name as an interjectory phrase, it is a sin against the second commandment. In some sense, blaspheming is the same as making a public proclamation against God, denouncing Him and His works.

If the sin of blasphemy is rampant in your home, it will surely perish.
Saint John Vianney

The need to gossip, detract, slander, calumniate use

vulgarity, curse or blaspheme often stems from a wound inside of you. Envy is the usual culprit. You feel you can build yourself up by tearing others down. Satan is happy to continually remind you of your wound inside if you will continually respond to his prodding by attacking others, committing sin or giving in to despair.

> The envious man invents all sorts of wickedness; he has recourse to evil speaking, to calumny, to cunning, in order to blacken his neighbor; he repeats what he knows, and what he does not know he invents, he exaggerates. Through the envy of the devil, death entered into the world; and also through envy we kill our neighbor; by dint of malice, of falsehood, we make him lose his reputation, his place. Let us, then, be good Christians and we shall no more envy the good fortune of our neighbor; we shall never speak evil of him; we shall enjoy a sweet peace; our soul will be calm; we shall find paradise on earth.
> Saint John Vianney

Sins of the Eyes

Besides being "window of the soul," the eyes are the primary way most of humanity experiences the world. Like any of your senses, the eyes can be used in a manner that tends toward virtue or vice. When you fix your gaze upon beauty, goodness and truth you open yourself up to a life of holiness. When you fix your gaze upon objects of temptation and worldliness you open yourself up to a life of sin. Custody of the eyes is such an important virtue to cultivate because of the many, involuntary images you are exposed to on a daily basis. These images remain stored in your mind. Even worse, any inappropriate images you actively consent to view are fair game for Satan to make use of in order to tempt you to do evil at a later time.

It is virtually impossible to avoid every image that presents itself to your eyes. You are constantly bombarded with visual stimulus. An inadvertent look, even at an objectively sinful object, is not a sin. There is no sin if there is no consent of the will. The sin arises when you intentionally place yourself in an environment that is conducive to sin and will likely cause you to lose custody of your eyes. Sin would also arise when you take a second look, that is, you consent to continue to view the inappropriate image, whether the initial look was voluntary or involuntary.

Often the eyes notice those objects or traits that you have strong feelings toward. This can easily lead to sins of envy or greed for those items you are desirous of or judgment and condemnation for those traits you find unappealing. Seeing a fancy car you can't afford can lead to jealousy toward the person driving the car. Seeing a homeless person shabbily dressed and unkempt can easily lead to judgment regarding their situation. Both jealousy and judgment are seeds of evil.

> Whenever you envy your neighbor you give demons a place to rest.
> Saint Ephraem the Syrian

> Do you not know that often a root has split a rock when allowed to remain in place? Give no place to the seed of evil, seeing that it will break up your faith.
> Saint Cyril of Jerusalem

Another way to sin with the eyes is from the inside out and can be summed up in the expression "If looks could kill...," The emotion attached to your look is sensed by others. When you glare at someone or have anger in your eyes or judge or condemn another by a look, you can easily sin by "killing" another person's spirit. You must gain custody of your eyes, both in what you take in and what you give off. Temptations to the sins of avarice, envy, gluttony and lust are the chief avenue of sins of the eyes, followed closely by sins of pride and judgment.

> The enemy is standing and observing day and night directly against our eyes to detect which entrance of our senses will be opened to him to enter. Once he enters through one of our senses because of our lack of vigilance, then this devious shameless dog attacks us further with his own arrows.
> Saint Isaac of Syria

Do not condemn, even with your eyes, for they are often deceived.
Saint John Climacus

Sins of the Ears

Sins of the ear can be as simple as listening to music, movies, speeches or conversations that are illicit, provocative or inclined toward evil. Eavesdropping would also be a misuse of the faculty of hearing. More often than not, sins of the ear are sins of omission. That is, you hear something said that is inappropriate, especially in regard to gossip, calumny etc. and rather than speaking up, or at the very least walking away, you say nothing. Unfortunately, by your silence you are speaking volumes.

Sins of omission can easily lead to scandal. By your lack of action, in this case not speaking out, you have given implicit approval to the sin spoken by another. The act of not saying something is usually not by itself sinful; but it becomes so when truth and charity require that you speak. One simple word from you might have ended the discussion before it turned into a sin of omission on your part.

Satan's role here is twofold, first to stir up apprehension or fear, then to excite or arouse your baser instincts to participate in the gossip, calumny, etc.

Never forget that souls are poisoned through the ear as much as bodies through the mouth.
Saint Francis de Sales

It is not enough to forbid our own tongue to murmur; we must also refuse to listen to murmurers.
Venerable Louis of Granada

The other two senses, touch and smell, can also contribute to sin. Clearly, the sense of touch can easily lead to sins of the flesh; that is detailed throughout the book. But even the sense of smell can be a contributing factor to sin. Gluttony is the most obvious link, but there are others. The sense of smell is unique among the senses in that it permits the strongest of recalls. Instantly a smell can seemingly transport

103

you back in time.

Whether it is freshly cut grass, ocean air, or a wood burning fireplace, your sense of smell has strong recall ability. The subtlety and strength of this sense does not escape the notice of Satan. Memories of past sins, often linked with strong feelings, can be triggered by the recall of a smell. A seemingly harmless scent suddenly fills you with feelings of lust, anger or rebellion and you don't even know why.

> Anyone, then, who desires to live chastely in Christ Jesus, must flee not only the mouse of lust, but even from its very scent.
> Saint Anthony of Padua

The mere recall of a scent, even one that is linked to past sins, is not sinful so long as the will is not engaged. However, placing yourself in an environment where the recall of problematic scents is likely is to occur is placing yourself in proximity to the near occasion of sin. Satan understands the mechanism of this linking and recalling perfectly well and exploits this as often as he can.

> The Lord has spoken, I believe, about all the senses, so that the one who touches and the one who uses every inner power in us to serve pleasure has actually committed the sin in his heart.
> Saint Gregory of Nyssa

> We must also struggle to protect our senses because it is not only through curious eyes that we fall into the sin of desire and commit fornication and adultery of the heart, as the Lord noted. There is also the fornication and the adultery of the sense of hearing, the sense of smell, the sense of taste, the sense of touch, and of all the senses together.
> Saint Nicodemos of the Holy Mountain

Your senses can be gateways to grace or sin. Stimulus passes through the senses, arouses the emotions and enters your thought process. These thoughts and emotions can serve one of three kingdoms, God's kingdom, the worldly kingdom or

Satan's kingdom. Serving the latter two will keep you out of the former. Satan knows this well and is waiting only for an opportunity, the tiniest of openings, in order to taint your thoughts and emotions. Give him no opening; on the contrary shut the door to him by rejecting the vice he proposes and embracing the virtue that will draw you in closer to God.

> If any bad thoughts come to you, make the sign of the cross, or say an Our Father, or strike your breast and try to think of something else. If you do that, the thought will actually be winning you merit, because you will be resisting it.
> Saint Teresa of Avila

> Vice mimics virtue.
> Saint Cyril of Jerusalem

> When we are assailed by some vice we must, as afar as possible, embrace the practice of the contrary.
> Saint Francis de Sales

The conclusion, then, is to guard all of your senses all of the time. The next time you bless yourself with holy water, bless your senses as well. Make the sign of the cross with the holy water over your eyes, your ears, your nose, your hands and your mouth. Beg God's grace upon each of your senses. Ask Him to wipe clean past sins and to protect you from new ones. Do your part, as well, to cooperate with God's grace. Speak the truth in love. Remain silent when appropriate. Fix your gaze upon Jesus. Listen only to that which uplifts your soul. Imitate Jesus in all you say and do and Satan's efforts will be futile.

> He [the devil] flies from a drop of holy water.
> Saint Francis de Sales

> You have before you constantly the instigations of sins and day and night all of your senses are being attacked by their evil desires.
> Saint Basil the Great

> When you feel the assaults of passion and anger, then

is the time to be silent as Jesus was silent in the midst of His ignominies and sufferings.
Saint Paul of the Cross

I think that man is called a peacemaker par excellence who pacifies perfectly the discord between flesh and spirit in himself and the war that is inherent in nature, so that the law of the body no longer wars against the law of the mind but is subjected to the higher rule and becomes a servant of the divine ordinance.
Saint Gregory of Nyssa

Three things I cannot escape: the eye of God, the voice of conscience, the stroke of death. In company, guard your tongue. In your family, guard your temper. When alone guard your thoughts.
Venerable Matt Talbot

Chapter 9
Toehold, Foothold, Stronghold I

Yet truly, each one is tempted by his own desires, having been enticed and drawn away. Thereafter, when desire has conceived, it gives birth to sin. Yet truly sin, when it has been consummated, produces death.
James 1:14-15

Satan operates on the principal of toehold, foothold, stronghold. Enticement leads to desire, which leads to sin and left unchecked, eventually, death. Give Satan a toehold and he'll turn it into a stronghold before you've had time to catch your breath. A seemingly innocuous suggestion becomes a full blown mortal sin in no time.

When Satan tempts you to be bad, bored, busy or boastful, he'll usually begin with a toehold, not a stronghold. An unconfessed venial sin might be an example of a toehold. An unconfessed mortal sin is definitely an example of at least a foothold. Ongoing and or multiple mortal sins can easily become a stronghold.

Whoever is drawn into sin against his will should understand that, because he allowed himself to be mastered by another sin committed previously, he is now, as a consequence of this first sin, led into another against his will.
Saint Basil the Great

When we are in deadly sin we do blindly sell ourselves to the devil. I beg you, for the love of Christ crucified: let's get out of such slavery.
Saint Catherine of Siena

The delineation among toehold, foothold and stronghold is somewhat subjective, though the sin behind them is not. Toeholds are those initial entry points. These entry points may not necessarily be sinful. They are more frequently disordered tendencies, personal peculiarities, perhaps even a good taken to an extreme. Whether sinful or not, they provide cover for Satan to begin to, almost imperceptibly, exert leverage in the form of temptation or harassment.

Toeholds

Provide no place for the devil.
Ephesians 4:27

Excessive clutter or cleanliness
God is a God of order, not of clutter or chaos. The spirit of disorder or chaos is a subtle, yet reliable toehold. If your bedroom is buried underneath a pile of dirty clothes, if your family room is strewn with empty pizza boxes and old newspapers, if your desk is submerged under piles of paper, then Satan has an opening. Clutter and chaos do not come from God. Clutter and chaos are a derivative of sin and therefore, where there is chaos there you will find a potential home for evil spirits.

Equally, a compulsion toward cleanliness or order can be an entry point for Satan and can easily lead to judgment. To demand sterility and spotlessness, to be overly concerned with outward appearances, to be obsessed with cleanliness can be an opening. Don't let Satan use good virtues like cleanliness or orderliness to draw you away from God. Proper order usually includes cleanliness, but proper order always puts God first.

The spirits of chaos, disorder, perfectionism, compulsion, sloth, anxiety, etc., operate here.

For all that the demons produce is disorderly. In common with the godless and the unjust, the demons

have but one purpose: to destroy the souls of those who accept their evil counsel.
Saint Peter of Damaskos

Poverty has always pleased me, but dirt, never.
Saint Bernard of Clairvaux

Compassion, my dear brother, is preferable to cleanliness. Reflect that with a little soap I can easily clean my bed covers, but even with a torrent of tears I would never wash from my soul the stain that my harshness toward the unfortunate would create.
Saint Martin de Porres

Accumulation of goods

Whether it is money, shoes, purses, tools, religious articles, golf clubs, music, books, etc., excess accumulation of goods lends itself to spirits of greed, gluttony and self-reliance. If you feel absolutely compelled to have the latest model or version of an item, then that is a potential entry point for evil spirits. If you financially strain yourself to keep up appearances, then that is a potential entry point. If you hoard money, seeking earthly security above eternal security, then that is a potential entry point. If you have a wardrobe that is sufficient to clothe a small army, then that is a potential entry point. The amassing of earthly honors and rewards can also become a point of pride.

A simple, humble lifestyle is one of the best defenses against Satan. Possessing things and not letting things possess you is the first step. Desiring to possess only those things you ought to possess is the second step. A holy indifference to all possessions is the third step. Cultivating a spirit of detachment will promote true happiness and prevent Satan from gaining a toehold in this area.

The spirits of gluttony, envy, pride, greed, worldliness, scarcity, etc., operate here.

He is truly happy who has all that he wishes to have and wishes to have nothing that he ought not to wish.
Saint Augustine

The evil spirits keep us in terror, because we expose ourselves to the assaults of terror by our attachments to honors, possessions, and pleasures. For then the evil spirits, uniting themselves with us — we become our own enemies when we love and seek what we ought to hate — do us great harm. We make them fight against us with our own weapons, which we put into their hands when we ought to be using them in our own defense

Saint Teresa of Avila

Excessive, non-essential use of the television or computer

Neither the television nor the computer is by itself inherently evil; neither is either necessarily a toehold. They can become so to the degree that either one moves you away from God. If used prudently and discriminately, they can be an edifying source of entertainment and education. If used imprudently or indiscriminately, they can become the devil's tabernacle.

Technology, used properly, can be a source of blessing. Used improperly it can become a curse. You must not run from progress, nor should you let progress run you. You should embrace technology to the degree that it brings you closer to God and is appropriate for your vocation. You do not need to be a hermit in order to encounter God. Take a look at the non-essential time you use the computer and television and compare that to the amount of time you spend in prayer and service to God.

The spirits of boredom, addiction, idolatry, lust, violence, addiction, pornography, etc., operate here.

Don't you see that Satan and his agents take possession of all inventions and all achievements of progress to convert them to evil? All the more reason to finally wake up and get to work in order to reconquer the positions taken up by the enemy.

Saint Maximilian Kolbe

Like the new frontiers of other times, this one too is full of the interplay of danger and promise and not without the sense of adventure which marked other great

periods of change. For the Church the new world of cyberspace is a summons to the great adventure of using its potential to proclaim the Gospel message.
Pope John Paul II

Secularization and paganization of holidays

The word holiday is simply a contraction of two old English words, "holy" and "day." Any holiday that is not also a holy day, at the very least, detracts from the glory and honor that is due God. At the worst, it pays homage to Satan in his quest to secularize the sacred.

In your life, to the extent that Christmas is not about Christ, it is a potential toehold. If Easter is more about chocolate bunnies than Jesus' resurrection, then an opening exists. Halloween, culturally the most hazardous, is a problem to the degree it imitates and promotes evil. If Saint Patrick's Day is about drinking green beer and Holy Week signals the start of "Spring Break," then Satan may have more influence in your life than you think he does. If the holidays are about good times to the exclusion of God, or fun to the exclusion of faith then Satan has gained a toehold.

The spirits of worldliness, mockery, false gods, etc., operate here.

As a mere exchange of material goods, Christmas is coming under the power of wanting-for-oneself; it is becoming the instrument of an insatiable egoism and has fallen under the sway of possessions and of power — whereas this event in fact brings us exactly the opposite message. Pruning back Christmas so that it is once again simple would be an enormous achievement.
Joseph Cardinal Ratzinger

It is the duty of Christians to spread through a witness of life the truth of Christmas, which Christ brings to every man and woman of good will.
Pope Benedict XVI

Not keeping holy the Sabbath

Sunday is intended by God to be a day set aside for you to direct your heart and minds toward Him and to rest in Him.

Attending Sunday Mass only meets the minimum requirements of the third commandment; you should also recognize Sunday as a day of rest. (It must be noted that missing Sunday Mass without a grave reason is a mortal sin and, therefore, a foothold.) It is Satan who desires to turn Sunday into a day of shopping, a day of separation from the family, a day spent watching endless hours of sports on television, etc. Sunday is to be a day of intentional to worship, rest and refresh.

Sunday is the Lord's Day, a day of worship and rest. It is a day set aside for faith, family, friends and fun. If your Sundays are not centered on worship and rest, then Satan has an entry point, whether through neglect, busyness or fatigue.

The spirits of disobedience, confusion, worldliness, false gods, etc., operate here.

> I entreat you, keep Sundays holy. Working on Sunday will not make you rich; on the contrary, you will bring down misfortunes on yourselves and your children.
> Saint Bernadette Soubirous

> Eucharistic assembly is the heart of the Day of the Lord. Therefore to observe Sunday properly, our first task is to take part in Holy Mass. This is a serious obligation, as the *Catechism of the Catholic Church* has recalled but, yet more important, it is a deep need which cannot but be felt by Christian souls.
> Pope John Paul II

> We hope for rest from three things [on Sunday]: from the labors of the present life, from the struggles of temptation and from servitude from the devil.
> Saint Thomas Aquinas

> We need to remember that it is Sunday itself that is meant to be kept holy, lest it end up as a day "empty of God."
> Pope Benedict XVI

Posters, statues, charms, clothing that promote idolatry

Objects can be blessed or cursed. Posters that incline the senses toward the baser instincts, or promote things of the occult are potential open doors. Images of celebrities posed provocatively or of bands that enjoy an association to the occult provide ongoing visual stimulus that is a portent of idolatry. Good luck charms provide an opportunity to stray from the love and protection of the one, true God. Clothing which promotes that which is profane is doubly problematic as it admits personal assent and bears public witness to others and can be a source of scandal.

Ultimately, any object (or person) can become a source of idolatry. If your attachment to an object or a person is disordered, then your relationship with God is compromised. The greater the attachment, the more the relationship is compromised. What you should properly seek from Him, you attempt to seek elsewhere. Any and all attachments or relationships, whether objects or persons, should give glory to God, not offend Him.

The spirits of false gods, false religion, pride, deceit, etc., operate here.

> My child, be not an observer of omens, since it leads to idolatry. Be neither an enchanter, nor an astrologer, nor a purifier, nor be willing to look at these things, for out of all these idolatry is engendered.
> *Didache*

> This appeal to shun idols, dear brothers and sisters, is also pertinent today. Has not our modern world created its own idols? Has it not imitated, perhaps inadvertently, the pagans of antiquity, by diverting man from his true end, from the joy of living eternally with God? This is a question that all people, if they are honest with themselves, cannot help but ask. What is important in my life? What is my first priority?
> Pope Benedict XVI

Chain letters, chain e-mails and superstitions

Many pass chain e-mails back and forth without a second thought. These e-mails promise a blessing if the chain remains unbroken and often threaten a curse if they are discontinued. Superstitions pay homage to a view of the world that is not Christian, as if ladders, mirrors, black cats and the

113

number thirteen have any inherent power. The only power that resides in superstitions is the power you give to the evil one by believing in them. (It is interesting to note that so often those who place their trust in such nonsense would ridicule the use of relics, holy water, blessed salt, etc. They believe that the power of the evil spirits can inhabit material items, but not the power of the Holy Spirit.) Superstition grows where faith declines.

Superstitions have as their origin and their end the worship of pagan gods. Believing in superstitions, even for fun, is a toehold, bordering on a foothold.

The spirits of the occult, witchcraft, magic, New Age, superstition, false gods, etc., operate here.

> Superstition is a vice opposed to religion by way of excess. It offers Divine worship to beings other than God or offers worship to God in an improper manner.
> Saint Thomas Aquinas

> From silly devotions and sour-faced saints, good Lord, deliver us.
> Saint Teresa of Avila

Self-help books

While God certainly can and likely has, reached people through this type of material, many more have been lost on the endless treadmill of self-improvement, self-help and self-exploration. Without God as the foundation, there is no self. To look for self, without an acknowledgement of God as God, is like trying to do advanced math without acknowledging that one plus one equals two.

Don't seek self-help, seek God-help. Go to the source for the answers, not to the imitators. Seek out those who have successfully completed the journey to God, go to the Saint-help section of your bookstore. Read about and imitate their lives; there you'll find all the help you need.

The spirits of the New Age, self-deceit, pride, ego, deception, mockery and false gods, etc., operate here.

> You will not see anyone who is really striving after his advancement who is not given to spiritual reading. And as to him who neglects it, the fact will soon be observed

by his progress.
Saint Athanasius

Often read spiritual books; then, like a sheep ruminate
the food you have taken.
Saint Antoninus

Membership in anti-Catholic organizations

Whether they exist outside the confines of the Church
or inside of the Church, membership in any organization not in
line with the teachings of the Church is an open door to Satan.
The more you value these memberships, the more your heart is
away from God (cf. Matthew 6:21), the more disobedience sets
in and hardens your heart.

Disobedience is Satan's calling card; disobedience to
proper authority flings the door wide open to Satan. He needn't
worry about sneaking in; he's got easy access to the mind and
will of the disobedient. Saint Augustine says obedience "rules
and restrains the intellect and the will."

Membership in Freemasonry is wrong because it
promotes indifferentism, the belief that all attempts to seek
God are equally valid. This leads to syncretism, the blending of
various rites, rituals and dogmas, which taken to its logical
conclusion, leads to the undermining of the Catholic Church.
Membership in any organizations that violate Church teaching
is not compatible with full membership in the Catholic Church.
Whether it is in regard to promotion of abortion, euthanasia,
homosexual lifestyle, female ordination, etc., you should not
associate yourself with these groups.

The spirits of false gods, idolatry, occult, Jezebel,
witchcraft, mockery, deceit, etc., operate here.

And Polycarp himself replied to Marcion, who met him
on one occasion, and said, "Do you know me?" "I do
know you, the first-born of Satan." Such was the horror
which the apostles and their disciples had against
holding even verbal communication with any corrupters
of the truth.
Saint Iranaeus

A reckless hand felt no repugnance in writing: Satan

will rule in the Vatican and the Pope will serve him in the uniform of a Swiss Guard and other things of that kind. This mortal hatred for the Church of Jesus Christ and for His Vicar was not just a prank on the part of deranged individuals, but a systematic action proceeding from the principle of Freemasonry: Destroy all religion, whatever it may be, especially the Catholic religion.
Saint Maximilian Kolbe

Supporting organizations with an anti-Catholic agenda

Almsgiving is a necessary part of the life of any Catholic. You are to share with others the bounty of grace and goods that God has bestowed upon you. You are to make prudential judgments regarding investing, charitable donations and volunteering. To invest your money with companies that promote or support lifestyles contrary to Catholic moral teaching is a toehold. To profit from businesses that promote a culture of death: abortion, homosexuality, gay marriage, cloning, infant stem cell research, etc., is to accept blood money. To donate time or money to organizations that endorse or encourage values in opposition to natural, moral or Church law is to contribute to the building up of Satan's kingdom. Spending money at restaurants, stores and businesses that condone and court immorality in their beliefs and practices is to dine, shop or do business with the devil.

Good stewardship requires more than profitability, it requires adherence to God's truth. The reality of living in a culture that flaunts God's commandments is not an excuse. To the extent possible, your involvement with organizations that contradict the teachings of the Church should be minimized or eliminated altogether.

The spirits of false gods, death, lies, murder, malice, blood money etc., operate here.

> Even the decision to invest in one place rather than another, in one productive sector rather than another, is always a moral and cultural choice.
> Pope John Paul II

I willingly grant that you may take care to increase

your wealth and resources, provided this is done not only justly but properly and charitably.
Saint Francis de Sales

Misuse of Religious Articles

When blessed religious articles are perceived as nothing more than lucky charms, Satan has at least a toehold. If you view religious articles through the eyes of superstition more than through the eyes of the Church, then their use can be counterproductive. If you start to put your faith and trust in the items themselves, as if they have any power apart from God, then you open the door to evil. Do not see them as an end apart from the Church who graciously gives them to you.

Blessed religious articles, such as relics, holy water, blessed salt, blessed palm branches, scapulars, rosaries, icons, etc. are simply tools of God's kingdom, support for the journey. Like any tool, they can be used properly or improperly. Always uses religious articles in the manner that brings glory and honor to God. Let these blessed items draw you closer to Him; let them draw you closer to His Church.

The spirits of false gods, magic, superstition, etc., operate here.

Q. 474. How should we make use of sacramentals?
A. We should make use of the sacramentals with faith and devotion, and never make them objects of superstition.
Baltimore Catechism

2111. Superstition is the deviation of religious feeling and of the practices this feeling imposes. It can even affect the worship we offer the true God, e.g., when one attributes an importance in some way magical to certain practices otherwise lawful or necessary. To attribute the efficacy of prayers or of sacramental signs to their mere external performance, apart from the interior dispositions that they demand, is to fall into superstition.
Catechism of the Catholic Church

When the Bishop Projectius brought the relics of Saint

Stephen to the town called Aquae Tibiltinae, the people came in great crowds to honor them. Among there was a blind woman, who entreated the people to lead her to the bishop who had the holy relics. They did so, and the bishop gave her some flowers which he had in his hand. She took them, and put them to her eyes, and immediately her sight was restored, so that she passed speedily on before all the others, no longer requiring to be guided.
Saint Augustine

The evil one is weakened in the face of cleanliness and order, mortification and sacrifice, purity and chastity, unity and truth. Do not give him even the slightest toehold. Do not let Satan's temptation or harassments gain any traction for his cause. Do not fight against God. Be humble, accept correction. Confess your sins; enter into His peace.

To be pleased at correction and reproofs shows that one loves the virtues which are contrary to those faults for which he is corrected and reproved. And, therefore, it is a great sign of advancement in perfection.
Saint Francis de Sales

I realize so clearly now how little power the devils have, if I am not fighting against God, that I am hardly afraid of them at all: for their strength is nothing unless they find souls surrendering to them and growing cowardly, in which case they do indeed show their power.
Saint Teresa of Avila

The confession of evil is the first beginning of good works.
Saint Augustine

If I confide in you, Mother of God, I shall be saved. Under your protection I shall fear nothing. With your help I shall rout all enemies. For devotion to you is a weapon of salvation God gives to those He wishes to save.
Saint John Damascene.

Chapter 10
Toehold, Foothold, Stronghold II

☩

I will not now speak at length with you. For the prince
of this world is coming, but he does not have anything
in me.
John 14:30

Footholds and strongholds are further down the path of
destruction than a toehold. It is as if you are floating on the
surface of the ocean looking to get back to shore, all the while
the demons are grabbing at you. First your toe, now your foot,
soon your entire body will be dragged down ever deeper,
descending into the cold dark abyss of sin.

An evil inertia seems to grip your very soul, almost
preventing you from fighting back. Your strength sapped, your
energy depleted, Satan's grip is life threatening. Such is the life
of a soul absent God's grace.

Footholds / Strongholds

Now the works of the flesh are manifest; they are:
fornication, impurity, homosexuality, self-indulgence,
the worshiping of idols, drug use, hostility,
contentiousness, jealousy, wrath, quarrels, dissensions,
divisions, envy, murder, inebriation, carousing, and
similar things. About these things, I continue to preach
to you, as I have preached to you: that those who act in

this way shall not obtain the kingdom of God.
Galatians 5:19-21

Or do you not know that your bodies are the Temple of
the Holy Spirit, who is in you, whom you have from
God, and that you are not your own? For you have been
bought at a great price. Glorify and carry God in your
body.
1 Corinthians 6:19-20

Unconfessed mortal sin

Persistent, unconfessed mortal sin is deadly. It is a
stranglehold on your soul. More than an open door, it is an
open invitation for Satan to enter and take up residence in your
soul. For as long as the sin is unconfessed, your life of grace is
forfeited. Mortal sin attacks your relationship with God, with
self and with others.

God's mercy beckons you to return to a life of grace.
God's mercy, like mortal sin, is something you can freely choose
to accept or reject. Repent and return to His mercy or reject His
mercy and remain in mortal sin? The choice is yours to make.
As a soldier for Christ there is only one choice. His mercy is
yours for the asking; simply repent and believe in the Gospel
(cf. Mark 1:15).

The spirits of spiritual murder, spiritual suicide,
indifference, rebellion, Satan, etc., operate here.

Repentance is returning from the unnatural to the
natural state, from the devil to God, through discipline
and effort.
Saint John Damascene

Misuse and abuse of drugs and alcohol

Drugs and alcohol are two of Satan's preferred entry
points. As they lower your defenses and impair your judgment,
they lead to many other toeholds, footholds and strongholds.
Plus they have the added bonuses of being addictive, destroying
the family, creating financial ruin and causing death. Whether
your goal is to numb pain, free inhibitions or fit in, Satan's
pharmacy is there to help you medicate yourself to death.

God's pharmacy, with its prescription of faith, hope and

love is there to help nurse you back to life. He is the Divine Physician; He can heal any wound. Ultimately, drug and alcohol abuse stems from woundedness that only God can heal. No amount of numbing the pain will bring relief; only He can.

The spirits of addiction, strongholds, rebellion, rage, death, gluttony, guilt, etc., operate here.

> Wine is the first weapon that devils use in attacking the young.
> Saint Jerome

> Never look down on a man who cannot give up the drink, it is easier to get out of Hell.
> Venerable Matt Talbot

Immoral sexual activity.
This includes pre-marital, extra-marital and homosexual activity; basically anything outside the covenant bonds of a marriage. It would also include any act not open to life, e.g., contraceptive sex, masturbation, etc., whether within the covenant bonds of a marriage or not. God created the sexual act to be love-giving and life-giving, unitive and procreative. When either one or both are missing a vacuum is created and the destructive nature of Satan enters into the act turning something beautiful into something deadly. Sex, a life-giving, sacred gift from God is a favorite entry point for Satan.

Satan delights in misrepresenting your purpose here on earth. Your purpose here on earth is to know, love and serve God (cf. *Baltimore Catechism*, Lesson 1, Question 6). That is your purpose; it is not the pursuit of perverted pleasure, no matter how much the world, the flesh or the devil try to tell you otherwise.

The spirits of lust, mockery, death, homosexuality, blasphemy, perversion, self-hatred, etc., operate here.

> The sins that lead more souls to Hell are the sins of the flesh.
> Our Lady of Fatima to Blessed Jacinta Marto

> Our relentless enemy, the teacher of fornication, whispers that God is lenient and particularly merciful

to this passion, since it is so very natural. Yet if we watch the wiles of the demons we will observe that after we have actually sinned they will affirm that God is a just and inexorable judge. They say one thing to lead us into sin, another thing to overwhelm us in despair.
Saint John Climacus

Contraception is to be judged objectively so profoundly unlawful as never to be, for any reason, justified. To think or say to the contrary is equal to maintaining that, in human life, situations may arise in which it is lawful not to recognize god as God.
Pope John Paul II

Pornography
Once confined to the seedy part of town and once imbued with a societal stigma, pornography has risen to a new level of accessibility and acceptability. From daytime soap operas to primetime television, from cable TV to motion pictures, pornography is seemingly ubiquitous. Even worse, pornography has overtaken the internet.

Pornography, in all its forms, is degrading, exploitative and destructive. It is a distortion of the truth; it is objectively evil and, as far as Satan is concerned, a solid foothold leading to further diabolical influences.

In many ways, because of the anonymity and accessibility of the internet to bring pornography into the home and office, it is one of the greatest threats to souls, especially men's. It is more so because of the nature and potency of the physiological addiction it creates. Pornography has as its end the destruction of marriage and families. It objectifies both viewer and participant. It demeans, debases and demoralizes. The lie that it is victimless or therapeutic is straight from the lips of the evil one.

The spirits of murder, lust, death, homosexuality, perversion, self-hatred, etc., operate here.

It is in the theatres that the demons of impurity display their pomp with greatest advantage. Nothing can be more opposed to the spirit of Christianity which is a

spirit of purity, prayer and penance.
Saint John Baptist de la Salle

Eros, reduced to pure "sex," has become a commodity; a mere "thing" to be bought and sold, or rather, man himself becomes a commodity.
Pope Benedict XVI

False religions, movements and cults

Islam, Hinduism, Buddhism, Taoism, Sikhism, Jehovah's Witness, Mormonism, Bahaism, Christian Scientists, Scientology, Seventh Day Adventism, atheism and agnosticism, et al., are all false religions, movements or cults. While it is true that outside of the structure of the Catholic Church there exist elements of sanctification and truth, it is equally true that the fullness of truth subsists only in the Catholic Church (cf. *Dominus Iesus*). For a baptized Catholic these false religions are to be avoided like the plague, for that is what they are, a plague to the soul. Any rites or ritual associated with them are to be repented from, rejected and renounced. There may be many ways up the mountain, but only way one reaches the top; too many lead off a cliff.

False religions all flow from Satan. He has done a mighty work in deceiving many good and decent people about the nature of religion. The light of Christ's truth needs to shine bright in and through you and be a witness to others.

The spirits of Satan, false gods, false religions, idolatry, false consolation, occult, etc., operate here.

We consider another abundant source of the evils with which the Church is afflicted at present: indifferentism. This perverse opinion is spread on all sides by the fraud of the wicked who claim that it is possible to obtain the eternal salvation of the soul by the profession of any kind of religion, as long as morality is maintained.
Pope Gregory XVI

Also perverse is the shocking theory that it makes no difference to which religion one belongs, a theory which is greatly at variance even with reason. By means of this theory, those crafty men remove all distinction

between virtue and vice, truth and error, honorable and vile action.
Pope Pius IX

Yoga

Yoga deserves its own paragraph because it is growing in popularity and it appears harmless. The word "yoga" is Hindu for union. The goal of yoga is to unite oneself with one of the false gods of Hinduism, Brahman. Some see the postures and breathing exercises associated with yoga as harmless. Viewed purely from a physical viewpoint, the stretching and breathing exercises can be beneficial. Yet, it is these very postures and breathing exercises that Hinduism teaches are the final two steps toward union with a false god.

You cannot separate the physical from the spiritual in yoga. The movements and breathing are designed to prepare body, mind and soul for Samadhi, the (alleged) union of man with the divine. Practicing yoga is akin to inviting thieves to secure your treasures for you. It is an invitation fraught with danger. Any benefit you might derive from yoga can be achieved apart from it.

The spirits of false gods, false religions, occult, idolatry, etc., operate here.

Yoga is incompatible with Catholicism.
Servant of God John Hardon

Whoever identifies, by pantheistic confusion, God and the universe, by either lowering God to the dimensions of the world, or raising the world to the dimensions of God, is not a believer in God.
Pope Pius XI

New Age novelties and health practices

Prana, crystals, enneagram, reiki, EST, gestalt therapy, primal scream therapy, transactional analysis, centering prayer, ayurveda, rebirthing, past life regression, transcendental meditation, rolfing, huna, reflexology, etc., are just some of the practices of the supposed New Age. It must be noted that not all of the practices of the New Age are equal in their rejection of what is true. Some of the practices and practitioners are adamantly opposed to God, some are merely ignorant of who God is, some try and incorporate Christianity into their work. Even if the latter is the case, that is insufficient reason to participate in these false practices. False healings can occur through these practices and practitioners and are the work of the evil one. Satan can cure sicknesses or diseases that were caused by diabolical influence; thereby giving the illusion of healing. It is these false healings that are more likely to flow from the

> First of all, they [the demons] make you ill; then to get a miracle out of it, they prescribe remedies either completely novel, or contrary to those in use, and thereupon withdrawing hurtful influence, they are supposed to have wrought a cure.
> Tertullian

True healing only comes from God; to the degree that God is behind the healing then it is of no concern. If it is not God who is being invoked and a healing occurs, you are, on some level, strongly indebted to the entity that is being invoked. This is the problem, the discerning of spirits. Better to avoid this question entirely than to discern wrongly.

New Age is simply a term for old heresies that have been recycled. It is the offspring of paganism and Gnosticism. With Satan as its spiritual leader, the New Age promotes the two lies he espoused in the Garden of Eden, "You certainly will not die," and "You will be like gods." Pope Pius X exposed and condemned what he called Modernism which he believed was infecting the Church. A combination of rationalism, secularism and humanism, the New Age is Modernism updated. By whatever name, it is the devil's doctrine and is to be avoided.

The spirits of occult, false religions, false healing, Satan, etc., operate here.

> Modernism is the synthesis of all heresies.
> Pope Saint Pius X

Satan has all the skill in the world to induce people to deny his existence in the name of rationalism and of every other system of thought which seeks all possible

means to avoid recognizing his activity.
Pope John Paul II

Books that contradicts the truths of the Catholic faith
This includes works of fiction, New Age books, extra-biblical gospels, etc. Equally off limits would be books that promote blasphemy, heresy or indifferentism from supposed Catholic authors. Inauthentic feminism, false morality, pseudo-liturgy and disobedience to proper Church authority are the frequent topics of such books. When read, the lies and half-truths that are proposed remain in your memory. There they can later be manipulated by Satan in a manner that seems palatable.

Books, especially those written for teens, often serve as an entry point and, ultimately, as a leverage point for the evil one. While disguising themselves as well written fantasy, they serve as an indoctrination to an evil agenda. Let not the shiny packaging deceive; evil is evil regardless.

Some might ask if this is not a case of censorship. It is not; it is a matter of prudence. G.K. Chesterton, a noted 20th century English convert to Catholicism, once said, "Merely having an open mind is nothing. The object of opening the mind, as of opening the mouth, is to shut it again on something solid." The truth, as taught by the Catholic Church, is solid.

The spirits of false religion, lies, mockery, blasphemy, etc., operate here.

> Never read books you aren't sure about... even supposing that these bad books are very well written from a literary point of view. Let me ask you this: Would you drink something that you knew was poisoned just because it was offered to you in a golden cup?
> Saint John Bosco

> The reading of bad books fills the imagination with bad thoughts. Through the mind poison passes and there begets ruin and death.
> Saint John Baptist de la Salle

> We are horrified to see what monstrous doctrines and

prodigious errors are disseminated far and wide in countless books, pamphlets, and other writings which, though small in weight, are very great in malice. We are in tears at the abuse which proceeds from them over the face of the earth.
Pope Gregory XVI

Movies, television, music or games that promote the occult

Many would argue that the seemingly endless fascination with the occult that permeates entertainment choices is harmless fun. Yet these choices introduce your soul to the concepts of magic and moral relativism and re-introduce Gnostic principles. Movies and television are incredibly powerful and persuasive mediums. When used to promote a morality that is anti-Christian, whether strident or subtle in doing so, they cause tremendous harm to souls.

Many musical artists openly and actively promote anti-Christian and pro-demonic concepts in their music; others do so more subtlety; beware of both. Many musicians use their God-given talent to promote personal agendas contrary to God's plan. Music's influence is turned more quickly into a stronghold because it can move the soul without any sort of filtering mechanism slowing the process down. Computer games which glorify violence and create an alternative and addictive culture attempt to create a world where the God of Christianity has no place.

Cries of "You're too old, you don't understand!" are irrelevant whether spoken to parents or to the Church. It's really the devil's cry of "*Non serviam!*" all over again. God made parents to be older for a reason. He gave authority to the Church for a reason. Be humble. Submit yourself to proper authority and you will be protected.

The spirits of false gods, false religions, Satan, occult, idolatry, magic, deceit, etc., operate here.

Everyone knows that damage is done to the soul by bad motion pictures.
Pope Pius XI

The watching of birds, divination, omens, or amulets, or charms written on leaves, sorceries, or other evil arts,

127

and all such things, are services of the devil; therefore shun them. For if after renouncing Satan and associating thyself with Christ, you fall under their influence, you shall find the tyrant more bitter; perchance, because he treated you of old as his own, and relieved you from his hard bondage, but has now been greatly exasperated by you; so you will be bereaved of Christ, and have experience of the other.
Saint Cyril of Jerusalem

Objects that promote divination

"But, I just read them for fun. They don't mean anything." "I don't really believe in them, they're harmless." Horoscopes are not harmless; neither is consulting with a medium, psychic, palm reader or astrologer. They are a perfect foothold precisely because so many people think they are harmless. Too many souls avail themselves of Tarot cards, I Ching, numerology, Ouija boards, Magic 8 balls, etc., without any sense of the doors they are flinging open. All attempt, with varying degrees of sophistication, to connect with other-worldly spirits. Seemingly, this is done in order to tell the future. This is a direct affront to God's sovereignty and a clear violation of the first commandment.

While ignorance might lessen your culpability here, ignorance will do nothing in terms of lessening your exposure to demonic influence. It will also not prevent a foothold from turning into a stronghold.

The spirits of false gods and religions, magic, New Age, Satan, witchcraft, occult, idolatry, blasphemy, lies, addiction etc., operate here.

> The good Christian should beware of mathematicians [astrologers] and all those who make empty prophecies. The danger already exists that the mathematicians [astrologers] have made a covenant with the devil to darken the spirit and to confine man in the bonds of Hell.
> Saint Augustine

2116. All forms of divination are to be rejected: recourse to Satan or demons, conjuring up the dead or other

practices falsely supposed to "unveil" the future. Consulting horoscopes, astrology, palm reading, interpretation of omens and lots, the phenomena of clairvoyance, and recourse to mediums all conceal a desire for power over time, history, and, in the last analysis, other human beings, as well as a wish to conciliate hidden powers. They contradict the honor, respect, and loving fear that we owe to God alone.
Catechism of the Catholic Church

Magic, Witchcraft or Wicca

The spirits of witchcraft, magic and the occult are some of the hardest spirits to overcome. Where divination is done to tell the future (allegedly), magic is performed to change the future through seals, curses, spells and hexes. Witchcraft employs magic, aligned with the forces of the evil one, toward the destruction of God's people and His kingdom. Wicca is a modern revival and repackaging of ancient, pagan witchcraft. Claiming to be harmless, even beneficial, some of Wicca's followers maintain that they perform only white magic, not black magic. This is a distinction without a difference for any Christian. The explosion in numbers of those claiming to be witches today cannot be ignored. While it is true that some change can flow from those who dabble in the occult, e.g. physical healing, solving of crimes, etc., you need to discern from where their power originates. Satan is more than willing to bring about a good if it will lure or lull you into complacency toward him, or worse, complicity with him. A far greater evil lurks just underneath the surface where Satan does a good. (He can never do a good as an end, only as a means to a greater evil.)

Steer clear of any connection to magic or witchcraft. Curiosity in this area can kill. It is far better to err on the side of caution than curiosity. It is far better to err on the side of Sacred Scripture than Satan's lies. Don't let the popularity of television shows that whitewash or glorify witchcraft or the occult fool you. Don't let alleged psychic mediums seduce you into selling your soul for an alleged glimpse into the afterlife or an alleged word from the "other side." Don't believe in the lie of white magic or the benevolence of Wicca. You have a specific, safe means of contacting God, praying to Jesus Christ.

The spirits of false gods, false religions, New Age, Satan, witchcraft, occult, idolatry, etc., operate here.

> You shall not practice magic, you shall not practice witchcraft. My child, flee from every evil thing and from everything like it.
> *Didache*

> 2116. All practices of magic or sorcery, by which one attempts to tame occult powers, so as to place them at one's service and have a supernatural power over others — even if this were for the sake of restoring their health — are gravely contrary to the virtue of religion. These practices are even more to be condemned when accompanied by the intention of harming someone, or when they have recourse to the intervention of demons.
> *Catechism of the Catholic Church*

This is a partial listing of potential toeholds, footholds and strongholds. It neither pretends nor intends to be an exhaustive list. It is a sampling of some more common openings.

Whether it is a toehold, foothold or stronghold that is gripping you, recourse to God through prayer and the sacraments is the answer. Sometimes your prayers are sufficient. Sometimes it is the power of communal prayer that is needed. Other times it may be the prayer of the Church that is required to free you.

The simplest way to ensure your actions are not providing Satan an opening is to remain in the state of grace and when necessary, return to the state of grace through sacramental confession.

Obviously, the weaker the grip, the easier the hold can be broken. That is why it is important to protect, and not neglect, any openings lest they be exploited by the evil one.

> However great the temptation, if we knew how to use the weapon of prayer well, we shall come off conquerors at last, for prayer is more powerful than all devils.
> Saint Bernard of Clairvaux

Chapter 11
Pride, Anger & Unforgiveness

☩

> Let all bitterness and anger and indignation and outcry and blasphemy be taken away from you, along with all malice. And be kind and merciful to one another, forgiving one another, just as God has forgiven you in Christ.
> Ephesians 4:31-32

Three potential tools of Satan deserve special mention. Thoughts and corresponding actions of pride, anger and unforgiveness are like a giant crowbar in Satan's hands. He will leverage the tiniest of openings to create a gaping wound that is not easily healed. He will manipulate your thoughts and inflate your emotions, stirring them against your will until you are no longer responding, but reacting. If he can incite your emotions to the point where reason and will are not in control or are not even being consulted, then he has a hold over you, a very strong hold over you. Not surprisingly, his favorite emotion to try and leverage is pride.

Pride

> Arrogance precedes destruction. And the spirit is exalted before a fall.
> Proverbs 16:18

Let nothing be done by contention, nor in vain glory. Instead, in humility, let each of you esteem others to be better than himself.
Philippians 2:3

Pride is thee sin. Pride is death. Satan is the prince of pride. Pride turns you from things divine toward things demonic. Pride was at the root of the temptation and sin of Adam and Eve. Pride is the root and beginning of all sin. Pride fosters disobedience and rebellion. It is the most dangerous of the sins because it is self-deluding. What is evil is called good when trapped in pride.

As a protective mechanism, pride often denies its own existence. Those most firmly in its grip seemingly have no awareness of their condition. They often think they are faultless and exceedingly humble. Despite this false persona, pride has a great need to defend and protect itself. It is as if part of them knows the façade is fragile and fleeting. Pride fears being exposed; it hides its inherent weaknesses under a false armor of bluster, confidence and arrogance. At its core pride is a fear based response masquerading as confidence and authority.

Those who love to be feared fear to be loved, and they themselves are more afraid than anyone, for whereas other men fear only them, they fear everyone.
Saint Francis de Sales

Pride isn't only about the obvious arrogance; it also shows itself in more subtle ways. If you're easily offended or exaggerate, that's a form of pride. If you need constant affirmation or recognition, that's a form of pride. If you need to be right or be heard, that's a form of pride. If you need to compete over everything or if you need to be the first to know or seek exclusivity, that's a form of pride. If you are hypercritical or judgmental, that's a form of pride. If you find yourself rebelling against the teachings of the Church, picking and choosing as if off a menu, that's a form of pride.

Pride seeks control above all else: control of self, others, situations, even of God. It seeks to control because it doesn't want to die. Pride's hidden motive is self-preservation and the seeking of earthly prominence and permanence. Pride is about attachment to the here and now. It knows it has no future, so it attempts to cling to the present.

> When a man is filled with pride his guardian angel, who is near him, withdraws from him. And when a man has offended this angel and the angel withdraws from him a stranger draws near.
> Saint Isaac of Syria

Pride can have no friends because pride is ever suspicious, ever selfish. It must demean others in order to survive; it feeds off humiliating others, it conquers by dividing. Pride cannot serve, pride cannot pray, pride cannot love. Pride is, in every way, antithetical to God.

The punishment for pride is death. It is a self-imposed death penalty, but death nonetheless. For the sin of pride, Satan lost Heaven forever. For the sin of pride, Adam and Eve lost their preternatural blessing and were banished from God's presence. For your every unconfessed sin of pride, you draw closer to Satan.

A momentary flash of pride that moves through your mind is no sin. In order to sin, your will must consent to do so. Because pride is deadly, the moment the will is involved it becomes a certain toehold, likely, a foothold. In the continued presence of pride, it takes little for that toehold or foothold to become a stronghold. There is no graver sin to your soul than pride. Pride leads to the only unforgivable sin, the grieving of the Holy Spirit.

Pride kills. Like crab grass taking over a lawn and leaving the landscape barren, pride will take over your soul. It steadily snuffs out the flame of the Spirit that flickers inside of you. Pride hardens, chills and eventually deadens hearts. Do not succumb to pride; humble yourself and God will lift you up. Your humble cooperation with God's grace can overcome any hold of Satan.

> Humility is the only virtue no devil can imitate. If pride made demons out of angels, there is no doubt that humility could make angels out of demons.
> Saint John Climacus

A man should know that a devil's sickness is on him if he is seized by the urge in conversation to assert his opinion, however correct it may be. If he behaves this way while talking to his equals, then a rebuke from his elders may heal him. But if he carries on in this way with those who are greater and wiser than he, his sickness cannot be cured by human means.
Saint John Climacus

Prayer is the counter poison of pride; the antidote to the passion of hatred.
Saint Ephrem of Syria

Anger

Be angry, and do not be willing to sin. Do not let the sun set over your anger. Provide no place for the devil.
Ephesians 4:26-27

A short-tempered man provokes quarrels. And whoever is easily angered is more likely to sin.
Proverbs 29:22

You know this, my most beloved brothers. So let every man be quick to listen, but slow to speak and slow to anger. For the anger of man does not accomplish the justice of God.
James 1:19-20

Anger is one of the seven deadly sins and a gateway to other sins. Anger is not necessarily sinful, nor is it necessarily an open door. It can be a virtue or a vice. Anger arising from holy zeal is virtuous; anger arising from worldly or evil passion is sinful. Virtuous anger is almost never related to self; it almost always is directed at the protection or defense of that which is holy: God, His Church, His people or that which requires justice. Don't be too quick to assume your anger is virtuous; it may be a prideful deception.

It is better to deny entrance to just and reasonable anger than to admit it, no matter how small it is. Once

let in it is driven out again only with difficulty.
Saint Augustine

Anger is never without a reason, but seldom with a good one.
Saint John Chrysostom

There is a holy anger, excited by zeal, which moves us to reprove with warmth those whom our mildness failed to correct.
Saint John Baptist de la Salle

Anger is an emotional response to a particular stimulus, often a perceived injustice. The stimulus can either be physical or verbal, internal or external, directed at you or others. The stimulus triggers an internal and emotional response followed by a physical and external response. Your response to the stimulus, what your will consents to, will determine the sinfulness of what follows.

Anger, like any emotion, gains traction when you consent to it. Prior to your consent, there can be no sin. Though Satan's whisperings may be heard, if there is no assent there is no toehold. Once your will assents, and assuming the anger is not arising from holy zeal, you are in a potential toehold area, a potentially venial sin.

Allowed to continue unimpeded the emotion takes over from reason and goes beyond it. Retaliation and revenge replace justice as the motivation. This is the mortal sin of anger and a certain foothold. An increase in intensity of emotion, from anger to hatred can create a stronghold. Habitual and frequent footholds of anger can also create a stronghold. This is a danger to your soul and a threat to your neighbor's body.

Anger not only hurts the body; it even corrupts the health of the soul.
Saint John Chrysostom

There is no wrong which gives man a foretaste of Hell in this life as anger and impatience.
Saint Catherine of Siena

Anger is an emotion of the soul, which leads us violently to repel whatever hurts or displeases us. This emotion, my children, comes from the devil: it shows that we are in his hands; that he is the master of our heart; that he holds all the strings of it, and makes us dance as he pleases. See, a person who puts himself in a passion is like a puppet; he knows neither what he says, nor what he does; the devil guides him entirely.
Saint John Vianney

Sinful anger is any anger that does not have holy zeal as its foundation. Sinful anger clouds your image of God, yourself and others. You act differently; you're less patient and more easily perturbed. You very often redirect your anger to a less threatening victim, thereby increasing the injustice and complicating the sin.

This deadly cancer of anger from which so much harm grows, it makes us unlike ourselves, makes us like furies from Hell, drives us forth headlong upon the points of swords, makes us blindly run forth after other men's destruction as we hasten toward our own ruin.
Saint Thomas More

He took over anger to intimidate subordinates, and in time anger took over him.
Saint Albert the Great

Sinful anger can express itself as unforgiveness, bitterness, sarcasm, stubbornness, sadness, impatience, etc. It may take the opposite side, hold grudges, nit pick, insult or seek revenge. When combined with pride, anger can come across as a calculated coldness. Where sinful anger exists, division and contradiction abound. The roots of sinful anger are most often based in pride. Sinful anger is rarely a singular incident; it frequently leads to further sinful anger.

From what does such contrariness arise in habitually angry people, but from a secret cause of too high an opinion of themselves so that it pierces their heart when they see any man esteem them less than they

esteem themselves? An inflated estimation of ourselves is more than half the weight of our wrath.
Saint Thomas More

It may seem that the second fit of anger does away with the first, but actually it serves to open the way for fresh anger on the first occasion that arises.
Saint Francis de Sales

Satan will happily exploit your woundedness in order to arouse your anger. For he knows that old wounds properly prodded will often give way to sinful anger. He'll gladly leverage any fear, pain or frustration of yours in order to turn a simmer into a boil. He'll bring to mind old betrayals, broken promises and bad experiences to serve as fuel for the fire and cause your anger to become sinful. He's hoping that your sinful anger will distract you from the holy path you desire to follow.

When we are perturbed, the enemy's attacks are more frequent and direct, for he takes advantage of our natural weakness, which prevents us from following the straight path of virtue.
Saint Pio of Pietrelcina

Anger should never remain suppressed or bottled up. If it rises up it needs to be acknowledged and dealt with at the appropriate time and place. Bring your anger to the Lord. Ask Him what the root cause of your anger is. Ask Him for the healing graces to overcome it. Ask Him for the grace to forgive yourself and others. Saint Francis de Sales claimed it took him more than twenty years to control his temper! Don't become discouraged or worse, angry, if you happen to slip and become angry. Don't lash out at others in an attempt to feel better about yourself. Instead, hurriedly turn toward God, repent and receive His mercy. Don't leave an open door; don't risk posioning your soul.

When we have found we have been aroused to anger we must call for God's help like the apostles when they were tossed about by the wind and storm on the waters.
Saint Francis de Sales

Do not let rancor toward others become poison for the soul.
Pope Benedict XVI

No one heals himself by wounding another.
Saint John Chrysostom

Unforgiveness

And Jesus said, "Father, forgive them. For they know not what they do."
Luke 23:34

And forgive us our debts, as we forgive our debtors.
Matthew 6:12

Support one another, and, if anyone has a complaint against another, forgive one another. For just as the Lord has forgiven you, so also must you do.
Colossians 3:13

Unforgiveness is a rejection or denial of God's mercy. It hardens your heart and turns you away from God. When you willfully choose to not forgive, you give Satan a toehold, perhaps a foothold. Either way, unforgiveness is a leverage point for Satan.

Forgiveness is a healing for your soul. The Greek word used for forgiveness in Scripture, "*aphesis*," connotes a sense of release. When you forgive there is a release of sin away from you and a movement of grace toward you. There is often also a release of physical, mental or emotional pain. Holding on to unforgiveness is a type of bondage. It is not healthy; it is not healing; it is not hopeful. Forgiveness you withhold is freedom you do not experience. Unforgiveness is a bind and a weight.

I will be like a tiny violet hidden in the grass, which does not hurt the foot that treads on it, but diffuses its fragrance and, forgetting itself completely, tries to please the person who has crushed it underfoot.
Saint Faustina Kowalska

Forgiveness is a biblical imperative. Scripture is clear, God forgives in like measures. The word "as" in the Our Father can have eternal consequences. It would be hypocritical to expect God's forgiveness if you were to voluntarily withhold it from others (cf. Matthew18:23-35).

Forgiveness is of God. You are not capable of forgiving on your own; you need God's grace to do so. Forgiveness is a supernatural virtue. It is Christ's death on the cross and subsequent resurrection which makes forgiveness possible. Forgiveness is unconditional love in action and, like love, it is a decision you make, not a feeling you get.

> 1449. The formula of absolution used in the Latin Church expresses the essential elements of this sacrament: the Father of mercies is the source of all forgiveness. He effects the reconciliation of sinners through the Passover of his Son and the gift of his Spirit, through the prayer and ministry of the Church:
>
> God, the Father of mercies, through the death and the resurrection of his Son has reconciled the world to himself and sent the Holy Spirit among us for the forgiveness of sins; through the ministry of the Church may God give you pardon and peace, and I absolve you from your sins in the name of the Father, and of the Son and of the Holy Spirit.
> *Catechism of the Catholic Church*

Unforgiveness causes you to continue to feel victimized, to continue to blame. With unforgiveness there can be no resolution, no peace. It keeps you far from the mind of Christ. Unforgiveness can stem from a variety of sources, not all of which are sinful. Some of the sources of unforgiveness are pride, anger, personal sin, self-righteousness, power, revenge, woundedness, lack of faith, fear and influence of the evil one. Amidst all that, it is sometimes difficult to hear God's call to forgive. That is why this virtue must be practiced frequently.

Very often a misunderstanding about the difference between forgiveness and reconciliation allows unforgiveness to fester. Forgiveness and reconciliation are related, but distinct. The biblical imperative is to forgive, not necessarily to reconcile; though if at all possible, that is the ideal. Part of the reason why reconciliation is not a requirement is because reconciliation depends upon the free will of another. It would be unjust for God to predicate your salvation upon the free will choice of another. That does not, of course, relieve you of your obligation to at least attempt to "reconcile with your brother" before you bring your gift to the altar (cf. Matthew 5:21-26).

Forgiveness is personal; reconciliation is interpersonal. You can forgive someone else without their knowledge or consent. Reconciliation, though, requires the other person's consent. Forgiving someone else requires no act of repentance, amends, regrets or repayments on their part; reconciliation likely will. Forgiveness is between you and God; reconciliation is between you, God and another person. Forgiveness does not necessarily mean the re-establishment of the relationship, especially if doing so would place you in harm's way. Reconciliation would be the re-establishment of the relationship. Ultimately, forgiveness is a gift that you give yourself; reconciliation is a gift you offer to another.

Read

> Remembrance of wrongs is the consummation of anger, the keeper of sin, hatred of righteousness, ruin of virtues, poison of the soul, worm of the mind. You will know that you have completely freed yourself of this rot, not when you pray for the person who has offended you, not when you exchange presents with him, not when you invite him to your table, but only when, on hearing that he has fallen into bodily or spiritual misfortune, you suffer and weep for him as for yourself.
> Saint John Climacus

Feelings of unforgiveness can be directed at self, others or God. Each is damaging in its own way, each causes division. If you are in the habit of not forgiving God it speaks to pride. It is pride that can't forgive. When you refuse to forgive God, you are expressing your belief that you know better than He does. This was Satan's sin; don't let it be yours. This is initially a toehold. If you persist, it will quickly become a stronghold. If you relent and repent, there is no hold, only God's mercy. If you still find yourself unable or unwilling to forgive, then pray to God for the desire and grace to forgive. Your prayer for the desire and grace can weaken any opposition.

If you are in the habit of not forgiving others, recall how often God has forgiven you or simply recite the Our Father to yourself. Focus on the words "and forgive us our trespasses as we forgive those who trespass against us," especially the word "as." In like measure, how you forgive others is how God will forgive you. This is a toehold, heading toward a foothold.

> Forgive as I forgive. Therefore He does not forgive, unless you forgive. Forgive as I forgive. You wish to be forgiven when you ask; forgive him that asks of you. He that is skilled in heaven's laws has dictated these prayers: He does not deceive you; ask according to the tenor of His heavenly voice: say, Forgive us, as we also forgive, and do what you say.
> Saint Cyprian of Carthage

> I cannot believe that a soul who knows how many sins God has forgiven her should not instantly and willingly forgive others.
> Saint Teresa of Avila

If you are in the habit of not forgiving yourself, you are in a sense rejecting God's forgiveness, placing your sins outside of His mercy. It can even be sinful, a form of false humility. In a sense, you are telling God that your sins are greater than His mercy. It is an affront to His omniscience and His omnipotence. It doesn't matter what you did, it can be forgiven. The only one who benefits by your lack of accepting forgiveness is Satan.

> For nothing is so loved of the devil as to find a person who has not forgiven another.
> Saint Theodore the Studite

> Resentment is like taking poison and hoping the other person dies.
> Saint Augustine

> The recollection of an injury is a rusty arrow and poison for the soul.
> Saint Francis of Paola

The root cause of pride, anger and unforgiveness is fear. Wherever you find Satan operating, you will find fear; either his fear of you or your fear of him. Satan is a fear-monger and merchant. He attempts to exploit wounded souls, to turn them into a place of wicked respite. Seek God's perfect love and Satan will fear you. Commit to Jesus and the coward will flee. For it is by the death and resurrection of Jesus that Satan is defeated. Climb up into the arms of Jesus and no harm will come to you. You may have to suffer, but you will not be harmed. Fear not and the evil one will flee. Be bold and courageous in the Lord.

> Fear is a greater evil than the evil itself.
> Saint Francis de Sales

> Let us rush with joy and trepidation to the noble contest and with no fear of our enemies. They are invisible enemies, but they can see the condition of our soul. If they see our spirits cowering and trembling, they will make a more vigorous attack against us. Let us arm ourselves against them with courage. They hesitate to grapple with a bold fighter.
> Saint John Climacus

> How consoling it is to know one is always under the protection of a heavenly spirit who never abandons us. Who is to be feared when accompanied by such an illustrious warrior? Was he not, perhaps, one of the multitude who joined with Saint Michael in the heavens to defend God's honor against Satan and against all the other rebellious angels, to vanquish them in the end and drive them down to Hell? Well, then, let me tell you that your Guardian Angel is still powerful against Satan and his evil satellites.
> Saint Pio of Pietrelcina

> "Oh the devil, the devil," we say when we might be saying "God! God!" and making the devil tremble.
> Saint Teresa of Avila

Part II
Basic Warfare Training

✛

And lead us not into temptation. But free us from evil.
Amen.
Matthew 6:13

Spiritual warfare is an ordinary part of any Christian's life, not
only those who acknowledge it. It is, in fact, the very act of
becoming a Christian that creates a lasting enmity between
you and the devil.

Ordinary spiritual warfare entails the ongoing, daily
battle against the world, the flesh and the devil. It
encompasses those thoughts, words and deeds that are proper
to all Christians. The struggles, fears, temptations and trials
that are part of the human experience are all part of ordinary
spiritual warfare.

You either choose to serve God or the evil one. There is
no other option. The choice is ever before you. You either choose
Christ and His eternal kingdom or you choose Satan and his
infernal kingdom.

The chapters following will detail how to best protect
and defend yourself from falling prey to Satan's devices and
making the wrong choice.

Christianity is warfare and Christians are spiritual
soldiers.
Saint Robert Southwell

143

The Lord gives the signal for us to stand guard in camp, to build the tower for which we may be able to discern and ward off the enemy of our eternal life. The heavenly trumpet of Christ urges the soldier on to battle.
Saint Augustine

Christians can only be slaves of the devil or slaves of Christ.
Saint Louis de Montfort

This world and the world to come are two enemies. We cannot therefore be friends to both; but we must decide which we will forsake and which we will enjoy.
Pope Saint Clement I

Chapter 12
Rules of Engagement

But solid food is for those who are mature, for those who, by practice, have sharpened their mind, so as to discern good from evil.
Hebrews 5:14

In boot camp, recruits are transformed into soldiers. It is in boot camp that they are taught how to discharge their duties. Only after boot camp does battle come. It is ordered this way for a reason, to save lives. A new recruit is raw and untrained and is not yet a productive member of the unit. A boot camp graduate is skilled and ready to serve, able to distinguish good from evil. As a spiritual warrior, it is necessary to complete boot camp before proceeding into battle. You must learn when and how to engage the enemy.

Follow these rules of engagement, corresponding scriptural references and saintly words of wisdom. They are not mere suggestions; they are spiritual commands designed to protect you from spiritual harm.

Pray, pray, pray

Jesus told his disciples a parable about the necessity for them to pray always without becoming weary.
Luke 18:1

Pray always. Pray before you start any mission the Lord calls you to and pray all the way through to the end. Remain in prayer especially during battle. Pray without ceasing. Make your very act of engaging in battle a prayer to the Lord by seeking out and following His will for you in every moment.

Nothing pleases the Lord more than your wholehearted desire to do His will. Let your every act be a prayer. Before, during or after your time of spiritual warfare, whether you are at work or rest, prayer is essential to your success.

> O Christian, who is in continual battle with Amalek, that is, a multitude of demons, learn how to fight. The enemy is only conquered on the mountain of perfection, on the peak of virtue, with prayer as the arms of battle. The humility of prayer is better than the might of all human preparation,
> Saint Thomas of Villanova

> Prayer is the protection of holy souls; a consolation for the Guardian Angels; an insupportable torment to the devil; a most acceptable homage to God; the best and most perfect praise for penitents and religious; the greatest honor and glory; the preserver of spiritual health.
> Saint Augustine

> To saints, their very slumber is a prayer.
> Saint John of the Cross

Await the invitation

> Then, even some of the traveling Jewish exorcists had attempted to invoke the name of the Lord Jesus over those who had evil spirits, saying, "I bind you by oath through Jesus, whom Paul preaches." And there were certain Jews, the seven sons of Sceva, leaders among the priests, who were acting in this way. But a wicked spirit responded by saying to them: "Jesus I know, and Paul I know. But who are you?" And the man, in whom there was a wicked spirit, leaping at them and getting

the better of them both, prevailed against them, so that they fled from that house, naked and wounded.
Acts of the Apostles 19:13-16

Do not overstep your bounds. To best be protected you must have a personal relationship with Jesus and a personal invitation from Jesus, before you enter into battle. Humility, not pride, is the calling card of a spiritual warrior. Humility, not pride, protects. Humility, not pride, waits for an invitation. The humble spiritual warrior cannot be subdued by the enemy.

As the Lord calls and as you respond affirmatively, He will provide you with all you need, preparing you as only He can. He will surround you with the right people and the right circumstances. He will even go before you and prepare the hearts and minds of others.

Satan defeats only the proud and cowardly, because the humble are strong. Nothing will confuse or frighten a humble soul.
Saint Faustina Kowalska

The basic need without which we are helpless in the face of the devil, the basic need for overcoming the evil spirit, is humility.
Servant of God John Hardon

True humility lies in obedience and the most literal compliance with His will.
Saint Francis de Sales

Never walk ahead of the Lord

And he said to me: "My grace is sufficient for you. For virtue is perfected in weakness." And so, willingly I will glory in my weaknesses, so that the virtue of Christ may live within me.
2 Corinthians 12:9

Once you are invited, the next step is to allow the Lord to lead. This rule requires humility. As a spiritual warrior you'll need to learn this sooner rather than later. Early on it may be curiosity or ignorance that has you proceed prematurely. This is normal and is part of the learning curve. To a degree, your innocence is your protection. Continued efforts to proceed prematurely are prideful and potentially void your protection.

Pride cannot overcome pride. You are no match for Satan in your pride. He is vastly stronger, smarter and more prideful. Do not venture even a single step ahead of the Lord. In your pride, Satan will seduce you before you know it. It is only with humility that you can begin to match up against Satan because it is only in humility that God's power can begin to have an effect. Let the Lord lead; let Him direct your path. Cloak your self and your actions in the humility of your Lord and savior.

> Do not examine the roads down which I lead you.
> Our Lord to Saint Faustina Kowalska

> Proud people are no match for Lucifer.
> Servant of God John Hardon

> You think that you will take in only a spark but you will be amazed to see that in a moment it has seized your whole heart and reduced your resolutions to ashes and your reputation to smoke.
> Saint Francis de Sales

Have faith in Jesus

> And when he had arrived at the multitude, a man approached him, falling to his knees before him, saying: "Lord, take pity on my son, for he is an epileptic, and he suffers harm. For he frequently falls into fire, and often also into water. And I brought him to your disciples, but they were not able to cure him." Then Jesus responded by saying: "What an unbelieving and perverse generation! How long shall I be with you? How long shall I endure you? Bring him here to me." And Jesus rebuked him, and the demon went out of him, and the boy was cured from that hour. Then the disciples approached Jesus privately and said, "Why

were we unable to cast him out?" Jesus said to them: "Because of your unbelief. Amen I say to you, certainly, if you will have faith like a grain of mustard seed, you will say to this mountain, 'Move from here to there,' and it shall move. And nothing will be impossible for you. But this kind is not cast out, except through prayer and fasting."
Matthew 17:14-20

Weak and ineffectual is the spiritual warrior who does not have faith in Jesus. Faith, a gift from God, needs to be nurtured. Faith is the relationship between you and God. It needs to grow through prayer, praise and worship. Faith needs to be active and alive or it will decline and die. Faith not wielded is like a sword in its sheath, useless. The gift of faith that has been given to you is a grace beyond compare, don't allow it to atrophy.

Spiritual warfare requires a decisive, certain faith in Jesus. As doubt opposes faith, any doubt can become a point of leverage for Satan, one he can manipulate to his advantage. A seed of doubt can grow into a huge weed in no time, choking off the seeds of faith. Trust in God. Tend to your garden often, being careful what seeds you plant. If a weed appears, yank it up from its roots. Trust in Jesus is not optional for those who desire salvation.

I will not delude you with prospects of peace and consolations, on the contrary, prepare for great battles. Fight like a knight, so that I can reward you. Do not be unduly fearful, because you are not alone.
Our Lord to Saint Faustina Kowalska

Cast away those fears and dispel those shadows which the devil is increasing in your soul in order to torment you.
Saint Pio of Pietrelcina

Christ said, "I am the Truth"; he did not say "I am the custom."
Saint Toribio

Do not see demons everywhere

> A dissension occurred again among the Jews because of
> these words. Then many of them were saying: "He
> [Jesus] has a demon or he is insane. Why do you listen
> him?"
>
> John 10:19-20
> For John the Baptist came, neither eating bread nor
> drinking wine, and you say, "He has a demon."
> Luke 7:33

One of the risks associated with spiritual warfare,
especially in the beginning, is the excessive focus and
overemphasis on Satan and his demons. It is easy to become
hypersensitive to the point of seeing demons everywhere and
blaming demons for everything. Remember, there are three
sources of evil, the world, the flesh and the devil. There needs
to be a healthy balance between the false extremes of Satan's
non-existence and his omnipresence. Some struggles are a
matter of life itself and have no attachment to the demonic;
their origin is your free will choice of evil.

Don't see demons where they are not. Don't misuse
your imagination. Don't assume differences in behavior equal
demonic possession. Don't let false fears paralyze you. Discern
properly; don't deny the demonic, but don't fabricate it either.
Be anxious about nothing; fix your sight upon the Lord.

> It will be enough to receive the evils which come upon
> us from time to time, without anticipating them by the
> imagination.
> Saint Francis de Sales

> Do not see enemies everywhere... Do not lose time as
> Satan wants, but offer everything up for the good of the
> works of the cross.
> Venerable Concepcion Cabrera de Armida

> This unresting anxiety is the greatest evil which can
> happen to the soul, sin only excepted. If our heart be
> disturbed and anxious, it loses power to retain such

graces as it has, as well as strength to resist the temptations of the evil one, who is all the more ready to fish in troubled waters.

Saint Francis de Sales

Seek the protection of the Lord

The Lord has freed me from every evil work, and he will accomplish salvation by his heavenly kingdom. To him be glory forever and ever. Amen.

2 Timothy 4:18

As a spiritual warrior, you need protection. The Lord will protect and preserve you provided you desire His will. Any other source of protection will eventually fail. If you seek your own will or the will of the evil one, you are stepping out from underneath God's mantle and rejecting His protection. Out of respect for your free will, He will not impose Himself or His protection upon you. Out of His great love for you, He will always provide the grace necessary for you to return to His fold. You simply need to be open to it.

He will protect you by providing you a means to grow in humility and obedience. Perhaps He will place you in the midst of a prayer community or with a prayer partner. Perhaps He will provide you with a spiritual director or mentor. Perhaps His protection will take the form of an excitement of the gifts of the Holy Spirit within you. Perhaps He will draw you closer to His mother or one of the saints. Provide Him with your "Yes," and He will take care of the rest. With your surrender to God's will, you will be drawn into His holiness.

My daughter, I want to teach you about spiritual warfare. Never trust in yourself, but abandon yourself totally to My will.

Our Lord to Saint Faustina Kowalska

Once we have asked for and obtained protection against evil, we are safely sheltered against everything the devil and the world can contrive.

Saint Cyprian of Carthage

Let the storm rage and the sky darken, not for that shall we be dismayed. If we trust as we should in Mary, we shall recognize in her, the Virgin Most Powerful, "who with virginal foot did crush the head of the serpent."
Pope Saint Pius X

Do not lose perspective

Yet truly, do not choose to rejoice in this, that the spirits are subject to you; but rejoice that your names are written in Heaven.
Luke 10:20

Spiritual warfare is nothing, salvation is everything. If the practice of spiritual warfare draws you closer to spending eternity with God, it is good to embrace it no matter what the cost. If it leads you away from God, it is to be shunned. Far greater than success in this or any ministry is faithfulness to God's will. Ignore false praise and feigned flattery; that is the language of the evil one.

In your humanity, it can be tempting to get carried away with spiritual warfare as a type of contest between you and the evil one, a contest you desire to win. Any attachment to an outcome is an earthly, temporal response. It is pride put into practice and it is also a potential toehold, or worse, for Satan to use. God sees the big picture, you cannot. He can bring ultimate triumph from ultimate tragedy. He doesn't need your advice, only your assent. He doesn't need you to do battle; you need Him. Keep proper perspective and you'll keep His peace.

It is a bigger miracle to eject passion from your own body than it is to eject an evil spirit from another's body. It is a bigger miracle to be patient and refrain from anger than it is to control the demons which fly through the air.
Saint John Cassian

But today we fight an insidious persecutor, an enemy who flatters. He does not stab us in the back but fills

our stomachs. He stuffs our pockets to lead us to death.
He imprisons us in the honors of the palace.
Saint Hilary of Poitiers

Our Lord needs from us neither great deeds nor
profound thoughts, neither intelligence nor talents. He
cherishes simplicity.
Saint Therese of Lisieux

Realize not all temptation or harassment is to be removed

You should fear nothing amid those things which you
will suffer. Behold, the devil will cast some of you into
prison, so that you may be tested. And you will have
tribulation for ten days. Be faithful even unto death,
and I will give to you the crown of life.
Revelation 2:10

What God permits, He can redeem. What He allows can
ultimately serve His will. What He sustains, He uses for good.
Satan's strategy of harassment and temptation can be used by
God to bring about His will. Satan hates when the evil he
perpetrates is redeemed, yet the most he can do about it is
whimper away. He is powerful only to the extent that God
allows him to be.

Much as the Apostle Paul's thorn in his side remained
with him throughout his life (cf. 2 Corinthians 12) God permits
certain temptations and harassments to remain. If He does
this, He will also provide you with the grace necessary to
endure.

I have sent him [the devil] in this life to tempt and
molest my creatures that they may conquer, proving
their virtue and receiving from me the glory of victory.
Our Lord to Saint Catherine of Siena

These enemies have not the courage to assail any but
those whom they see ready to give in to them, or when
God permits them to do so, for the greater good of His
servants, whom they may try and torment.
Saint Teresa of Avila

153

Temptation is necessary to make us realize that we are nothing in ourselves.
Saint Josemaria Escriva

Heed these rules of engagement, these spiritual guidelines; they will help you to safely engage in spiritual warfare. They will help you maintain a layer of protection around you and your loved ones.

The devil is like a mad dog tied to a chain. Beyond the limit of the chain the dog cannot go, so you should stay far from where the chain reaches or you will be hurt.
Saint Pio of Pietrelcina

Every morning during meditation, I prepare myself for the whole day's struggle. Holy Communion assures me that I will win the victory; and so it is. I fear the day when I do not receive Holy Communion. This bread of the Strong gives me all the strength I need to carry on my mission and the courage to do whatever the Lord asks of me. The courage and strength that are in me are not of me, but of Him who lives in me — it is the Eucharist. O my Jesus, the misunderstandings are so great; sometimes, were it not for the Eucharist, I would not have the courage to go any further along the way You have marked out for me.
Saint Faustina Kowalska

The Lord who has taken away your sin and pardoned your faults also protects you and keeps you from the wiles of your adversary the devil, so that the enemy, who is accustomed to leading into sin, may not surprise you. One who entrusts himself to God does not dread the devil. "If God is for us, who is against us?"
Saint Ambrose

Chapter 13
Know Your Enemy

Most beloved, do not be willing to believe every spirit, but test the spirits to see if they are of God. For many false prophets have gone out into the world.
1 John 4:1

And no wonder, for even Satan presents himself as if he were an Angel of light.
2 Corinthians 11:14

Spiritual warfare is a battle for your soul, fought on the battlefield of your mind and body. The reality is that spiritual warfare is most often a hidden, silent, interior war. It is only infrequently a visible, noisy, exterior battle. Whispers, not exploding weapons, are the sounds of this war. It is important to be able to discern who is doing the whispering so you know whether to proceed or retreat. You must be able to discern and describe the enemy on a spirit level, not a human level.

They never turn back to admit their sins or to ask for My mercy, so they come to the gate of falsehood because they follow the teaching of the devil, who is the father of lies. And this devil is their gateway through which they come to eternal damnation.
Our Lord to Saint Catherine of Siena

To discern humanly is to create a devil of your own doing, a devil of your own creation. It is important that you discern and describe the devil that God has revealed. And as God has revealed the reality of Satan as a creature and not just a concept, it is a truth you are obligated to accept. (An equally valid truth is the reality of the good angels who can act as a spiritual counterbalance to Satan's evil, and draw you closer to God. Their role will be discussed further in chapter 19)

You must spiritually discern the enemy

The purpose of discernment of spirits is to determine which ideas, inspirations and inclinations are from the Holy Spirit, which are from the human spirit and which are from the evil spirit. You should never desire to do what the evil spirit desires. Nor should you desire to do what the human spirit desires, especially in the context of spiritual warfare. Rather you should always seek to do what the Holy Spirit desires. As a spiritual warrior, the more you conform your will to His, the more protected you will be and the more peace you will experience. Prayer is the primary means by which your will can be conformed to His.

As you pray, realize that all three spirits may be present. Also realize that the Holy Spirit and His good angels can only do that which will ultimately bring about your union with God. Satan and the other bad angels can only do that which will ultimately bring about your separation from God. (Of course, God can order any and all acts of the evil one to bring about His plan. Nonetheless, the demons can not, by their intention, act in your best interest.)

Your free will allows you to choose from among the three spirits. That is why it is important to discern properly. If you discern that the Holy Spirit is operating, then proceed prayerfully and prudently. If you discern that the evil spirit is operating, then reject any such inspiration immediately and completely. If you discern that the human spirit is operating, then you need to discern if the inspiration is in conformity with God's will for you at that time. If it is, then proceed. If it is not, then the inspiration needs to be rejected.

A most powerful and efficacious remedy for all evils, a

means of correcting all imperfections, of triumphing over temptation and preserving our hearts in an undisturbed peace, is conformity with the will of God.
Saint Vincent de Paul

Saint Ignatius of Loyola is well known for his principles of discernment of spirits. The standard that Saint Ignatius uses is one of consolation and desolation. Saint Ignatius teaches that in a grace-filled soul, the promptings of the Holy Spirit produce peace and joy in the soul. This is what is known as consolation. The promptings of the evil spirit produce the opposite effect in one who is in a state of grace and fervently seeking God's will — disturbance and selfishness. This is what is known as desolation.

In a soul absent of sanctifying grace, the opposite effect is produced by each set of spirits. That is, the Holy Spirit's promptings will tend to create dissonance and guilt or desolation and the evil spirit's promptings will create a fleshy, false pleasure or a false consolation. This is only true in a soul that is devoid of sanctifying grace. Never be overly attached to consolation, nor disturbed by desolation; allow both consolation and desolation to draw you closer to God.

> Spiritual life is made up of desolations and consolations, and Saint Ignatius says that the right thing to do during desolation is to make no changes, and in a time of consolation not to cling too steadfastly to it, but to strengthen yourself for the next period of desolation.
> Venerable Concepcion Cabrera de Armida

> To every man there are two attending angels, the one of justice and the other of wickedness. If there be good thoughts in our heart, and if righteousness be welling up in our soul, it can scarcely be doubted that an angel of the Lord is speaking. If, however, the thoughts of our heart be turned to evil, an angel of the devil is speaking.
> Origen

The process of discernment begins and ends with

prayer. Place yourself in the presence of God, pray and listen. You might pray the scriptures, pray a formal prayer, pray a spontaneous prayer, pray aloud or pray silently. You might pray alone, with a partner or in community. Communal discernment, (minimum of two or three), is preferable when the discernment is an important one (cf. Matthew 18:18-19).

Pray to the Lord. Ask Him, "Lord, is this of You?" "Do You want me to do this?" "Lord, I want to hear Your voice. Are these whispers of You?" However you are led to pray, whatever questions you choose to ask, your prayer is only half done if you have not yet listened.

> What we need most in order to make progress is to be silent before this great God with our appetite and with our tongue, for the language he best hears is silent love.
> Saint John of the Cross

After you ask, sit with the silence. Silently await and expect an answer from God. In the silence, in the absence of sound, you will hear Him speak. The Lord has not left you an orphan; He has not left you without a means of knowing His will for your life. Sometimes God will speak to you in images or thoughts or a Scripture verse. He might even use another person or certain circumstance you find yourself in or a word you hear or see. Be open to the manner and timing of His choosing about the answering of your prayer. However He makes His will known to you, be assured if you seek Him with an honest heart, He will not lead you astray. Be patient and allow God the time to mold you. If you do your part, God will find a way to help you understand.

Pray to know His will for you. Pray to be able to serve Him according to His will. Pray for the courage, wisdom and strength to continue in His will. Don't allow Satan to steal your peace. Don't allow his cunning to bear fruit in your mind. Don't allow his whisperings to dampen your resolve. Don't give him a place to dwell. Don't give in to the father of lies. Do praise God in all things. Do surrender to His will. Do trust your Lord with your life.

> When you intend to do something and see that your thought is perturbed, and if after invoking God's name

it remains perturbed even by a hair's breadth, know from this that the action you mean to commit is from the evil one and refrain from committing it.
Saint Barsanuphius

By the anxieties and worries of this life Satan tries to dull man's heart and make a dwelling for himself there.
Saint Francis of Assisi

Sometimes a man desires something good, but God does not help him. This happens because at times a similar desire comes from the devil and is harmful instead of useful. Yet the devil uses all of his wiles to offer this activity in a favorable light, to incite us to it and thus disturb our peace of soul or cause harm to the body. So we must carefully examine even our good desires.
Saint Isaac of Syria

You must spiritually describe the enemy

To verbalize the actions of the enemy does not bring undue attention to him. It does the exact opposite; it exposes him to the light which he fears. In this light, you can begin to more easily recognize the traps of the evil one.

The enemy can be obvious or understated. The enemy can use temptation or harassment or both. The enemy can use your enemies or your friends, either knowingly or unknowingly, to carry out his plan. Good intentions and good relationships are not respected by Satan. He'll use whatever opening serves his malicious will. Be careful, know your enemy.

The enemy can be described as a liar

For the devil sins from the beginning.
1 John 3:8b

When he speaks a lie, he speaks it from his own self. For he is a liar, and the father of lies.
John 8:44e

He is a liar from the beginning. Satan's nature, while

created good, has been eternally corrupted. His character is to lie; he has no truth in him. Since he is now the enemy of good, he is also the enemy of truth. What proceeds from his mouth are lies and half-truths. He tells no more truth than he needs to tell you in order to win you over.

Here the spirits of lies, deception, confusion, envy and jealousy are active.

> He is the friend of lies, and a lie himself.
> Saint Teresa of Avila

> We can presume that his [the evil one's] sinister action is at work where the denial of God becomes radical, subtle and absurd; where lies become powerful and hypocritical in the face of evident truth; where love is smothered by cold, cruel selfishness; where Christ's name is attacked with conscious, rebellious hatred, where the spirit of the Gospel is watered down and rejected, where despair is affirmed as the last word; and so forth.
> Pope Paul VI

The enemy can be described as a murderer

> He was a murderer from the beginning. And he did not stand in the truth, because the truth is not in him.
> John 8:44c-d

He is a murderer from the beginning. His lies are designed to kill your soul, your spirit, your will, your mind and your body. He wants to kill the life of grace in your soul, wipe it away. Though a murderer, he is not necessarily repulsive to the eyes and ears. He can speak quite smoothly and seductively and appear pleasing to the eyes. He's a patient assassin, a ruthless and relentless killer. Here the spirits of murder, suicide, lies, envy and jealousy are active.

> The devil flatters that he may deceive us, he charms that he may injure us; he allures that he may slay us.
> Saint John Climacus

The enemy can be described as an accuser

> And I heard a great voice in Heaven, saying: "Now have arrived salvation and virtue and the kingdom of our God and the power of his Christ. For the accuser of our brothers has been cast down, he who accused them before our God day and night."
> Revelation 12:10

Satan's name means accuser. He accuses you before God, before yourself and before other men. He delights in disparaging your name, shaming your conscience and causing scandal in the Church. He accuses the innocent and the guilty, the humble and the proud. He knows your wounds and weaknesses. He'll exploit you with accusations of unworthiness and shame.

Here the spirits of guilt, shame, judgment and pride are active.

> The devil will try to upset you by accusing you of being unworthy of the blessings that you have received. Simply remain cheerful and do your best to ignore the devil's nagging. If need be even laugh at the absurdity of the situation. Satan, the epitome of sin itself, accuses you of unworthiness! When the devil reminds you of your past, remind him of his future.
> Saint Teresa of Avila

> I ask that from now on, you never let your past sins be an obstacle between you and Jesus. It's a ruse of the devil to keep putting our sins before our eyes in order to make them like a screen between the Savior and us.
> Saint Therese of Lisieux

The enemy can be described as tolerant of all things

> In this way, the sons of God are made manifest, and also the sons of the devil. Everyone who is not just, is not of God, as also anyone who does not love his brother.
> 1 John 3:10

Satan loves to spread the lie that tolerance is a virtue and intolerance is a sin. He wants to replace truth with tolerance. Tolerance is an affront to justice for justice permits only that which is of God; tolerance permits everything except intolerance. Under the banner of tolerance love is devoid of truth and truth is devoid of love. Where the weeds of tolerance grow truth and love get choked off. Tolerance is one of Satan's most effective lies. The reality of tolerance is that when you stand for everything, you stand for nothing. Dante, the great Italian poet, stated that those who were apathetic and indifferent to good and evil suffer eternally in Hell.

Here the spirits of lies, indifference, apathy, self-righteousness and self-importance are active.

> The most deadly poison of our time is indifference.
> Saint Maximilian Kolbe

> Tolerance that does not know how to distinguish between good and evil would become chaotic and self-destructive.
> Saint Maximus

> Holy steadfastness is not intolerance.
> Saint Josemaria Escriva

> How can God, who is truth, approve or tolerate the indifference, neglect, and sloth of those who attach no importance to matters on which our eternal salvation depends; who attach no importance to pursuit and attainment of necessary truths, or to the offering of that proper worship which is owed to God alone?
> Blessed John XXIII

The enemy can be described as a seducer

> However, the serpent was more crafty than any of the creatures of the earth that the Lord God had made.
> Genesis 3:1a

Satan is a master of seduction. He is able to make what is deadly to the soul seem appealing. With a well-placed whisper or thought, he is able to create an opening where previously there was none. He is able, by his clever ways, to knock you off balance, to obscure the warning signs and to gain a toehold before you realize what has happened. The flesh, because of concupiscence, is especially vulnerable. Your senses are not safe; guard them with care. Clothe yourself in God's protection and the Blessed Mother's mantle and Satan will be unable to seduce you.

Here the spirits of addictions, seduction, lust, impurity, gluttony, alcohol and drugs are active.

Let us not succumb to temptation, free us from evil, from the evil one, O Lord; let us not fall into the infidelity to which we are seduced by the one who has been unfaithful from the beginning.
Pope John Paul II

He undermines man's moral equilibrium with his sophistry. He is the malign, clever seducer who knows how to make his way into us through the senses, the imagination and the libido, through utopian logic, or through disordered social contacts in the give and take of our activities, so that he can bring about in us deviations that are all the more harmful because they seem to conform to our physical or mental makeup, or to our profound, instinctive aspirations.
Pope Paul VI

The enemy can be described as a deceiver

And he was thrown out, that great dragon, that ancient serpent, who is called the devil and Satan, who seduces the whole world. And he was thrown down to the earth, and his angels were cast down with him.
Revelation 12:9

Satan deceives at every opportunity without any shame; he is the great liar. He'll tell a partial truth to get you to believe a greater lie — and he does it so well. His angelic attributes, though tainted, still remain intact; he is very skilled in the art of deception. His greatest deception is to convince you he doesn't exist. This allows him to operate almost unimpeded. Alternately, he tries to convince you that he is God's equal so he can control you by fear. Whatever deception he employs, he cannot overcome a grace-filled life.

Here the spirits of distortion, lies, guilt, confusion, mockery and pride are active.

> Those spirits are deceivers, not by nature, but by malice. They make themselves gods and souls of the departed, but they do not make themselves devils for they really are so.
> Saint Augustine

> With what infamous lucidity does Satan argue against our Catholic faith. But, let us tell him always, without entering into debate: I am a son of the Church.
> Saint Josemaria Escriva

> The enemy cares not whether what he says is true or false, but only whether he conquers us.
> Saint Ignatius of Loyola

The enemy can be described as anti-authority

> The Spirit of God may be known in this way. Every spirit who confesses that Jesus Christ has arrived in the flesh is of God; and every spirit who contradicts Jesus is not of God.
> 1 John 4:2

Satan refused to acknowledge God as God; he was prideful and disobedient. Obedience and humility are not in his vocabulary. He hates authority and tries to inspire similar feelings in you. He desires to destroy the Church and undermine its God-given authority. He has waged many successful campaigns in this area, but ultimately he will not prevail. Jezebel, Satan's powerful right hand woman, aids Satan in his efforts. She is an anti-authority spirit, an inciter of passions, a seductress, a mocker of truth, a false prophet and is filled with pride and envy.

The spirits of pride, envy, arrogance, false humility and

Jezebel are active here.

> Knowing the devil fell from Heaven through pride, for
> this cause the demons attack first those who have
> attained to a very great measure, seeking by means of
> pride and vainglory to turn them against one another.
> They know that in this way they can cut us off from
> God.
> Saint Antony of the Desert

> Q. 229. What was the devil's name before he fell, and
> why was he cast out of Heaven?
> A. Before he fell, Satan, or the devil, was called Lucifer,
> or light-bearer, a name which indicates great beauty.
> He was cast out of Heaven because through pride he
> rebelled against God.
> *Baltimore Catechism*

Do not be deceived, the enemy is deadly. He wants you
to die with the stain of mortal sin on your soul. He doesn't want
you to be able to perceive him or recognize him. He knows the
better you can spiritually discern and describe him, the better
you can defend against and deter him. Let prayer and Holy
Eucharist be your strength.

> What defense, what remedy should we use against the
> devil's action? We could say: everything that defends us
> from sin strengthens us by that very fact against the
> invisible enemy. Grace is the decisive defense.
> Innocence takes on the aspect of strength. Everyone
> recalls how often the apostolic method of teaching used
> the armor of a soldier as a symbol for the virtues that
> can make a Christian invulnerable.
> Pope Paul VI

> When the devil cannot enter with sin into a soul's
> sanctuary, he wants the soul to be at least unoccupied
> with no Master, and well removed from Holy
> Communion.
> Saint Therese of Lisieux

We should all realize that no matter where or how a man dies, if he is in the state of mortal sin and does not repent, when he could have done so and did not, the devil tears his soul from his body with such anguish and distress that only a person who has experienced it can appreciate it.
Saint Francis of Assisi

If you say the Rosary faithfully until death, I do assure you that, in spite of the gravity of your sins 'you shall receive a never-fading crown of glory.' Even if you are on the brink of damnation, even if you have one foot in Hell, even if you have sold your soul to the devil as sorcerers do who practice black magic, and even if you are a heretic as obstinate as a devil, sooner or later you will be converted and will amend your life and will save your soul, if and mark well what I say, if you say the Holy Rosary devoutly every day until death for the purpose of knowing the truth and obtaining contrition and pardon for your sins.
Saint Louis de Montfort

We ourselves put weapons into their [the demons] hands, that they may assail us; those very weapons with which we should defend ourselves. It is a great pity. But if, for the love of God, we hated all this, and embraced the cross, and set about His service in earnest, Satan would fly away before such realities, as from the plague.
Saint Teresa of Avila

The devil often transforms himself into an angel to tempt men, some for their instruction and some for their ruin.
Saint Augustine

In anything that is for the service of the Lord, the devil tries his arts, working under the guise of holiness.
Saint Teresa of Avila

Chapter 14
Armor of God

Concerning the rest, brothers, be strengthened in the Lord, by the power of his virtue. Be clothed in the armor of God, so that you may be able to stand against the treachery of the devil. For our struggle is not against flesh and blood, but against principalities and powers, against the directors of this world of darkness, against the spirits of wickedness in high places. Because of this, take up the armor of God, so that you may be able to withstand the evil day and remain perfect in all things. Therefore, stand firm, having been girded about your waist with truth, and having been clothed with the breastplate of justice, and having feet which have been shod by the preparation of the Gospel of peace. In all things, take up the shield of faith, with which you may be able to extinguish all the fiery darts of the most wicked one. And take up the helmet of salvation and the sword of the Spirit (which is the Word of God). Through every kind of prayer and supplication, pray at all times in Spirit.
Ephesians 6:10-18a

If you are to succeed as a spiritual warrior you must first be properly equipped and trained. In the above Scripture citation, Paul uses the imagery of an earthly soldier and his equipment to help explain a spiritual concept. This is probably the most well-known verse of Scripture relating to spiritual warfare. It is filled with vivid imagery and vital information.

Though the armament Paul speaks of is not meant as a physical reality, it is meant to be taken as a spiritual reality. Keep in mind that the term spiritual does not mean imaginary. Don't allow your visible, fleshy existence to overlook your invisible, spiritual existence. As the battle is not with the fleshy world but the spirit world, the spiritual armor Paul calls you to put on is both real and necessary. Each verse from Ephesians chapter 6 is detailed below.

10 Concerning the rest, brothers, be strengthened in the Lord, by the power of his virtue.

This is the step where you acknowledge that God is everything and you are nothing. Nowhere is this more important than in a spiritual battle. It is prayerfully waiting to be cloaked with His power from on high. You wait on the Lord and move only when He tells you. If He doesn't tell you to move, you wait until He does. Complete and total submission to and compliance with His will is essential for your protection as you battle in His name.

Satan, by use of trickery, will try and draw you out from under the Lord's power and protection. He will try to manipulate you into thinking that you can wage war under your own power. A lack of humility exposed, he will seek to destroy you by virtue of your pride. He'll also try and draw you out prematurely, before you are fully prepared, leaving you vulnerable. You need to let God's power, the power that has already vanquished Satan, run through you. Silence, prayer and contemplation need to precede the putting on of God's armor. This is a time of pondering, preparing and of resting in Jesus.

> Isn't our God more concerned about our salvation than we are ourselves? Isn't He stronger than Hell itself? Who can resist and overcome the King of Heavens? What are the world, the devil, the flesh and all our enemies before the Lord?
> Saint Pio of Pietrelcina

The soldier of Christ, trained by Christ's commands

and instructions, will not tremble at the thought of battle, but will be ready to receive the crown of victory.
Saint Cyprian of Carthage

11 Be clothed in the armor of God, so that you may be able to stand against the treachery of the devil.

The purpose of the armor as revealed by Paul, is to stand firm against the devil's tactics, harassment and temptation among them. Notice it is God's armor that you are to put on, not your armor. It's not even armor that God gives to you; it is God's very armor. He graces you with the virtues of truth, righteousness, peace and faith which flow from His very essence.

Don't be fooled by Satan attempting to fit you with false armor, a cheap imitation of the real thing. He'll try to get you to put on pride, arrogance, self-sufficiency, judgment and over-confidence. Though it may look good, the false armor will expose you and make you vulnerable to Satan. God has created armor, tailored made by His hand with His love, which fits you perfectly. He knows every hair on your head (cf. Luke12:7); He is your creator. It is His nature to love and protect you. Run to Him, secure His armor about you and realize it is His will that you prepare for battle.

> If you would do any good, it will not do for you to stand still and say "I shall lose my peace." Follow the call of God and His Vicar, quit your solitude and run to the field of battle.
> Saint Catherine of Siena

> If we have taken stock of the enemy's forces, this would be the right moment to make war on them. But one would have no confidence against the ranks of the opponents unless he was protected by the whole armor of the Apostles. One piece of armor separated from another cannot by itself be a protection.
> Saint Gregory of Nyssa

12 For our struggle is not against flesh and blood, but against principalities and powers, against the directors of this world of darkness, against the spirits of wickedness in high places.

Paul speaks of the struggle you face as being against and as originating with the evil spirits. Paul states both who the enemy is and who the enemy is not. Knowing both is vital to the success of any battle and war. If you do not know who you are supposed to be at war with, you are in trouble. Imagine being fully prepared to do battle and then finding out your allies were your enemies or your enemies were your allies.

The evil spirits, as Paul states, are your enemies. To deny that evil spirits exist and that they are engaged in an ongoing struggle with God's people is to deny Scripture. To deny that evil spirits exist is often the first step of the slippery slope of not acknowledging Jesus as God. It is also to aid and abet the enemy. Satan couldn't be happier to hear the silence, and sometimes even contradiction, regarding his existence. As God is creator of the principalities, powers, world rulers and evil spirits in the heavens, you have nothing to fear. God is on your side, or more to the point, you are on His.

> The battle against the devil, which is the principle task of Saint Michael the Archangel, is still being fought today, because the devil is still alive and active in the world. The evil that surrounds us today, the disorders that plague our society, man's inconsistency and brokenness, are not only the results of original sin, but also the results of Satan's pervasive and dark action.
> Pope John Paul II

> The peace of Jesus is the fruit of a constant struggle against evil. The battle that Jesus has decided to fight is not against men or human powers but against the enemy of God and man, Satan.
> Pope Benedict XVI

13 Because of this, take up the armor of God, so that you may be able to withstand the evil day and remain perfect in all things.

The purpose of the armor is primarily defensive. It is to hold ground, not to advance. You only advance if and when the Lord asks you to do so. In spiritual warfare you never precede the Lord. It is His timing, His way. The armor is meant to help you resist the enemy; it is not meant to help you conquer the enemy. It is meant to help you hold your ground; it is not meant to help you take new territory. It is to resist to the end so that you may find your eternal reward in Heaven. It is not for earthly treasures that you are engaged in this battle.

Satan would have you do nothing to prepare for this battle. His boot camp would consist of having you serve and spoil your flesh in every way possible. That way, you would be so big the armor wouldn't fit and you would be so weak you wouldn't be able to bear its weight. God wants you to prepare and will give you the grace necessary to do so. Prayer, fasting and almsgiving will prepare your spirit and flesh to desire only the Father's will. It is then your mission will seem easy; your armor will seem light.

> Let us humble ourselves profoundly and confess that if God were not our breastplate and our shield, we should at once be pierced by every kind of sin.
> Saint Pio of Pietrelcina

> For neither the devil nor anyone else can force me to commit a single deadly sin against my will. We can never be overcome unless we give up this armor and turn it over to the devil by our willing consent.
> Saint Catherine of Siena

14a Therefore, stand firm, having been girded about your waist with truth

This is the belt of truth; it holds everything together. The Holy Spirit is the belt. He is the spiritual glue. In ancient times, the belt served as the foundation for sword and breastplate. No soldier would have gone into battle without the belt secured. And so it should be for you as well. You receive the belt when you are humble. Humility is truth. Standing firm gives the sense of being stationary. It is much more a defensive posture, a posture of patiently waiting, not of advancing. No matter the sense of urgency you may perceive, always wait on the Lord.

Satan's foundation is one of shifting sand. It is undergirded by lies. It is impossible to surround yourself in truth when you are surrounded by the father of lies. God's foundation is solid rock. His Church is the "pillar and foundation of truth" (cf. 1 Timothy 3:15). It is undergirded by truth. It is impossible to surrender to lies when you put on the belt of truth.

> We must declare the truth and not keep silence out of fear, but be ready generously to give our life for Holy Church.
> Saint Catherine of Siena

> He [Satan] will have nothing to do with those who walk in the truth.
> Saint Teresa of Avila

14b and having been clothed with the breastplate of justice

The breastplate covers the heart and other vital organs. You don't want your heart to be vulnerable to an external attack or an internal infection; either can be deadly, whether due to your own sin or Satan's influence. You can't be a bleeding heart; you need to stand in truth. Nor can you be a heart of stone; you need to stand in charity. As with any protective device, there needs to be a balance between protection and functionality. It is useless to wear armor that is so heavy that it impedes movement; likewise it is useless to wear armor that is so light that it affords you no protection against the weaponry of the enemy. The breastplate of justice (righteousness) will help you maintain a proper perspective and a balanced, pure heart. The breastplate righteousness will help you maintain a heart of truth and love, of mercy and justice.

Satan attempts to upset your equilibrium at every turn. You cannot protect yourself so much that you disengage from the world, nor can you engage the world without proper protection. God is your equilibrium. Hungering and thirsting for His righteousness will satisfy you and bring His blessing upon you. Let His blessing and righteousness be your protection. Commit to engaging the world in service to His will.

> Let us take this armor and defend ourselves with these spiritual defenses from Heaven, so that when the evil day comes we may be able to resist the threats of the devil, and fight back against him. Let us put on the breastplate of righteousness so that our breasts may be

protected and kept safe from the arrows of the enemy.
Saint Cyprian of Carthage

As the breastplate is impenetrable, so also is righteousness. Such a life no one shall ever be able to overthrow; it is true, many wound him, but no one cuts through him, no, not the devil himself.
Saint John Chrysostom

15 and having feet which have been shod by the preparation of the Gospel of peace.

In ancient times, a soldier's sandals were well secured. The straps of his sandals would wrap around his legs several times in an upward spiral. This created a solid foundation from which to do battle. The foundation of every battle you engage in needs to be a foundation of peace. Peace needs to integrate itself into every aspect of your life as a spiritual warrior.

Satan attempts to pervert every rule in order to create chaos. If you attempt to play by his rules, you will lose. You can be at peace in the midst of chaos only if you focus upon Christ. If you are consumed by Christ (and consuming Him) you can be at peace. You can fight with holy boldness, holy confidence and holy perseverance only if you are in His peace. Be little. Be humble. Be obedient. Be at peace. Fight with truth and love, not pride and hatred. Let His victory be your peace.

Let our feet be shod in the teaching of the Gospel, and armored so that when we begin to trample on the serpent and crush it, it will not be able to bite us or trip us up.
Saint Cyprian of Carthage

Peace consists in having achieved victory over the world, the devil, and our own passions.
Saint Pio of Pietrelcina

16 In all things, take up the shield of faith, with which you may be able to extinguish all the fiery darts of the most wicked one.

The shield Paul is referring to is a whole body shield, roughly four feet by two feet. It provided individual protection for each soldier. When overlapped with other shields, it also provided protection for many soldiers at once. Two-by-two is the rule for all spiritual warriors. Check to see whose authority you are operating under. Keep an eye on your flank; know with whom you enter into battle. Don't proceed into battle if you or your partner is under the bondage of mortal sin and never proceed into battle alone.

Satan will try and draw you away from your surety, faith in Christ Jesus. He will shoot flaming arrows your way when and where you are most vulnerable. He will do his best to isolate and insulate you from the truth.

He will try to separate you from community. Alone, your shield is limited in its effectiveness. Alone, you are at risk of being wounded by his flaming arrows. Fear not, God will counter with His grace to strengthen your faith. He will place you alongside faith-filled soldiers so collectively you will create a virtually impenetrable shield of faith to protect against flaming arrows.

> Thanks be to the highest God Eternal, who has placed us in the battlefield as knights to fight for His bride with the shield of holiest faith.
> Saint Catherine of Siena

> When the soul is clothed in faith the devil is ignorant of how to hinder it, neither is he successful in his efforts, for faith gives the soul strong protection against the devil, who is the mightiest and most astute enemy.
> Saint John of the Cross

> Whoever is armed with faith need fear nothing; this is the only armor necessary to repel and confound our enemy; for what can harm him who says Credo, "I believe" in God, who is our Father, and our Father Almighty?
> Saint Francis de Sales

17a And take up the helmet of salvation

The helmet protects the mind, the point of entry for most temptations. Spiritual warfare's main battlefield is the mind. Temptation's door is through the imagination. This is prime territory; Satan's whispers are strong here. Satan wants you to put on the mind of the times, situational ethics, subjective truths, indifference, tolerance, compromise, etc. All are subtle entry points for Satan; all pervert what is true. They are the equivalent of removing your helmet in the middle of a raging battle. The helmet only protects the head which wears it. If you're filled with self (ego) your head will be too big for the helmet and you won't be able to wear it. Satan will gladly swell your head with false praise and delusions of grandeur if it will prevent your helmet from fitting properly.

Put on the mind of Christ and let Jesus show you the way, the truth and the life. Put on the mind of Christ and the helmet of salvation will fit you like a glove. It will be snug and secure. Control access to your mind; avoid pride of the mind. Be careful about who is whispering in your ear and targeting your imagination and intellect. Always wear your helmet.

Let us wear on our head the helmet of the Spirit, to defend our ears against the proclamations of death, to defend our eyes against the sight of accursed idols, to defend our foreheads so that God's sign may be kept intact, and to defend our mouths so that our tongues may proclaim victoriously the name of Christ the Lord.
Saint Cyprian of Carthage

Pride of mind is much worse than pride of will. When the mind is firmly grounded in the self-relying thought that its own judgments are better than all others, who can cure it in the end? This is why you must hasten to oppose this pernicious pride of mind, before it penetrates into the marrow of your bones.
Saint Nicodemos of the Holy Mountain

17b and the sword of the Spirit (which is the Word of God).

The last part of the armor listed is the only offensive weapon Paul mentions. The sword Paul speaks of is a double edged, short, slicer type of sword, perhaps the kind used by Peter in the Garden of Gethsemane. As in verse eleven, the armor to be used is not to be your own, but the Spirit's. It is to be the sword of the Holy Spirit that you use. The sword of the Spirit is the Word of God, both Scripture and Jesus. You wound Satan when you claim and cling to the promises made to you by

God, both in His written word and in His Son. Let the Word be your weapon. Let the sword of the Spirit do the fighting, not you.

Satan knows Scripture, do not be deceived. He is not the author of Scripture; but he is its unofficial, unauthorized interpreter. Satan will distort Scripture to try and entrap you. He'll include just enough truth in his interpretation to make it seem plausible, almost pleasant. Don't be fooled, the lie is always just below the surface.

The Book of Hebrews speaks of the word of God as being living and active, as being sharper than any two-edged sword (cf. Hebrews 4:12). It has the ability to penetrate hearts and minds. It is powerful, incisive and discerning. It knows the difference between the truth and a lie. Trust in His Word.

> And let us arm our right hand with the sword of the spirit so that it may courageously refuse the daily [pagan] sacrifices, and, remembering the Eucharist, let the hand that took hold of the body of the Lord embrace the Lord himself, and so gain from the Lord the future prize of a heavenly crown.
> Saint Cyprian of Carthage

> You have aroused this fierce beast; but do not fear. You have received a greater power, a sharper sword. Pierce the serpent with it.
> Saint John Chrysostom

18a Through every kind of prayer and supplication, pray at all times in the Spirit.

You are to take all of your prayer, all of your entreaties and pleas and pray in the Spirit. You are to do this early and often. Pray in the Spirit; pray with the Spirit; pray as led by the Spirit. Pray while at work, pray while at play. Let your every action become a prayer. Pray at every opportunity in the Spirit.

Satan wants to distract you from prayer, distract you from your faith in God. He wants to make you believe you are independent and that God is unnecessary and irrelevant. He wants you to neglect the gifts and fruits you received from the Holy Spirit at baptism. He wants to penetrate your armor and render it unusable. More than that, he wants to penetrate your soul and render it unusable.

Prayer draws you in to the Father. Prayer, because it is an act of humility, helps you to strengthen your resistance to the evil one. Prayer brings you full circle; it is how you "draw your strength from the Lord" as Paul speaks of in verse ten. In and through prayer you become one with God the Father and have access to His power and authority. In faith, cry out to the Lord.

"Prayer makes the soul one with God."
Blessed Julian of Norwich

Put on the garment of holiness, gird yourself with the belt of chastity. Let Christ be your helmet, let the cross on your forehead be your unfailing protection. Your breastplate should be the knowledge of God that he himself has given you. Keep burning continually the sweet smelling incense of prayer. Take up the sword of the Spirit. Let your heart be an altar.
Saint Peter Chrysologus

Almighty and merciful God, Who in the person of the Blessed Virgin Mary provided never-ending assistance for the defense of the Christian people grant, we beg of you, that, strengthened by such help, we may do battle during life and be able to obtain victory over the treacherous foe in death.
Prayer for the Feast of Mary, Help of Christians

Clothe yourself daily in the armor of God. Every morning pray each piece of God's armor onto yourself and onto your loved ones. "Lord, I place your helmet of salvation upon my head, your breastplate of righteousness upon my chest, your belt of truth around my waist, your shoes of peace upon my feet, with your shield of faith in one hand and the sword of the Spirit in the other."

As you are suiting up, pray for the gifts of the Holy Spirit to be stirred up in you: wisdom, understanding, knowledge, piety, fortitude, counsel and fear of the Lord. Pray for the fruits of the Holy Spirit to come alive in you. They are charity, joy, peace, patience, kindness, goodness, generosity, gentleness, faithfulness, modesty, self-control and chastity. Pray for the humility, obedience, surrender and trust to be a soldier of the Lord. Stand firm in His armor, draw your strength from Him, pray in Him and you will receive the crown of glory that awaits you.

> Woe to me if I should prove myself but a halfhearted soldier in the service of my thorn-crowned Captain.
> Saint Fidelis of Sigmaringen

> The devil strains every nerve to secure the souls which belong to Christ. We should not grudge our toil in wresting them from Satan and giving them back to God.
> Saint Sebastian

> Take up the shield of faith and fight the battles of the Lord vigorously. You especially must stand as a wall against every height which raises itself against the knowledge of God. Unsheath the sword of the spirit, which is the word of God, and may those who hunger after justice receive bread from you.
> Pope Gregory XVI

Chapter 15
Resisting Satan

☨

Therefore, be subject to God. But resist the devil, and he will flee from you. Draw near to God, and he will draw near to you. Cleanse your hands, you sinners! And purify your hearts, you duplicitous souls! Be afflicted: mourn and weep. Let your laughter be turned into mourning, and your gladness into sorrow. Be humbled in the sight of the Lord, and he will exalt you.
James 4:7-10

In Ephesians, Paul details the armor of God, the external battle gear. The purpose of the armor is to be able to stand firm and resist Satan. In this verse from Scripture, James explains of the necessity to freely submit to God in order to be able to resist the devil. A submission not freely given, whether due to pride, fear, indifference, etc., creates a reluctant soldier. A reluctant soldier is a dangerous soldier.

A reluctant soldier may still look like a soldier, but will rarely act like one. A reluctant soldier will meet the minimum standards, but will never exceed them. He will do just enough to keep from getting killed, but ironically, not enough to stay alive. A reluctant soldier, because he does not possess the fighting spirit, will resist the battle, not the enemy. The sword of the Spirit remains sheathed.

A reluctant spiritual soldier is a worldly soldier, more concerned with earthly respite than heavenly reward. The methods of resisting Satan the world and the flesh proffer are vastly different than the method of resisting Satan spoken of in Scripture and by the saints.

The world and the flesh say, "Resist Satan by pretending he doesn't exist."

> And it was not enough for them to go astray concerning the knowledge of God, but also, while living in a great war of ignorance, they call so many and such great evils "peace."
> Wisdom 14:22

"I'll pretend he's not there and he'll leave me alone." Ignoring what is true does not change the truth; neither does ignoring Satan make him go away. Ignoring Satan brings a false peace, a false calm. Ignoring Satan is tantamount to submitting to him; it only serves to empower and embolden him. And like the schoolyard bully, Satan has an ability to detect and target those who are easily intimidated and vulnerable.

Resisting Satan by pretending he doesn't exist is no resistance at all. In fact, it makes it easier for Satan, because all he has to do is glance your way and he controls you by controlling which way you are looking.

> This matter of the devil and of the influence he can exert on individuals as well as on communities, entire societies or events, is a very important chapter of Catholic doctrine which should be studied again, although it is given little attention today.
> Pope Paul VI

> Remember the devil never sleeps, but seeks our ruin in a thousand ways.
> Saint Angela Merici

> The devil does not sleep, but works hard to make you lose your soul. Will you then continue to rest when your eternal salvation is at stake?
> Saint Augustine

The world and the flesh say, "Resist Satan by will power."

> I am the vine; you are the branches. Whoever abides in me, and I in him, bears much fruit. For without me, you are able to do nothing.
> John 15:5

"I'll just focus my energy and my mind and I'll be fine." Most people can't resist a dessert they shouldn't have or an item on sale they don't really need, to say nothing of the sins they commit time after time. If you can't resist these temptations, how are you going to resist the prince of this world? He is so clever, so seductive; you stand no chance on your own. Positive thinking is no match for the Prince of Darkness. Those who think they do stand a chance against Satan are worshipping at one of his side altars, that of ego. You cannot resist Satan without God. You can do nothing without God. The spiritual warrior who thinks otherwise is foolish and prideful.

Being filled with pride is a prerequisite to believing this lie. A little temptation, a little whisper in your ear and your will power is gone. Abide in God's will, not your own, and then you can resist Satan.

> The field of battle between God and Satan is the human soul. This is where it takes place every moment of our lives. The soul must give free access to our Lord and be completely fortified by Him with every kind of weapon. His light must illuminate it to fight the darkness of error. He must put on Jesus Christ, His truth and justice, the shield of faith, the word of God to overcome such powerful enemies. To put on Jesus Christ we must die to ourselves.
> Saint Pio of Pietrelcina

> Nowadays they prefer to appear strong and unprejudiced to pose as positivists, while at the same time lending faith to many unfounded magical or popular superstitions or, worse still, exposing their souls, their baptized souls, visited so often by the Eucharistic Presence and inhabited by the Holy Spirit,

to licentious sensual experiences and to harmful drugs, as well as to the ideological seductions of fashionable errors. These are cracks through which the evil one can easily penetrate and change the human mind.
Pope Paul VI

The world and the flesh say, "Resist Satan by deceiving yourself."

Are you so foolish that, though you began with the Spirit, you would now end with the flesh?
Galatians 3:3

"I'll simply change the rules and trick myself into thinking that things aren't really that bad." All deception, including self-deception, is from the father of lies. He wants you to live a life of deception, of falsehoods and of un-reality. Satan doesn't want you to live in God's world. He attempts to lure you in to his world, a world of falsity, lies and evil. He doesn't care if he lies or tells the truth as long as he ensnares you. Trapped in his world, in no time he'll have you distorting, denying, justifying, excusing, rationalizing, overlooking and eventually, sinning. The spiritual warrior who tries this tactic is destined for destruction.

Satan's alternative lifestyle is not life at all. Its only end is death and eternal separation from God. Don't be fooled by his euphemisms or your own.

He who pretends to amuse himself with the devil will not rejoice with Christ.
Saint Peter Chrysologus

Oppose the devil and try to discern his wiles. He usually hides his gall under an appearance of sweetness, so as to avoid detection, and he fabricates various illusions, beautiful to look at — which in reality are not at all what they seem — to seduce your hearts by a cunning imitation of truth, which is rightly attractive. All his art is directed to this end, to oppose by all possible means every soul working well for God.
Saint Antony of the Desert

The world and the flesh say, "Resist Satan by playing now and repenting later."

> But God said to him: "Foolish one, this very night they require your soul of you. To whom, then, will those things belong, which you have prepared?"
> Luke 12:20

"God will forgive me, it's what He does." It's true that God is love and that forgiveness is love in action. It is not necessarily true that "later" will ever come. Most often you die as you habitually live. The inertia of sinful habits makes it harder to break free. Inactive muscles atrophy. If you freely choose to embrace sin while you are living, sin is apt to wield a grip on your soul as you die. The spiritual warrior who tries this tactic risks hardening of the heart.

God's mercy is infinite, but it is not indiscriminate. Presumption upon God's mercy is a sin and a poor strategy for resisting the evil one. The spiritual warrior who indulges in this lifestyle is compounding his sin.

> To sin with the intention of persevering in sin and through the hope of being pardoned, is presumptuous and this does not diminish, but increases sin.
> Saint Thomas Aquinas

> If the devil tempts me by thoughts of divine justice, I think of God's mercy; if he tries to fill me with presumption by the thoughts of His mercy, I think of His justice.
> Saint Ignatius of Loyola

> The fervid enemy of the human race hurls some down because of reckless despair, but others he trips up with the deception of a false hope.
> Saint Fulgentius

The world and the flesh say, "Resist Satan by negotiating with him."

> For how does it benefit a man, if he gains the whole

world, yet truly suffers damage to his soul? Or what shall a man give in exchange for his soul?
Matthew 16:26

"I'll negotiate a settlement, a pleasant middle ground." With Satan, there is no negotiation, there is no middle ground; there is only abdication and surrender. You can attempt to justify, excuse or rationalize all you like, but a compromise with Satan is a single-sided suicide pact. Satan will be glad to have you enter into such a pact. He'll be more than willing to forgot about you and leave you alone as long as you are willing to forget about God and leave Him alone. Negotiating a compromise with Satan is like Christianity without the cross, useless.

Don't be fooled, Satan is an expert negotiator. He'll ask from you only those things he knows he can get. A Faustian bargain will never end well for you; it is an eternal death sentence. Since he does not possess what you require, he can never quench your soul's desire. No matter what the alleged benefit received, no price is worth your soul.

> Do not bargain with any temptation; lock yourself immediately in My heart and, at the first opportunity, reveal the temptation to the confessor and then the temptation will lose all of its force.
> Our Lord to Saint Faustina Kowalska

> There is no better explanation for the massive evils that are plaguing the modern world than to say that the devil is extraordinarily effective in seducing otherwise intelligent people with his deceptive snares.
> Servant of God John Hardon

> It is safer for mankind to deserve the hatred of the devil than his peace.
> Pope Saint Leo the Great

The world and the flesh say, "Resist Satan by tolerating him."

> Why do you look upon the agents of iniquity, and remain silent, while the impious is devouring one who

is more just than himself?
Habakkuk 1:13b

"Whatever makes you happy. I'm not here to tell anybody else how to live." G.K. Chesterton once said, "Tolerance is the virtue of the man without convictions." Tolerance is a misguided act of love accepting what is not true or it is a misguided act of truth accepting what is not love. Tolerance cannot tolerate truth and love together, for tolerance is a lie. As easily as it passes off the lips, it pollutes the soul.

To tolerate sin is to begin to slowly poison yourself. When you accept love without truth, you pay homage to Satan's kingdom. When you accept truth without love, it leads you away from the heart of truth and into the mushy middle of tolerance.

Truth and love are the two stakes of the cross, they go together. They cannot be separated; they can admit no compromise. Truth and love are what separates those in Hell from those in Heaven. Truth and love are what you are called to embrace and how you are called to act. The spiritual warrior who lacks one or the other is not one with the heart and mind of Christ.

> Do not accept anything as the truth if it lacks love. And do not accept anything as love which lacks truth. One without the other becomes a destructive lie.
> Saint Teresa Benedicta of the Cross

> Sacred pluralism must coexist with the love of the Church and the authentic mind of the Church.
> Pope John Paul I

> Compromising is a sure sign of not possessing the truth. When a man yields in matters of ideals, of honor, or of faith, that man is without ideals, without honor, and without faith.
> Saint Josemaria Escriva

The world and the flesh say, "Resist Satan by giving in."

For it is necessary for you to be patient, so that, by

doing the will of God, you may receive the promise. So then, we are not sons who are drawn away to perdition, but we are sons of faith toward the securing of the soul. Hebrews 10:36, 39

"Why bother? It's no use." Often, the final act of the reluctant soldier is to resist by giving in. This one is doubly harmful. Not only does it give in to Satan, it despairs of God's mercy. When you hand over your will to Satan you are committing spiritual suicide. Even in this darkest of moments Satan's victory can be fleeting; God's grace awaits.

Never despair of God's mercy. No sin is too great, no time is too late. God's love and mercy trumps Satan's hate. Cry out and He will hear you. Do not be discouraged by the many ways the world and the flesh tell you to resist Satan. God allows all of them. And if God allows them, He can use them to bring about His will. If you doubt that Satan's plans can be used to bring about God's plans, simply take a look at the crucifix. Satan's "crowning glory" became his sure and certain demise. The spiritual warrior who gives in to Satan gives up on God. Even when all around you seems lost, especially when all around you seems lost, trust in God. Even when others commit spiritual murder, do not commit spiritual suicide.

> It is the devil who wanders around our spirit, rummaging about and causing confusion, trying to find an open door if he can. Keep all the entrances well closed. Satan will tire and if he doesn't, God will make him remove his siege.
> Saint Pio of Pietrelcina

> The spiritual combat in which we kill our passions to put on the new man is the most difficult struggle of all. We must never weary of this combat, but fight the holy fight fervently and perseveringly.
> Saint Nilus the Younger

So much for how the flesh and the world would have you resist. How does God want you to resist? Submit your will wholly, completely, freely and fully. You cannot resist Satan unless you submit to God.

Jesus resisted by saying, "Not My will be done, but Yours."

> Father, if you are willing, take this chalice away from
> me. Yet truly, let not my will, but yours, be done.
> Luke 22:42

In His deepest moment of agony, Jesus teaches all of
humanity the ultimate prayer of submission. Egoless and
emptied of self, Jesus submits to the will of the Father. He
subordinates His will to the Father's, not for the purposes of
achieving a certain outcome, but in obedience to the Father and
out of love for the Father. It was obedience that brought Jesus
to the cross; it was love that kept Him there.

This prayer serves as a kind of litmus test for sanctity
and sainthood. When you pray this prayer with conviction,
especially in the face of adversity, you become Christ-like. As a
spiritual warrior, you are called to obedience to God's will out of
love for God.

> Having no doubts about the true nature of my disease, I
> am calm, resigned and very happy in the midst of my
> people. God certainly knows what is best for my
> sanctification and I gladly repeat: Thy will be done.
> Saint Damien of Molokai

**Mary resisted by saying, "Be it done unto me according to your
word."**

> Then Mary said: "Behold, I am the handmaid of the
> Lord. Let it be done to me according to your word." And
> the Angel departed from her.
> Luke 1:38

Alone, troubled and now subject to an uncertain future,
Mary responds with grace and humility. With no regard for
herself, Mary submits to God's will. Mary's *"Fiat,"* countered
Satan's *"Non serviam."* Her "Yes," countered Eve's "No." Her
simple act of humility foiled Satan's elaborate act of pride. As a
spiritual warrior you are called, like Mary, to surrender your
will to the Father's will. Trust in Mary, the Mother of God and
you will one day, like her, be united with Jesus in Heaven.

What Lucifer lost by pride, Mary won by humility.
What Eve ruined and lost by disobedience Mary saved
by obedience.
Saint Louis de Montfort

Saint John the Baptist resisted by saying, "He must increase, I must decrease."

He must increase, while I must decrease.
John 3:30

Knowing that his mission was complete, John the
Baptist stepped aside and pointed his followers to Jesus. He
prepared their hearts, he witnessed to the truth and then he
humbly submitted to the Messiah. He, by the grace of God,
successfully fulfilled the mission given to him by the Father.
Having done so, John remarked that his joy was complete (cf.
John 3:29). As a spiritual warrior you are called to fulfill your
mission and lead others to Jesus. Do so and your joy will also
be complete.

"It is necessary for him to grow, but for me to
diminish." The one grew on the cross; the other was
diminished by the sword. So let man's honor diminish,
God's honor increase, so that the honor of man may be
found in the honor of God.
Saint Augustine

Saint Stephen resisted by saying, "Lord, do not hold this sin against them."

Then, having been brought to his knees, he cried out
with a loud voice, saying, "Lord, do not hold this sin
against them." And when he had said this, he fell
asleep in the Lord.
Acts of the Apostles 7:60

The first Christian martyr, in his last breath, begs the
Lord to show mercy on his killers. As he was being stoned to
death for speaking the truth, his last thought was not of
himself, but of his attackers. In imitation of Jesus on the cross,

Saint Stephen accepted his death and submitted to the Father's will. As a spiritual warrior, you may be called to surrender your life for the cause and to forgive those who are trying to kill you.

> The way to overcome the devil when he excites feelings of hatred for those who injure us is immediately to pray for their conversion.
> Saint John Vianney

Saint Paul resisted by saying, "For when I am weak, then I am powerful."

> And lest the greatness of the revelations should extol me, there was given to me a prodding in my flesh: an angel of Satan, who struck me repeatedly. Because of this, three times I petitioned the Lord that it might be taken away from me. And he said to me: "My grace is sufficient for you. For virtue is perfected in weakness." And so, willingly shall I glory in my weaknesses, so that the virtue of Christ may live within me. Because of this, I am pleased in my infirmity: in reproaches, in difficulties, in persecutions, in distresses, for the sake of Christ. For when I am weak, then I am powerful.
> 2 Corinthians 12:7-10

Saint Paul, after praying for the removal of his thorn, willingly accepted it from the Lord, not as punishment, but as a safeguard against pride. He trusted that the Lord knew what was best for him and submitted to this pain and many others. He embraced the cross that was given to him for he knew in dying to self, he could better bear witness to Jesus Christ crucified and the glory that awaits.

> Well, at any rate, in future when I preach, instead of saying , "My dear bretheren," I shall say, "My fellow lepers."
> Saint Damien of Molokai

> In all trials I will say always; "Lord, Your will be done."
> Saint Gerard Majella

This is the way that the martyrs and saints resisted Satan; by submitting themselves to God, even unto death. They realized that God is God and they are not; they recognized His mercy and sought to extend it to those who desired to kill their flesh. They were given the grace to realize that their martyrdom would hasten their reunion with God and grow His Church. They were willing to be a witness for God. In all things, at all times, they sought to do His will. By God's grace they lived as saints. By God's grace they died as saints.

> May God have mercy on you. May God bless you. Lord, You know that I am innocent. With all my heart I forgive my enemies. Viva Cristo Rey!
> Blessed Miguel Pro

> God be blessed; I'll pray for all of you in heaven. What more could I desire than to die for no other crime but that of being a religious and for having made my contribution to the Christian education of children. I have been judged and condemned to death. I accept the sentence with joy. No charges have been brought against me. I have been condemned to death only because I am a religious. Do not weep for me, I am not worthy of pity. I shall die for God and for my country. Farewell, I shall be waiting for you in heaven.
> Saint Jaime Hilario

> My lords, as the blessed Apostle Saint Paul, as we read in the Acts of the Apostles, was present and consented to the death of Saint Stephen, and kept their clothes that stoned him to death, and yet they be now both twain holy saints in Heaven, and shall continue there friends for ever, so I verily trust, and shall right heartily pray, that though your lordships have now here on earth been judges to my condemnation, we may yet hereafter in Heaven right merrily all meet together, to our everlasting salvation. And thus I desire Almighty God to preserve and defend the King's Majesty, and to send him good counsel.
> Saint Thomas More

He has real charity toward his enemies who, when he suffers injustice, thinks first of all the harm the unjust one has done to his own soul.
Saint Francis of Assisi

I know you have come to kill me. I make God my shield. If all the swords in England were pointed at my head, your threats could not move me. Foot to foot you will find me in the battle of my Lord. I accept death in the name of the Lord. And I commend my soul and the cause of the Church to God and His Blessed Mother and to the patron saints of this church. I shall not feel your swords.
Saint Thomas Becket

O God, if sacrifice of life is needed, accept it from us who are free from family obligations. Spare those with wives and children.
Blessed Mary Stella and her eleven companions

Christian people, I come to die for the faith of Christ's Holy Catholic Church, and I thank God my stomach has served me very well, so that yet I have not feared death. Wherefore I do desire you all to help and assist me with your prayers, that at the very point and instant of death's stroke, I may in that very moment stand steadfast without fainting in any one point of the Catholic faith free from anyfear; and I beseech Almighty God of His infinite goodness to save the king and this Realm, and that it may please Him to hold His holy hand over it, and send the king good Counsel.
Saint John Fisher

Chapter 16
Consuming the HOST

He humbled himself, becoming obedient even unto
death, even the death of the Cross.
Philippians 2:8

For this reason, the Father loves me: because I lay
down my life, so that I may take it up again. No one
takes it away from me. Instead, I lay it down of my own
accord.
John 10:17-18

Jesus was humble and obedient. He surrendered to His
Father's will. He trusted that His Father would bring ultimate
good out of the ultimate evil. The Son's once-for-all sacrificial
act of love opened up the gates of Heaven. Reparation for sin
against an infinite and perfect God required an infinite and
perfect sacrifice of an infinite and perfect victim. Jesus Christ
is that Sacrament and that victim. Each Eucharist is a re-
presentation of that same once-for-all sacrifice. In consuming
the Host, you are consuming the Body, Blood, Soul and Divinity
of Jesus Christ. No greater source of strength is there for a
spiritual warrior than Eucharist.

As a spiritual warrior, you are strengthened in Jesus
and can therefore resist Satan best by partaking of the
Eucharistic Host. You can also be strengthened in Jesus and
resist Satan by imitating Jesus in His humility, obedience,

surrender and trust. The acronym HOST, (Humility, Obedience, Surrender and Trust), can help you to remember the virtues necessary to be a courageous soldier of Christ. In imitation of Jesus, Mary and the saints, you need to submit to God in humility, in obedience, in surrender and in trust. You stand firm against Satan when you consume the HOST. A good soldier will frequently and faithfully consume and fully digest the HOST.

> The means of holiness and salvation are known to everybody, since they are found in the Gospel; the masters of the spiritual life have explained them; the saints have practiced them. These means are sincere humility, unceasing prayer, complete self -denial, abandonment to divine Providence and obedience to the will of God.
> Saint Louis de Montfort

HOST   Humility

> Take my yoke upon you, and learn from me, for I am meek and humble of heart; and you shall find rest for your souls. For my yoke is sweet and my burden is light.
> Matthew 11:29-30

A good soldier must be humble. If there is no humility, there is no following through on commands. A lack of humility leads to chaos and a lack of order. Disorder in times of battle causes dire consequences, up to and including death.

Humility is the foundational virtue, the one from which all the other virtues spring. And as a virtue, it is naturally opposed to a vice. Humility is an act of the will; it is something you can choose or not choose. It cannot be imposed on you or coerced from you. Humility must be freely chosen or else it cannot manifest itself. It is an internal disposition with external manifestations, not the other way around. Humility is, at its most basic level, an act of submission. It is a dying to self for the love of God. True humility requires proper intention; the act of submission need not only be done willingly, but also done for the glory of God. The prophet Micah reveals what the Lord

194

requires of man, to do what is right and to walk humbly with God (cf. Micah 6:8).

Humility is a confession and acknowledgement of the greatness of God. When you render to God what is truly His, you are left with nothing. If He were to withdraw His life-force, you would cease to exist and in doing so He would be doing you no wrong. He is Creator and Lord of all. All creatures are held into existence only by His consent, whether sinner or saint, angel or human.

> God dwells in a secret and hidden way in all souls, in their very substance. For if He did not, they could not exist at all.
> Saint John of the Cross

> If God did not remain present in the creatures He made, we would lapse into the nothingness from which we came.
> Servant of God John Hardon

You must, of course, balance this with the realization that God loves you and He chooses to allow you to exist. He has loved you into existence and loves through your existence. This, of course, should inspire you to an even deeper level of gratitude and humility, not to pride. All you possess is your nothingness. That means, in a certain sense, that humility is everything.

> Let us not deceive ourselves. If we have not humility, we have nothing.
> Saint Vincent de Paul

> The whole of the Christian religion is humility.
> Saint Augustine

> I saw the snares that the enemy spreads out over the world and I said groaning, "What can get through from such snares?" Then I heard a voice saying to me, "Humility."
> Saint Antony of the Desert

Humility is not weakness. The crucifix is the most powerful example of this. The Blessed Virgin Mary is also a great example of humility as strength. The height of Mary's sanctity is directly related to the depths of her humility. Her "*humilitatas*" or lowliness that she speaks of as the handmaiden of the Lord is actually her strength. In Heaven the practice of all the virtues, save charity and humility, cease. In the Book of Revelation, John speaks of the elders who prostrate themselves before God to worship Him (cf. Revelation 11:16). You should practice here on earth those virtues you will engage in when you are in Heaven.

When you willingly submit yourself to God and others, for the glory of God, you are acting with humility. No ego, no pride, no judgment and no desires — really a holy indifference as Saint Francis de Sales calls it. Fall down on your knees and beg for the grace of humility. Learn from the meek and humble heart of Jesus and you will find rest.

Humility is truth.
Saint Bernard of Clairvaux

The gate of Heaven is very low, only the humble can enter it.
Saint Elizabeth Ann Seton

The most powerful weapon to conquer the devil is humility. For, as he does not know at all how to employ it, neither does he know how to defend himself from it.
Saint Vincent de Paul

It is good that you are remaining in a state of holy indifference in everything that pertains to the will of God.
Our Lord to Saint Faustina Kowalska

HOST   **Obedience**

Be like sons of obedience, not conforming to the desires of your former ignorance, but in accord with him who has called you: the Holy One. And in every behavior, you yourself must be holy, for it is written: "You shall

be holy, for I am Holy."
1 Peter 1:14-16

A good soldier must be obedient. A soldier's lack of obedience can easily cause injury or death. A lack of obedience can cause harm to the body of the earthly warrior and to the soul of the spiritual warrior.

Satan fears obedience because it flows from humility and leaves no room for pride. Obedience is also a virtue, a moral virtue of the highest order. Obedience protects and preserves the other virtues. It is in many ways a mini-martyrdom; like humility, it is a dying to self. When you freely and lovingly subject your will to that of another, the ego part of you dies. As the human will is a prized possession, its surrender to proper authority yields tremendous graces.

In your act of obedience, you can rise higher than the fallen angels, who were disobedient. In your act of obedience, with God's grace, you can overcome the attacks of Hell. Obedience leads to freedom, obedience leads to knowledge and obedience leads you deeper into a relationship with Jesus. A deeper relationship with Christ will also lead you into suffering. So, in a sense, obedience also leads into suffering. Your "Yes," to this suffering, when done with humility, is imitative of Christ in His suffering.

When you are obedient to proper authority, you are protected. Disobedience to proper authority is an open invitation for Satan to set up camp. At one point during his short life, Blessed Miguel Pro was ordered by his superiors to go into hiding. He did not want to do so; he wanted to continue to serve God's people. Yet out of obedience he remained hidden in cramped quarters. As a loyal soldier of Christ, he chose obedience. Even though his desire to serve the people was good, and even though he was willing to die for his faith, he obeyed his superiors. He accepted their judgment that now was not the time for him to be tending to God's flock. Now was the time to wait in seclusion.

Obedience is superior to sacrifice which is why I haven't budged from where I am.
Blessed Miguel Pro

Similarly, Saint Pio of Pietrelcina was confined to his quarters, maliciously accused by envious brothers. Being the good soldier of God that he was, he responded to the accusations and punishment with utter humility. Rather than fight, grumble or retaliate he accepted his "assignment" as God's will and did so without bitterness. In doing so he provided not the slightest opening for Satan.

Through obedience you acknowledge your nothingness apart from God. Through obedience you imitate Christ. Through obedience you repel Satan. Through obedience you come to salvation.

> Thank God I always have work to do. Before I listened to confessions, now I pray. May God's will be done.
> Saint Pio of Pietrelcina

> The devil doesn't fear austerity but holy obedience.
> Saint Francis de Sales

> It is easy for those who obey to overcome all the attacks of Hell for by obedience they subject their will to men, they rise superior to the demons who fell on account of their disobedience.
> Pope Saint Gregory the Great

> The reward of obedience is similar to that of martyrdom. In martyrdom, we offer to God the head of our body; by obedience we offer Him our will, which is the head of the soul.
> Venerable Sertorius Caputo

HOST   **Surrender**

> Then he said to everyone: "If anyone is willing to come after me: let him deny himself, and take up his cross every day, and follow me. For whoever will have saved his life, will lose it. Yet whoever will have lost his life for my sake, will save it."
> Luke 9:23-24

A good soldier must be willing to surrender his life, not

to the enemy obviously, but to the cause. If he is not willing to give this ultimate sacrifice, he is a compromised soldier. A compromised soldier is an ineffective and dangerous soldier.

"Your will be done," is the perfect phrase of surrender. "Let it be done unto me," is equally perfect in its humility, charity and surrender. No quicker path to holiness exists than full surrender to the will of God. No path to the "peace that surpasses all understanding" (cf. Philippians 4:7), is more direct. Your surrender must be passive and active; it must be passive in your acceptance of God's will and active in your efforts to bring His will to fruition. With this total surrender comes joy, true joy, for in this total surrender you step into the very role for which you were created. Of course, hand in hand with your surrender must be an active prayer life, for it is during prayer that God will reveal His will to you.

As a soldier, there can be no more rewarding experience than doing exactly as you are commanded, exactly when you are commanded to do it, exactly how you are commanded to do it, yielding the exact results expected by the commander. With humility and obedience, your full surrender will allow you to be not only in full union with the commander, but in full unity with the commander. Full surrender leads to full unity with God.

Your surrender, in order to be full, must flow from the heart, not the head. Intellectual consent is not enough; the purest of motivations is required for full surrender, the motivation of faith, hope and love. This total surrender of self transcends any earthly rewards and yields the sweetest and most ripe heavenly fruit.

> Let us suppose that you turn to God with blind trust and surrender yourself unconditionally and unreservedly to Him, entirely resolved to put aside your own hopes and fears; in short, determined to wish nothing except what He wishes and to wish all that He wishes. From this moment you will acquire perfect liberty and will never again be able to feel troubled or uneasy, and there is no power on earth capable of doing you violence or giving you a moment's unrest.
> Saint Claude de la Colombiere

The other day I came across this striking passage: "To be resigned and to be united to the will of God are not the same; there is the same difference between them as that which exists between union and unity; in union there are still two, in unity there is but one." Yes, let us be one with God even in this life; and for this we should be more than resigned, we should embrace the cross with joy.

Saint Therese of Lisieux

In this life we cannot achieve union with God through our intellect, our imagination, or indeed, through any of our senses. We can achieve this union by faith, by hope and by love.

Saint John of the Cross

Faith, hope and love transform an ordinary soldier into a soldier for Christ. Faith, hope and love lead to perfection and sanctification. Satan, who is eternally imperfect and eternally unholy, will do whatever he can to keep you from entering onto the path of perfection and holiness. He will likewise do whatever he can to knock you off the path once you are on it. What allows Satan to knock you off balance and off the path is the weight of that which you have not yet surrendered. Total surrender to God renders you weightless, yet immovable and impervious.

Ego, or attachment, is weighty and unstable and easily knocks you off balance. It is easily distracted as it desires to be recognized and rewarded. Surrender, like humility and obedience, is a dying to self. It is an experience contrary to the world and the flesh; it is truly a participation in the Divine, for it is in the person of Jesus Christ that you learn how to die to self, so that you might rise in Him.

You can become who God created you to be only through full surrender. Partial surrender allows you to become only partially who God created you to be. Whatever part is not surrendered to God is serving either the human spirit or the evil spirit. Neither choice is very appealing.

Now the great means by which one may enter into the path of perfection and of holiness is to surrender oneself

to our good God.
Saint Therese Couderc

Lord Jesus Christ, take away my freedom, my memory, my understanding and my will. All that I have and cherish you have given me. I surrender it all to be guided by your will. Your love and your grace are wealth enough for me. Give me these, Lord Jesus and I ask for nothing more.
Saint Ignatius of Loyola

Let a prayer of surrender and hope rise up to God when your fragility causes you to fall, and thank the Lord for all the graces with which he enriches you.
Saint Pio of Pietrelcina

HOST   **Trust**

And indeed, these called upon almighty God, so that the trust that had been entrusted to them would be preserved with all integrity.
2 Maccabees 3:22

A good soldier must trust and be trustworthy. Doubt and dishonesty are like chinks in the armor. Where there is doubt, there is weakness. Where there is dishonesty, there is weakness. It is these types of openings that Satan will leverage to the fullest. Where doubt exists, pride is not far behind. Where dishonesty exists, division is not far behind. A lack of trust among soldiers can be deadly.

Without trust, relationships suffer. Without trust, suspicion and doubt weave their way into your mind and heart eroding the foundation of humility, obedience and surrender. Without trust, you start to question who and what you believe.

You trust in those whom you believe. You believe those in whom you have faith. You have faith in those whom you trust. Without trust the cycle breaks down and doubt seeps in, weakening your trust. The downward spiral continues, unless you trust once again in Him. Without trust, God's will is questioned and becomes subordinate to your own will. When that happens, chaos, disobedience and death are not far behind.

Trust in God fortifies and renews your humility, obedience and surrender. It is a living expression of your faith in God's divine will. Your trust in Him is a grace which activates and aligns your will with His will. Your trust in God's will gives Him permission to make adjustments to your will. Trust in Him is a portent of divine mercy. Trust in divine mercy leads you away from sin, away from struggle and away from Satan. Trust in divine mercy leads you to greater sacrifice, surrender and sanctity. Trust in Him leads to life eternal.

> The greatest sinners would achieve great sanctity, if only they would trust in My Mercy.
> Our Lord to Saint Faustina Kowalska

You are to trust God in all things, trust Him when the battle is going well and trust Him when the battle seems lost. Nothing can be counted as a loss that is surrendered totally to God, for in Him there is only life, love and victory. True trust in God necessarily leads to continual conversion. Drawn ever deeper into His will, ever closer to His perfection, you begin to see, feel and act differently. Your spiritual senses heighten; your desire to know, love and serve Him at an ever deeper level does as well. Also, your ability to be used as a vessel of His love and mercy increases correspondingly.

To trust in God seems at times to go against human nature, which is rather ironic since it was God who created human nature. You need to trust in Him more, not less; you need to trust in yourself less, not more. Be as if a little child.

> I trust in the Lord Jesus Christ, not in myself.
> Saint Catherine of Siena

Free your mind from all that troubles you, God will take care of things. You will be unable to make haste in this without, so to speak, grieving the heart of God, because He sees that you do not honor Him sufficiently with holy trust. Trust in Him, I beg you, and you will have the fulfillment of what your heart desires.
> Saint Vincent de Paul

Pray, hope and don't worry.
Saint Pio of Pietrelcina

The little way is the way of spiritual childhood, the way of trust and absolute surrender.
Saint Therese of Lisieux

When you consume the Host during communion, you receive the Body, Blood, Soul and Divinity of Jesus. There is no separating the Body from the Blood, or the Soul from the Divinity. They are inseparable and undividable. So it is with humility, obedience, surrender and trust. One flows into the other and is necessarily linked. Remove one from the equation and you're left with none. Without humility, you'll never fully obey. Without obedience, you'll never fully surrender. Without surrender, you'll never fully trust. Without trust, you'll never persist in your humility, obedience and surrender.

The virtues of humility, obedience, surrender and trust are the virtues that led Jesus to accept and embrace His death on a cross. Humility, obedience, surrender and trust are the same virtues that will allow you to accept and embrace your cross. When you are humble and obedient, when you surrender and trust, you will yield to God's will. In yielding to His will, you will not only have victory, but peace as well. There is no greater word to a spiritual warrior than peace.

Heart of Jesus, I love You; but increase my love. Heart of Jesus, I trust in You; but give greater vigor to my confidence. Heart of Jesus, I give my heart to You; but so enclose it in You that it may never be separated from You. Heart of Jesus, I am all Yours; but take care of my promise so that I may be able to put it in practice even unto the complete sacrifice of my life.
Blessed Miguel Pro

Humility is the true title of the glory of each person on earth since it imparts the recognition of God's law, a sincere acceptance of Christ's precepts and a noble involvement in the service of human brotherhood.
Blessed Pope John XXIII

A soul is obedient in proportion to her humility and humble in proportion to her obedience.
Saint Catherine of Siena

Do not let what is happening to me, daughter, cause you any grief, for it does not cause me any. What greatly grieves me is that one who is not at fault is blamed. Men do not do these things, but God, who knows what is suitable for us and arranges things for our own good. Think nothing else but that God ordains all, and where there is no love, put love, and you will draw out love.
Saint John of the Cross

May it [Holy Communion] purify me from evil ways and put an end to my evil passions. May it bring me charity and patience, humility and obedience, and growth in the power to do good. May it be my strong defense against all my enemies, visible and invisible, and the perfect calming of all my evil impulses, bodily and spiritual.
Saint Thomas Aquinas

Unclean I am but cleanse me in Your blood; of which a single drop, for sinners spilt, can purge the entire world from all its guilt
Saint Thomas Aquinas

Chapter 17
Prayer, Fasting & Almsgiving

⊕

Now, therefore, the Lord says: "Be converted to me with your whole heart, in fasting and weeping and mourning." And rend your hearts, and not your garments, and convert to the Lord your God. For he is gracious and merciful, patient and full of compassion, and steadfast despite ill will.
Joel 2:12-13

Therefore, when you give alms, do not choose to sound a trumpet before you, as the hypocrites do in the synagogues and in the towns, so that they may be honored by men. Amen I say to you, they have received their reward. But when you give alms, do not let your left hand know what your right hand is doing, so that your almsgiving may be in secret, and your Father, who sees in secret, will repay you. And when you pray, you should not be like the hypocrites, who love standing in the synagogues and at the corners of the streets to pray, so that they may be seen by men. Amen I say to you, they have received their reward. But you, when you pray, enter into your room, and having shut the door, pray to your Father in secret, and your Father, who sees in secret, will repay you. And when you fast, do not choose to become gloomy, like the hypocrites. For they alter their faces, so that their fasting may be

apparent to men. Amen I say to you, that they have received their reward. But as for you, when you fast, anoint your head and wash your face, so that your fasting will not be apparent to men, but to your Father, who is in secret. And' your Father, who sees in secret, will repay you.
Matthew 6:2-6, 16-18

The three traditional pillars of Catholic Lenten practices of prayer, fasting and almsgiving should be the three pillars of your life as a spiritual warrior.

The devil dreads fasting, prayer, humility and good works.
Saint Antony of the Desert

The Christian must at times make use of special ascetical practices to escape from certain diabolical attacks.
Pope Paul VI

Prayer

And when they had entered into the cenacle, they ascended to the place where Peter and John, James and Andrew, Philip and Thomas, Bartholomew and Matthew, James of Alphaeus and Simon the Zealot, and Jude of James, were staying. All these were persevering with one accord in prayer with the women, and with Mary, the mother of Jesus, and with his brothers.
Acts of the Apostles 1:13-14

For a spiritual warrior prayer is what sustains and nourishes. It is what draws you nearer to God. It is also the primary weapon of spiritual warfare. Whether it is for yourself or others, the means of surviving this war is through prayer. It is a necessary prerequisite to any and all spiritual battles. Prayer purifies and strengthens the mind, the most frequent point of attack for Satan and his evil minions. A healthy, active prayer life will allow you to be a healthy, active spiritual warrior for Christ.

Essentially, prayer is communicating with God. The foundation of prayer is humility, the very virtue that opposes Satan's sin of pride. That should give you some sense of how important a fruitful prayer life is to spiritual warfare. Prayer is not so much you seeking out God as it is your response to God's call. He has called you first and He awaits your response. He wants your "Yes," so that He can bring about His plan through you. He wants your "Yes," so you can fulfill the mission He has prepared for you in advance (cf. Ephesians 2:10).

As a spiritual warrior, there are several prayers to pray in order for you to fulfill your mission. The first prayer to pray is for discernment regarding your role in the battle, to know His will. The second prayer to pray is to embrace the battle, to love His will. The third prayer to pray is for strength and protection to be able to engage in battle, to live His will. Each prayer is predicated on and builds upon the prior prayer. As the foundation of prayer is humility, it is interesting to note that one of the results of these prayers is a deeper humility. This deeper humility leads, in turn, to further and deeper prayer.

As a spiritual warrior you may be often called to pray for others, to act as a prayer intercessor. Because the practice of prayer is lacking in many and is shaky in others, Satan is having a field day grabbing people's souls. To counteract Satan's grab for souls, God raises up spiritual warriors among His people to "stand in the gap," to pray on behalf of those in need. During Mass, the General Intercessions are prayed for the Holy Father, the local bishop, the Church and other needs. While these communal prayers are powerful, you may also be called as an individual to intercede for those in need.

> God is not being loved and honored as he should by the race He has elevated to the sublime dignity of adopted sons. God is looking for someone to stand in the gap before Him on behalf of this race and beg that He may not destroy it.
> Blessed Teresa of Calcutta

By the merits Christ won by His death and resurrection and by your cooperation with His grace, you will be able to grow in your ability to pray and intercede for others. You may be called on to intercede for a specific person in crisis for a limited time. You may also be called on to intercede for a specific person on an ongoing basis for their conversion, protection, release from purgatory, etc. You may also be called to intercede for a group of people, a parish, etc. Your intercessory prayer on their behalf can weaken their resistance to God's grace and the grip of Satan. So much of spiritual warfare is intercession. Your prayer, fasting and almsgiving offered on behalf of others can save souls. That is the heart of true spiritual warfare.

When you are called to intercede on behalf of a person and it seems as if your prayers are not working, one tactic is to change the way you're praying. Acknowledge the reality that the person you are praying for has a free will and may very well be exercising it. So, instead of praying for a conversion or a return to the faith, pray instead for a "desire" for a conversion or a "desire" to return to the faith.

When you pray for the desire you are, in a sense, working with the person's free will as opposed to, potentially, against it. Desire works before the free will is engaged. Praying for the desire, which etymologically means, "of the Father," is really praying that the person would allow God to work in and through him to bring about union with His will. For while God desires the person's conversion, He does not desire a coercive conversion; He desires a cooperative conversion.

> For it is God who works in you, both so as to desire, and so as to act, in accord with his good will.
> Philippians 2:13

> Christ does not force our will; He only takes what we give Him.
> Saint Teresa of Avila

> He who wills what God wills, possesses all that he desires.
> Saint Alphonsus Liguori

Like fasting and almsgiving which follow, all your prayers, whatever they may be, need to flow from your heart. Your heart is the source of prayer (cf. *Catechism of the Catholic*

Church 2562). Therefore, if your prayer is not from your heart, it is in vain. Satan wants you operating from your head, not your heart.

> When we pray the voice of the heart must be heard more than the proceedings from the mouth.
> Saint Bonaventure

> Usually prayer is a question of groaning rather than speaking, tears rather than words.
> Saint Augustine

When you operate from your head, Satan has an enormous advantage over you because of his superior intelligence. When you operate from the heart you have an advantage over Satan because of his lack of ability to love. When you operate from the heart you afford yourself God's protection. For it is the heart where love resides and it is love, "perfect love," that casts out fear. Pray from the heart, live from the heart, love from the heart, do all you do from the heart and Satan's efforts against you will all come to naught.

> If you would gain power and strength to overcome the temptations of the enemy, be a man of prayer. If you would mortify your will with all its affections and lusts, be a man of prayer. If you would understand the cunning devices of Satan and defend yourself against his deceits, be a man of prayer.
> Saint Bonaventure

> God refuses no one the gift of prayer. By it we obtain the help we need to overcome disorderly desires and temptations.
> Saint Alphonsus Liguori

> Let him never cease from prayer who has once begun it, be his life ever so wicked; for prayer is the way to amend it, and without prayer such amendment will be much more difficult.
> Saint Teresa of Avila

Fasting

> I humbled my soul with fasting, and my prayer will become my sinews.
> Psalm 34:13

Fasting can be defined as voluntary abstinence from food. This definition can be expanded to also include abstinence from other activities and behaviors as well, not just food. For example, you can fast from unnecessary leisure or luxury activities. You can also fast from gossip and judgment and other vices.

In a religious context, fasting is done not as an end, but as a means to grow in virtue, to counteract the weak nature of the flesh and as aid in conforming your will to God's will. It teaches your body to be subject to your will and ultimately, to conform to His will. Fasting is an act of mortification, of denying self and, ultimately, of dying to self. Fasting should be an integral part of a spiritual warrior's prayer life; it is good for the soul.

Fasting is not to be taken lightly; it should commence only after prayerful discernment and preparation as to the timing and method of fasting. Preparation for your fast should include praying for the grace from God to fast well and according to His will.

Fasting is a grace from God and as such, there should neither be boasting about your fast, nor any judging of another's fast. Fasting should always start with a pure intention and joy in your heart, keeping in mind this is your gift to the Father. Part of your intention should be to fast only as long as or intensely as God calls you to do. To fast beyond what and how God is calling you to do can lead to pride, which leads to your fast becoming an empty, vain offering.

In the same way that prayer attaches you to God, fasting detaches you from the world. In helping you separate the essential from the excessive, fasting can help you to purge from the memory and the flesh, any remnants of attachment to sin. Fasting can even help you heal from the consequences of past sin.

Fasting also increases the quality and efficacy of prayer. It activates God's power in your life. Prayer is essential

210

to proper fasting, both as a means of strengthening the will and of conforming it to the will of the Father. Fasting without prayer is simply deprivation.

From your act of fasting can come clarity and a fresh perspective. It reveals your dependencies, removes your fears and can help repel Satan. It also creates a void, a vacuum, a vulnerability, inside of you. Therefore, fasting may also initially intensify Satan's attacks upon you. That is why it is important to fast only according to God's plan, so you can endure the temptations and harassment that will likely come your way.

Remember that Jesus fasted for forty days just prior to being tempted by the evil one. Always call upon God and His holy angels and saints to strengthen and encourage you in accord with His will. Fasting, done in union with God's will, will protect you from harm, though not necessarily from suffering.

Fasting should be for you a sign of hope and expectation. It should be a reminder to you of your poverty, emptiness and dependence. Fasting should lead you into the arms of Christ. Its physical hunger and thirst should create in you a spiritual hunger and thirst. Whether your fast is one of bread and water, or of eliminating meat, or of skipping dessert, or if it lasts one day or three, is scheduled monthly, weekly or as needed, good works should always proceed from your fasting. Good works are a fruit of fasting.

> Fasting is a kind of wall, then, for the Christian, impregnable to the devil, inaccessible to the enemy.
> Saint Maximus of Turin

> When the stomach is full, it is easy to talk of fasting.
> Saint Jerome

> It is also the teaching of the saints, in fasting one must not only obey the rule against gluttony in regard to food, but refrain from every sin so that, while fasting, the tongue may also fast, refraining from slander, lies, evil talking, degrading one's brother, anger and every sin committed by the tongue. One should also fast with the eyes, that is, not look at vain things, not look shamefully or fearlessly at anyone. The hands and feet

should also be kept from every evil action. When one fasts through vanity or thinking that he is achieving something especially virtuous, he fasts foolishly and soon begins to criticize others and to consider himself something great.
Saint Ambrose

Almsgiving

But do not be willing to forget good works and fellowship. For God is deserving of such sacrifices.
Hebrews 13:16

Almsgiving can be defined as any material benefit given to assist those who are in need. It is both a sign of love and affection for your brothers and sisters in Christ and your gratitude to God. Almsgiving is closely linked to prayer and fasting; it should be the natural extension, or fruit of them. Almsgiving is both a source and a sign of Christian maturity. Almsgiving can also be directly linked to your act of fasting; the money saved by your acts of fasting can be given to those in need.

Almsgiving's origin should be love, not guilt; it should be seen as an act of compassion, not of obligation. It should be foremost in your mind that poverty is not a disease or a curse. Neither is it divine punishment; remember that Jesus was poor. Nor is poverty an evil that needs to be redeemed. Poverty is an opportunity to live out the love which you proclaim. Almsgiving can be a source of grace for both those who give and those who receive.

Almsgiving should always flow from what you can share, not just what you can spare. When you give alms, you should do so discreetly and to the degree possible, anonymously. (Anonymity here is to prevent the drawing of undue attention to yourself, not a need to unnecessarily disconnect yourself from the recipients of your charity.)

Almsgiving, to the degree possible, should be anticipatory, not reactionary. Timely, frequent and joyful acts of charity are good for the soul. Joy, as it is a sure sign of the Holy Spirit, is an important part of almsgiving. God does not need givers who are unhappy; He wants His givers to be cheerful (cf. 2 Corinthians 9:7). When you give alms, give with joy so that the gift you give is more than just a material gift, but a spiritual one as well.

Almsgiving needs to be an act of self-giving, otherwise it is false giving. Whatever goods or money are given, part of you needs to go with them. Almsgiving is not the spiritual equivalent of depositing money in the bank or mindlessly giving of your excess. It should always involve your prayerful presence, your humble sincerity, your genuine concern. It is this giving of self, the charitable concern for others and not simply the donation of money or goods, that helps strengthen you spiritually and deter Satan.

Almsgiving fosters humility which Satan opposes. Almsgiving builds up community which Satan opposes. Almsgiving is an act of charity which Satan opposes. Almsgiving animates your prayer life and strengthens your fasting, both of which Satan opposes. Almsgiving pleases and is remembered by God. Ongoing, individual almsgiving tends to create a climate of giving that can influence an entire culture, which Satan opposes. Satan opposes almsgiving because it is a sacrificial act of selfless giving which is imitative of Christ.

> The bread you store up belongs to the hungry; the cloak that lies in your chest belongs to the naked; the gold you have hidden in the ground belongs to the poor.
> Saint Basil the Great

> Especially anticipate the needs of those who are ashamed to beg. To make them ask for alms is to make them buy it.
> Saint Thomas of Villanova

> Do you wish your prayer to fly toward God? Give it two wings: fasting and almsgiving.
> Saint Augustine

The Lord calls you to be a soldier of the heart, not of the head. He wants you to have a heart that longs to know only Him, not the evil one, so He desires you to pray. He wants you to have a heart that longs to love only Him, not your flesh, so He desires you to fast. He wants you to have a heart that longs to serve Him, not yourself, so He desires you to give alms. And He wants you to do so with right intention and a pure disposition.

Prayer, fasting and mercy. These three are one and they give life to each other. Fasting is the soul of prayer; mercy is the lifeblood of fasting. Let no one try to separate them; they cannot be separated. If you have only one of them or not all together, you have nothing.
Saint Peter Chrysologus

It is impossible to engage in spiritual conflict unless the appetite has first been subdued.
Pope Saint Gregory the Great

During a time of disturbance and warfare of thoughts, one should lessen a little even the ordinary quantity of food and drink.
Saint Barsanuphius

The rich man who gives to the poor does not bestow alms but pays a debt.
Saint Ambrose

It would be considered a theft on our part if we didn't give to someone in greater need than we are.
Saint Francis of Assisi

We must be charitable and humble and give alms, because they wash the stains of sin from our souls.
Saint Francis of Assisi

Chapter 18
Sacraments & Sacramentals

✝

And God was accomplishing powerful and uncommon
miracles by the hand of Paul, so much so that even
when small cloths and wrappings were brought from
his body to the sick, the illnesses withdrew from them
and the wicked spirits departed.
Acts of the Apostles 19:11-12

Sacraments and sacramentals are indispensable tools
for you as a spiritual warrior. Though essentially different,
they are similar. They are, for the most part, uniquely Catholic.
They both support a grace-filled life; sacraments primarily and
essentially, sacramentals secondarily.

The efficacy of both flows from Jesus' Incarnation. The
act of God becoming man endowed the created world with an
even greater dignity and power.

Sacraments take precedence over sacramentals, as the
sacraments are first in the order of grace. Sacraments are the
primary and preferred means of overcoming the actions of the
evil one. Sacramentals are relegated to a secondary position
relative to the sacraments when engaging in spiritual warfare;
this even includes the sacramental of exorcism which is inferior
to the Sacrament of Penance. A spiritual warrior should make
proper, frequent and fervent use of the sacraments of the
Church (consistent with one's vocation and the laws of the
Church) and the various sacramentals of the Church.

Sacraments

The seven sacraments are the gateway to grace for Catholics. Since Christ's ascension into Heaven, the sacraments are the ordinary means by which Catholics encounter God. The seven sacraments are an actual encounter with Him. Assuming proper disposition, each sacrament allows you to access and grow in God's supernatural grace. God's grace is available to strengthen and guide you and is vital during spiritual warfare.

The seven sacraments of the Catholic Church are Baptism, Penance, Eucharist, Confirmation, Matrimony, Holy Orders and Anointing of the Sick. Except for Holy Matrimony, the conferring of the sacraments is the domain of the ordained, with the emergency baptism of a person in danger of death the only exception. (In the Sacrament of Holy Matrimony, it is the bride and groom who are the ministers of the sacrament to one another.)

Sacrament of Baptism

Baptism is the foundational Christian sacrament. It is the moment you first received God's sanctifying grace. It was then you were freed from the stain of original sin, established as an heir of God, received into His Church and baptized into the life and death of Jesus Christ (cf. Romans 6:3). In baptism, you were sealed with an indelible mark uniting you to Christ. Part of the baptismal rite includes an exorcism, called a minor exorcism by the Church. It was at the moment of baptism that a life of grace was initiated and that Satan first opposed you. Baptism signifies "liberation from sin and from its instigator the devil" (*Catechism of the Catholic Church* 1237).

The Sacrament of Baptism is like a shot fired across the bow of Satan's ship.

> Before Baptism, grace encourages the soul from the outside, while Satan lurks in its depths. But from the moment we are reborn through Baptism, the demon is outside, grace is within. Where before Baptism error ruled the soul, after Baptism truth rules it.
> Saint Diadochus of Photike

This is the water in which the flesh is submerged that all carnal sin may be washed away. Every transgression is there buried.
Saint Ambrose

Sacrament of Penance

Penance is an irreplaceable tool for those seeking to remain in the will of God and in His good graces. It is the sacrament of the infinite mercy of Jesus; it restores sanctifying grace for a soul that was dead. Through the Sacrament of Penance you are called to an ever deeper repentance and conversion of the heart. It is a sacrament that restores right relationship with God, with others and with self. Regular confession helps form your conscience, calls to mind your future judgment and is a source of "spiritual strength for the Christian battle" (*Catechism of the Catholic Church* 1496).

The Sacrament of Penance is an infinite supply line of God's mercy.

If the serpent, the devil, bites someone secretly, he infects that person with the venom of sin. And if the one who has been bitten keeps silence and does not do penance and does not want to confess his wound, then his brother and his master, who have the word [of absolution] that will cure him, cannot very well assist him.
Saint Jerome

Confession heals, confession justifies, confession grants pardon of sin. All hope consists in confession. In confession there is a chance for mercy. Believe it firmly. Do not doubt, do not hesitate, never despair of the mercy of God. Hope and have confidence in confession.
Saint Isidore of Seville

Sacrament of Eucharist

Eucharist is the preeminent sacrament. It is, as *Lumen Gentium* describes it, "the source and summit of the Christian life." Eucharist unites you to Christ, His Church and His cross. It purges you of your prior venial sins, protects you from future venial and mortal sins and points to the future glory that awaits you, if you persevere. It is a sacrament of faith, hope and love. Eucharist is the single greatest source of strength for you as a spiritual warrior. Whether you receive Jesus during Mass (the most powerful prayer that exists), adore Him at a Holy Hour or worship Him at Adoration and Benediction, let Him be your strength. Eucharist is the spiritual warrior's sustenance and the "medicine of immortality, the antidote for death" (*Catechism of the Catholic Church* 1405).

The Sacrament of Eucharist is the single greatest weapon ever imagined, Jesus Christ, love incarnate.

> Endeavour not to miss any Holy Communion. We can scarcely give our enemy, the devil, any greater joy than when we withdraw from Jesus, who takes away the power the enemy has over us.
> Saint Margaret Mary Alacoque

> The Sacrament of the Body of the Lord puts the demons to flight, defends us against the incentives to vice and to concupiscence, cleanses the soul from sin, quiets the anger of God, enlightens the understanding to know God, inflames the will and the affections with the love of God, fills the memory with spiritual sweetness, confirms the entire man in good, frees us from eternal death, multiplies the merits of a good life, leads us to our everlasting home, and re-animates the body to eternal life.
> Saint Thomas Aquinas

Sacrament of Confirmation

Confirmation seals the graces and gifts received in baptism. It also leaves an indelible mark on the soul, a mark that cannot be removed. It perfects you as a Christian and makes you a bold soldier of Christ. The traditional Gifts of the Holy Spirit are sealed during confirmation. They are wisdom, piety, fortitude, knowledge, understanding, counsel and fear of the Lord. These gifts play a significant role in the life of a spiritual warrior, especially in regard to the "promise of divine protection in the great eschatological trial" (*Catechism of the Catholic Church* 1296).

The Sacrament of Confirmation is the sound of

"Reveille" being played to awaken the troops.

> Forget not the Holy Ghost at the moment of your enlightenment; He is ready to mark your soul with His seal. He will give you the heavenly and divine seal which makes the devils tremble.
> Saint Cyril of Jerusalem

> Confirmation has not been instituted as necessary for salvation, but that by virtue thereof we might be found well-armed and prepared when called upon to fight for the faith of Christ.
> *Catechism of the Council of Trent*

Sacrament of Matrimony

Matrimony unites a man and a woman in a sacred, covenantal and lifelong bond. God, the creator of all life is the author of marriage. It is a communion of love made possible with the grace that only God can supply. Husband and wife can provide for each other opportunities to grow in holiness and God's grace. They can be a witness to and an image of God's love in a world decimated by sin. They can, by being open to life, populate Heaven. For this reason Satan attacks solid, God-centered marriages with extreme vigor. The same self-sacrificing love that defeated Satan on Calvary is the same love needed to build and strengthen marriages. Marriage perfectly combats the disease that Satan caught and desires to spread to humanity. Marriage helps "to overcome self-absorption, egoism, pursuit of one's own pleasure..." (*Catechism of the Catholic Church* 1609).

The Sacrament of Matrimony is the solidarity and the selflessness that exemplifies the strongest of corps.

> Marriage is the nursery of Christianity.
> Saint Francis de Sales

> In this entire world, there is not a more perfect, more complete image of God, unity and community than the marital embrace and the life it begets.
> Pope John Paul II

Sacrament of Holy Orders

Holy Orders sets apart and brings forth the ministerial priesthood, the means by which Christ tends to His earthly flock. Whether as bishop, priest or deacon, the Sacrament of Holy Orders leaves an indelible mark on the soul of the man who answers God's call. It confers upon him Christ's authority to carry out those ministries proper to his office; to teach, to govern or to sanctify.

The Sacrament of Holy Orders gives the priest the ability to make Jesus Christ present, Body, Blood, Soul and Divinity, something not even the angels can do. The Sacrament of Holy Orders gives him Christ's power, the power to defeat the evil one, "a 'sacred power' which is none other than that of Christ" (*Catechism of the Catholic Church* 1551).

The Sacrament of Holy Orders is Officer Training School for God's militia.

> The priest has the power of delivering sinners from Hell, of making them worthy of Paradise and of changing them from the slaves of Satan into the children of God.
> Saint Alphonsus Liguori

> The most high and infinitely good God has not granted to angels the power with which He has invested priests.
> Saint John Chrysostom

Sacrament of Anointing of the Sick

Anointing of the Sick heals and strengthens body and soul. It, too, is a sacrament of mercy. Through this sacrament sins are forgiven, healing is accomplished according to God's will and suffering is made redemptive. It is a sacrament of intercession and sanctification, both for the person anointed and for the Church. It helps prepare you for the final battle and helps you to claim Christ's victory as your own because it "strengthens against the temptations of the evil one..." (*Catechism of the Catholic Church* 1520).

The Sacrament of Anointing of the Sick is balm for the wounds of battle.

Let the sheep hasten unto the seal and that sign of the

cross which is a remedy against evils.
Saint Gregory of Nyssa

After the Council of Florence had described the
essential elements of the Anointing of the Sick, the
Council of Trent declared its divine institution: "This
reality is in fact the grace of the Holy Spirit, whose
anointing takes away sins, if any still remain to be
taken away and the remnants of sin; it also relieves and
strengthens the soul of the sick person, arousing in him
a great confidence in the divine mercy, whereby being
thus sustained, he more easily bears the trials and
labors of his sickness, more easily resists the
temptations of the devil 'lying in wait' and sometimes
regains bodily health, if this is expedient for the health
of the soul."
Pope Paul VI

The seven sacraments are an indispensable part of the
Catholic Church; they are the ordinary means of salvation.
They are equally an indispensable part of a spiritual warrior's
life.

Sacramentals

Sacramentals are those words, objects and actions
which resemble the sacraments, prepare you to receive grace or
sanctify a particular time and place. Sacramentals sanctify the
ordinary moments of life. God grants His grace to you through
sacramentals in relation to the intensity of the faith with which
you use them.

Sacramentals flow from the baptismal priesthood and,
as such, lay people may engage in the practice and use of
sacramentals. Some sacramentals, especially liturgical or
ecclesial rites, are reserved to the ministerial priesthood. They
are neither mandatory nor essential, though they are
recommended and beneficial. They are meant to accompany
and aid you in prayer, not to be viewed as collectibles or
amassed as some sort of religious trophies.

Sacramentals play an important role in the life of a
spiritual warrior. Not only are they prayer aids, they can also

221

provide protection against the evil one.

> By the sign of the cross all magic ceases; all
> incantations are powerless; every idol is abandoned and
> deserted; all irrational voluptuousness is quelled and
> each one looks up from earth to Heaven.
> Saint Athanasius

> All the martyrs are to be honored by us, but especially
> those whose relics we possess. They assist us by their
> prayers; they preserve us as to our bodies in this life,
> and receive us when we depart hence.
> Saint Maximus of Turin

The list of sacramentals is extensive. Some of the more
familiar and relevant sacramentals to spiritual warfare are
listed below.

Prayers
Rosary and Chaplets
Invocation of the Saints
Saint Michael Prayer
Blessing at Meals
Exorcism
Novenas

Actions
Eucharistic Adoration
Stations of the Cross
Sign of the Cross
Genuflection
Pilgrimages
Spiritual Communion

Objects
Blessed Water, Salt, Oil, etc.
Relics and Medals
Scapulars
Crucifix
Images, Icons, Holy Cards
Holy Ashes

Adoration, Benediction, Holy Hours
The Body, Blood, Soul and Divinity of Jesus, present
under the species of bread, is present in every consecrated
Host. The same Jesus that was crucified, died, buried and who
rose from the dead is the same Jesus that is present in every
tabernacle and monstrance of the Catholic Church. Whether
you worship Jesus in songs of praise, through the communal

prayers of the Church or in silent adoration, there is no greater source of peace, comfort and strength. Every spiritual warrior should commit to spend regular time in front of the Blessed Sacrament.

Satan fled rather than worship God; he will flee from you as you worship God, too.

> Do you want the devil to attack you? Visit Jesus rarely in the Blessed Sacrament. Do you want him to flee from you? Visit Jesus often. Do you want to conquer the devil? Take refuge often at the feet of Jesus. Do you want to be conquered by the devil? Forget about visiting Jesus.
> Saint John Bosco

> Adoration of the Blessed Sacrament is the end of the Church Militant just as adoration of God in His glory is the end of the Church Triumphant.
> Saint Peter Julian Eymard

> And what are we to do in the presence of the Blessed Sacrament? Love him. Praise him. Thank him. Ask of him. What does a poor man do in the presence of a wealthy man? What does a sick person do in the presence of a doctor? What does a thirsty person do at the sight of a fountain of sparkling water?
> Saint Alphonsus Liguori

The Name of Jesus

There is tremendous power in the name of Jesus. His name is the name above all names, the name at which every knee shall bend (cf. Philippians 2:10). Call upon His name when you are being attacked, when you are feeling down, whenever you feel like the enemy is gaining a toehold. Simple say, "Jesus, Jesus, Jesus," and watch the demons flee. It is the simplest and shortest prayer there is. It is a prayer that should be on the lips of every spiritual warrior.

Satan trembles at the invocation of the name of Jesus. May it be frequently on your lips.

Do not fear; Jesus is more powerful than all Hell. At the

223

invocation of His Name every knee in Heaven, on earth and in Hell must bend before Jesus; this is the consolation of the good and terror of the evil ones.
Saint Pio of Pietrelcina

The names of Jesus and Mary have special power to banish the temptations of the devil.
Saint Alphonsus Liguori

Baptism in the Holy Spirit

Baptism in the Holy Spirit, not a sacrament and not a repeat of baptism, is an antidote to the plague of spiritual lethargy, a plague that is reaching epidemic proportions. Unfortunately, for too many Catholics, the gifts and graces received in the sacraments remain dormant and inaccessible. Baptism in the Holy Spirit is one antidote to this plague of spiritual lethargy.

Baptism in the Holy Spirit is an invitation for the Holy Spirit to fan into flames those gifts previously received at baptism and sealed at confirmation. Baptism in the Holy Spirit does not detract from any of the seven sacraments; it simply calls upon the Holy Spirit to stir up within you the desire to live out your faith more fully and more fervently. It is an awakening, a call to arms, a renewal, a revival. The gifts of the Spirit were not meant to be received and then remain stagnant. They were meant to be continually refreshed and revitalized. Baptism in the Holy Spirit is recommended for every spiritual warrior.

Let us rediscover dear brothers and sisters, the beauty of being baptized in the Holy Spirit; let us be aware again of our baptism and of our confirmation, sources of grace that are always present.
Pope Benedict XVI

Come, Holy Spirit, and make ever more fruitful the charisms you have bestowed on us.
Pope John Paul II

That very charity, the Holy Spirit, with His hands has given and continues to give us God. He is constantly

serving us every grace and gift, spiritual as well as material.
Saint Catherine of Siena

To whom does the Spirit come? He comes to the ones who love him, who invite him, who eagerly await him.
Saint Bonaventure

Devotion to the Blessed Virgin Mary

True devotion to Mary begins and ends with true devotion to Jesus. Mary is the means, Jesus is the end. Mary is God's gift of grace to humanity. She is God's perfect intermediary and intercessor. Devotion to Mary, so often misunderstood, is devotion to Jesus. God the Father honored Mary in a way that no other person shall ever be honored by Him; He allowed His Son to be born of her womb. God the Holy Spirit honored Mary in a way that no other person shall ever be honored by Him; He overshadowed her and remains her spouse. God the Son honored Mary in a way that no other person shall ever be honored by Him; He allowed Himself to be born of her flesh and rightly calls her mother. As a spiritual warrior Mary is not only your mother; she is also the model soldier.

Satan, who rejected God's grace, cannot coexist with Mary, who embodies God's grace.

Where Mary is present, the evil one is absent.
Saint Louis de Montfort

O most sweet Mother, I beg you help me, lest the enemy rejoice over me or prevail against me by his snares.
Saint Bridget of Sweden

Satan, being so proud, suffers infinitely more in being vanquished and punished by a lowly and humble servant of God, for her humility humiliates him more than the power of God.
Saint Louis de Montfort

At every moment you must trust in Mary most holy, so that she can assist you and overthrow your every

enemy with her power.
Saint Gerard Majella

Our Father

The Our Father was the prayer given to humanity by Jesus. It is a simple, powerful prayer of love, honor and obedience. It is equally a prayer of petition and protection. Saint Augustine said that the recitation of it forgives venial sins. Saint Thomas Aquinas called it the perfect prayer. Saint Ignatius' advice was to close all discernment with this prayer. It is a prayer that should be recited frequently. When you pray the Our Father, do so with an acute awareness of the meaning of the words. As a spiritual warrior, submitting to and doing His will in all things is paramount. Whether good or bad, at battle or at rest, whether in life or death, remember you are blessed and privileged to be able to call God your Father. As a spiritual warrior, Abba, Father, daddy is your ultimate authority. "Your will be done, not mine," are the words that need to easily pass off the lips of every spiritual warrior.

I might die? What they might do or what they might not do to me, all that is in the hands of God. Would that I might be found worthy of suffering persecution for the Holy Name of Jesus. Do I not belong to His army? But let us repeat as in the Our Father: "Your will be done." Blessed Miguel Pro

With an awareness, therefore, of the opposition that individual souls, the Church and the world must face at the present time, we will try to give both meaning and effectiveness to the familiar invocation in our principal prayer: "Our Father . . . deliver us from evil." Pope Paul VI

Here we must observe that Christ teaches us to pray, not that we may not be tempted but that we may not be led into temptation — for if man overcomes temptation he deserves a crown. Saint Thomas Aquinas

The Sign of the Cross, Crucifix

With every trace of the hand, every time you repeat "In the name of the Father, and of the Son, and of the Holy Spirit" you are bearing witness to your faith in Jesus Christ crucified. It was the death of Jesus on the cross that defeated Satan. The power of that once and for all event is recalled every time you cross yourself. Both the signing of the cross and the crucifix remind Satan of his past defeat and his future ignominy. Meditate upon the crucifix and Christ's wounds.

When you feel overwhelmed in the midst of battle, take your pain and frustration to the cross. Saint Rita of Cascia once encountered a woman who was tormented by an evil spirit. Saint Rita looked up to Heaven, offered a prayer, made the sign of the cross on the woman's head and the demon fled. As a spiritual warrior you should meditate often upon the crucifix and make the sign of the cross fervently and frequently.

Satan recoils at the making of the sign of the cross and in the presence of the crucifix.

> Men can use no better arms to drive away the devil than prayer and the sign of the cross.
> Saint Teresa of Avila

> We Christians, by merely pronouncing the name of Jesus crucified, drive away those demons whom you worship as gods. Their charms and their influence lose all their power wherever the sign of the cross is formed.
> Saint Antony of the Desert

> Many have been crucified throughout the world but none of these do the devils dread, but Christ having been crucified for us. When they see but the sign of the cross, the devils shudder.
> Saint Cyril of Jerusalem

Rosary, Chaplets, Stations of the Cross, etc.

Second only to the Mass in efficacy as a prayer, the Rosary should be the weapon every spiritual warrior wields. The Rosary embodies the whole of the Gospel in its blessed beads. In the Chaplet of the Seven Sorrows of Mary you come face-to-face with the sorrows that Mary humbly bore out of love for God. By uniting her sufferings with her Son's, Mary teaches you how to sanctify your suffering. The Chaplet of Divine Mercy calls to mind God's infinite mercy, a message Satan doesn't want you to hear. Pray it often to counter the whispers of the evil one. Similarly, the many other approved chaplets and devotions bring to mind some aspect of God's truth and call you to closer union with Him. The Stations of the Cross remind us to walk in the way of the Lord always.

Satan, like the coward he is, fears simple, humble prayers the same way he fears simple, humble Mary.

> What the Eucharist is in the order of Sacraments, the Rosary is the same in the order of sacramentals.
> Servant of God Fulton Sheen

> Through the chaplet [of Divine Mercy] you will obtain everything, if what you ask for is compatible with My will.
> Our Lord to Saint Faustina Kowalska

> Always say your Rosary and say it well. Satan always tries to destroy this prayer, but he will never succeed.
> Saint Pio of Pietrelcina

Holy Water, Blessed Salt, Oil, Candles, etc.

Water, salt and oil are biblical symbols which variously bring to mind new life, cleansing, preserving, healing, etc. Jesus used simple elements of creation such as these to perform His miracles and to sanctify His people. It was and is the blessing given to the item by Christ and, subsequently, His Church that allows these common elements to be vehicles of grace. These items can be used offensively, as a preventive or deterrent or they can be used defensively, as a response to an attack. Liberal use of holy water and blessed salt in and around your home, work place and any gathering place is advisable. Making the sign of the cross over each of your senses with blessed oil is a great way to ward off the effect of the evil one. Blessed candles represent the light of Christ and can be used anywhere to dispel the darkness.

Satan flees from wherever holy water or blessed salt is sprinkled or where blessed oil is placed.

228

I often experience that there is nothing the devils flee from more, without returning, than holy water. They also flee from the cross, but they return. The power of holy water must be great.
Saint Teresa of Avila

Seal the cross openly on your forehead and on your children's, so that the demons, seeing the royal sign, will tremble and flee.
Saint Cyril of Jerusalem

Relics, Scapulars, Medals, Litanies, Images and Icons

Any item or prayer which helps remind you of the reality of the Communion of Saints and of the efficacy of praying with them is worthy of your focus. The saints in Heaven are more fully alive than anyone on earth. Their prayers on your behalf are powerful indeed. Wear their medals, meditate upon their icons, recite their Litanies, keep their Holy Cards close at hand and pray with their relics. Fill your home and your workplace with images of the saints as a loving reminder of those who have triumphed in Christ. In battle, it is wise to make use of every weapon at your disposal.

Satan fears when you call upon those saints who have attained their heavenly reward.

We do not worship, we do not adore, for fear that we should bow down to the creature rather than to the creator, but we venerate the relics of the martyrs in order to better adore Him whose martyrs they are.
Saint Jerome

Watchful with fatherly love over the heavenly treasures of the Church, and desirous of enriching with the grant of Indulgences the sacred medals known under the name of Crosses or Little Medals of Saint Benedict, we have gladly accorded to certain persons holding certain dignities the special power to bless the said Medals with rich indulgences, and to distribute them amongst the faithful.
Pope Benedict XIV

Sacraments and sacramentals, though essentially different, are both channels of God's grace and are both effective weapons for spiritual battle. They are a spiritual warrior's best friends. As best friends, they should be respected not abused; appreciated, not taken advantage of; and visited frequently, not ignored.

59. The purpose of the sacraments is to sanctify men, to build up the body of Christ, and, finally, to give worship to God; because they are signs they also instruct. They not only presuppose faith, but by words and objects they also nourish, strengthen, and express it; that is why they are called "sacraments of faith." They do indeed impart grace, but, in addition, the very act of celebrating them most effectively disposes the faithful to receive this grace in a fruitful manner, to worship God duly, and to practice charity.

It is therefore of the highest importance that the faithful should easily understand the sacramental signs, and should frequent with great eagerness those sacraments which were instituted to nourish the Christian life.

60. Holy Mother Church has, moreover, instituted sacramentals. These are sacred signs which bear a resemblance to the Sacraments: they signify effects, particularly of a spiritual kind, which are obtained through the Church's intercession. By them men are disposed to receive the chief effect of the Sacraments, and various occasions in life are rendered holy.

61. Thus, for well-disposed members of the faithful, the liturgy of the sacraments and sacramentals sanctifies almost every event in their lives; they are given access to the stream of divine grace which flows from the paschal mystery of the passion, death, the resurrection of Christ, the font from which all sacraments and sacramentals draw their power.
Sacrosanctum Concilium

Chapter 19
Mary, the Angels & Saints

☩

Furthermore, since we also have so great a cloud of
witnesses over us, let us set aside every burden and sin
which may surround us, and advance, through
patience, to the struggle offered to us.
Hebrews 12:1

Every soldier needs support. The fictional film hero, a
reclusive, muscular, fatigue clad soldier with an attitude, ready
to single-handedly take on the world, is not reality. This is
especially so in regard to spiritual warfare. Two-by-two is the
minimum requirement. Rest, reinforcements and
replenishment are a necessary part of the battle. Go it alone
and you may incur significant damage from the enemy. He is
too strong and too smart to face undermanned.

God has designed it so that you need not ever worry
about facing the enemy alone. You can ask God for His grace to
flow to you through the Blessed Mother. You can call upon the
mighty angels of God for protection and direction. You can tap
into the wisdom of the saints who have gone before you. You
can ask for the prayers of those suffering in purgatory. You
have God's Church and His shepherds to lead and guide you.
You can call upon your brothers and sisters in Christ to support
you in your trials and battles. Through Christ, each member of
His Church is connected to one another.

The Mystical Body of Christ unites all those in union

with God. This union is called the Communion of Saints and is composed of the Church Triumphant (those souls in Heaven), the Church Suffering (those souls in purgatory), and the Church Militant (those souls here on earth). Each member of the Church can, through prayer, intercede for one another.

As a member of the Church Militant, you should cultivate support from the Church Triumphant and be solicitous toward one another and of the Church Suffering.

> God takes care of the souls in purgatory in permitting that they be rescued by the desires of the Church Triumphant, by the prayers of the Church Militant and by the oblation of the priests.
> Saint Thomas Aquinas

> Just as in a physical body the operation of one member contributes to the good of the whole body, so it is in a spiritual body such as the Church. And since all the faithful are one body, the good of one member is communicated to another; everyone members, as the Apostle says, of one another. For that reason, among the points of faith handed down by the Apostles, is that there is a community of goods in the Church, and this is expressed in the words Communion of Saints.
> Saint Thomas Aquinas

Heavenly Support

The Church Triumphant

> But you have drawn near to mount Zion, and to the city of the living God, to the heavenly Jerusalem, and to the company of many thousands of Angels, and to the Church of the first-born, those who have been inscribed in the heavens, and to God, the judge of all, and to the spirits of the just made perfect, and to Jesus, the Mediator of the New Testament.
> Hebrews 12:22-24a

The Church Triumphant includes all of the righteous who have gone before you marked in the sign of faith. This includes those officially declared as saints as well as the countless number of undeclared saints. All of these saints, declared or undeclared, can pray for you and intercede on your behalf. There is nothing better than to have many righteous souls praying for you as you prepare to do battle. Think of them as friends in high places.

These friends in high places, knowing the glory of Heaven, desperately desire for you to share in God's glory with them. They can relate to the trials and tribulations of earthly life. Fully alive in God, they delight in assisting those who desire to serve God while here on earth. By God's design and grace, their death does not separate them from you. No longer bound by the constraints of original sin, they are free to serve God more fully. All who die in God's friendship are alive in Him, more alive than ever before. Having passed the test, they are eager to lend their support to those who ask. Such heavenly support is invaluable to you as a spiritual warrior.

Heavenly Spiritual Director

> His mother said to the servants, "Do whatever he tells you."
> John 2:5

Mary, the Mother of God is the Mediatrix of God's graces; it is she through whom all of God's graces flow. As the graces you need to do battle flow through the Blessed Virgin Mary, she is the ideal heavenly spiritual director for all spiritual warriors. A spiritual director should be someone who knows God intimately, who is a lover and seeker of His will and who is committed to helping you achieve salvation. Mary is all this and more. Her motherly love extends to all of God's children.

Never having been under the dominion of Satan, due to God's singular grace extended to her in the Immaculate Conception, Mary was and is always the devil's enemy. Mary, whose heart was pierced, who gave birth to a son destined to rule nations, who between herself and Satan an eternal enmity exists, against whose offspring Satan wages war knows how to do battle with the evil one. More than that, she knows how to best defeat the evil one, by keeping her eyes humbly fixed upon her Son. She knows when it is best to pull back and when it best to proceed. She knows when it is best to reflect and when it is best to respond. She knows how to encourage and embolden you. As her spouse is the Holy Spirit, her gifts and graces are boundless.

> Let us turn our gaze to Mary, Christ's first disciple, Spouse of the Holy Spirit and Mother of the Church, who was with the Apostles at the first Pentecost, so that she will help us to learn from her fiat docility to the voice of the Spirit.
> Pope John Paul II

The Blessed Virgin Mary, by virtue of God's grace, was always obedient to the will of the Father while on earth. Likewise, from her place in Heaven, she can only do and recommend that which is consistent with the Father's will. She is gentle, yet unyielding. She is God's perfect creature. She is the spouse of the Holy Spirit and the mother of Jesus. His will is her will; His desire for you is her desire for you. These attributes are what make the Mary the perfect heavenly spiritual director.

Prayer, devotion and consecration to Mary will allow her to spiritually direct your life. Surrender to her and she will guide your every move in such a way that it draws you in ever closer to her Son and gives glory to God. As a spiritual warrior, you could do no better than to be under the direction of your heavenly Mother.

> Modern times are dominated by Satan and will be more so in the future. The conflict with Hell cannot be engaged by men, even the most clever. The Immaculata alone has, from God, the promise of victory over Satan. She seeks souls who will consecrate themselves entirely to her, who will become, in her hands, effective instruments for the defeat of Satan and the spreading of God's kingdom upon earth.
> Saint Maximilian Kolbe

I am greatly indebted to our Mother Mary for her driving away these temptations of the enemy. I told you

that the strength of Satan is something terrible, but
may God be praised for Jesus has placed the cause of
my salvation and the ultimate victory in the hands of
our heavenly Mother.
Saint Pio of Pietrelcina

When the devil wishes to make himself master of a
soul, he seeks to make it give up devotion to Mary.
Saint Alphonsus Liguori

No man is delivered or preserved from the world-wide
snares of Satan save through Mary; and God grants His
graces to no one except through her alone.
Saint Germanus

Although it is very true that the Blessed Virgin loves
all that love her, nevertheless those who wish to have
the Blessed Mother as a helper at the hour of death
must in life merit such a signal favor by abstaining
from sin and laboring in her honor.
Pope Pius XI

Heavenly Prayer Partner

He is not the God of the dead, but of the living.
Mark 12:27

Those souls in Heaven are more alive now than they
ever were. Your Guardian Angel, your patron saint, a favorite
saint or some combination of these, make for great prayer
partners. Holy angels, with their eternal commitment to the
Father's will, can only respond to you in truth. They will
petition and intercede for you to know God's will and help you
to strive for it. Saints in Heaven, those who have completed the
race, make superb role models and mentors. They know the
race course well and will help you to victory. Your heavenly
prayer partner is at various times an intercessor, confidant,
protector, friend, moral compass and spiritual guide. By the
grace of God, they can be for you whatever He permits them to
be for you and what you, in a sense, permit them to be.

Patron Saint

> Remember your leaders, who have spoken the Word of
> God to you, whose faith you imitate, by observing the
> goal of their way of life.
> Hebrews 13:7

The saint or saints to whom you have a special
connection desire nothing more than for you to join them in
Heaven giving worship and glory to God. Whether the
connection is through your baptismal or confirmation name or
through your vocation or ministry or simply an affinity for a
particular saint, all the saints desire God's will for you. Being
human, they understand the struggles and foibles of humanity.
They know the power of the grace of God in their lives and they
know the reward awaiting you in Heaven.

At various times, God may place different saints in your
midst, corresponding to the different needs in your life. At
times you might feel more attracted to a saint with a mystical,
contemplative lifestyle. Other times it might be a saint who
was bold and zealous; still other times it might be a saint who
lived an ordinary life in an extraordinary way. When God
places a saint's name on your heart, seek out that saint in
prayer. Pray with the saint as if he or she is right there with
you. Through a grace granted to them by God, your chosen
saint can be with you in prayer. Feel free to seek counsel and
comfort from this "friend of God."

Many of the saints engaged in serious warfare with the
evil one. Saint Antony of the Desert, Saint Rita of Cascia, Saint
Benedict, Saint Faustina Kowalska, Saint Martin de Porres,
Saint Rose of Lima, Saint Catherine of Siena, Saint Francis
Xavier, Saint Teresa of Avila, Saint Francis of Assisi, Saint
Gemma Galgani, Saint John Vianney, Saint Therese of Lisieux,
Saint Pio of Pietrelcina and Blessed Teresa of Calcutta, among
many others, were all known to do battle — either physically or
spiritually — with the evil one. Their intercession, as well as
their counsel and comfort, is very strong in this area. As a
spiritual warrior it is a good idea to seek the wisdom of those
who have successfully battled the evil one. They not only can
help, they want to help.

I will spend my Heaven doing good on Earth.
Saint Therese of Lisieux

I will ask the Lord to let me remain at the threshold of Paradise and I will not enter until the last of my spiritual children has entered.
Saint Pio of Pietrelcina

Heavenly Prayer Community

And when he had opened the book, the four living creatures and the twenty-four elders fell down before the Lamb, each having stringed instruments, as well as golden bowls full of fragrances, which are the prayers of the saints.
Revelation 5:8

The Church Triumphant and the Church Suffering are your heavenly companions. (Members of the Church Suffering are not yet in Heaven; nor are they any longer on earth. They are, thus, include here as part of the "heavenly" realm.) Your prayers for the souls in purgatory rise like incense to Heaven. Your prayers seeking the intercession of the saints in Heaven are echoed to God. The saints can also initiate prayer on their own for your sake. Those in purgatory can pray for you as well. All of this is done by God's grace and for His glory. Prayer for one another within the Communion of Saints has as its source, and is an expression of, God's love.

When you perceive that God is chastening you, fly not to his enemies, but to his friends, the martyrs, the saints and those who were pleasing to him and who have great power in God.
Saint John Chrysostom

Angels

Then the devil left him. And behold, Angels approached and ministered to him.
Matthew 4:11

Sacred tradition relates that the angels in Heaven are also part of the Communion of Saints and therefore, part of the Church Triumphant. The name angel denotes what they do rather than who they are; angel means messenger. Angels are spirits whose primary role is to act as God's messengers. They also exist in service to humanity, to bring each person into closer union with God. As a spiritual warrior, considering who your enemy is, it would be prudent to establish a relationship with God's messengers.

> Make friends with the angels, who though invisible are always with you. Often invoke them, constantly praise them, and make good use of their help and assistance in all your temporal and spiritual affairs.
> Saint Francis de Sales

> An angel is put in charge of every believer, provided we do not drive him out by sin. He guards the soul like an army.
> Saint Basil the Great

Guardian Angel

> See to it that you do not despise even one of these little ones. For I say to you, that their angels in Heaven continually look upon the face of my Father, who is in Heaven.
> Matthew 18:10

It has been the constant teaching of the Church that each person has assigned to them a Guardian Angel. Your Guardian Angel is a gift given to you from God. This angel's purpose is to protect, prompt and pray for you. Out of love and obedience for God and love for you, your Guardian Angel seeks your eternal happiness.

While respecting your free will, your Guardian Angel will do whatever it can to protect your body and soul from danger. He will prevent you, if you will it, from entering into agreement with an evil thought, word or deed. He will prompt you to right judgment and to do good and avoid evil. Your Guardian Angel always prays for you, that you might surrender your will freely and fully to God. He will never leave your side, from conception until death. After God and the Blessed Mother, there is no greater friend to you than your Guardian Angel.

> Jesus has not left me alone; He makes my guardian angel stay with me always.
> Saint Gemma Galgani

As a whole, your Guardian Angel is likely underappreciated and underutilized. If you want to grow in the spiritual life, then build a relationship with your Guardian Angel. If you are called to do battle, then seek the protection and guidance of your Guardian Angel. As a spiritual warrior, your Guardian Angel is one of your most powerful allies.

> We should pray to the angel who is given to us as guardian.
> Saint Ambrose

> When tempted, invoke your angel. Ignore the devil and do not be afraid of him; he trembles and flees at your Guardian Angel's sight.
> Saint John Bosco

> In the warfare we carry on to remain strong against the evil powers, the angels are our helpers. For our weakness is such that, if the Guardian Angels had not been given to us, we could not resist the many and powerful attacks of the evil spirit.
> Saint Hilary of Poitiers

> Each and every member of the faithful has a guardian angel to protect and guard, and guide them through life.
> Saint Basil the Great

> These celestial spirits [guardian angels] have been placed at our side to protect us, instruct us and guide us.
> Saint Bernard of Clairvaux

Saint Michael the Archangel

> And there was a great battle in heaven. Michael and his Angels were battling with the dragon, and the dragon was fighting, and so were his angels.
> Revelation 12:7

Saint Michael the Archangel deserves special mention here. Among other patronage, he is the patron saint of battle. Drawn from Scripture, tradition speaks to the four roles that Saint Michael plays in God's plan. He is to fight against Satan, to liberate souls from the grasp of Satan, to advocate for God's people and to accompany the souls of those who have died to their judgment. He is a powerful intercessor for any spiritual warrior to call upon. As powerful as he is and as fearlessly as he fights against the evil one, he only does so according to God's will. In humility and obedience, unlike Satan, Michael awaits God's command.

> May prayer strengthen us for the spiritual battle we are told about in the Letter to the Ephesians: "Draw strength from the Lord and from His mighty power." The Book of Revelation refers to this same battle, recalling before our eyes the image of Saint Michael the Archangel. Pope Leo XIII certainly had a very vivid recollection of this scene when, at the end of the last century, he introduced a special prayer to Saint Michael throughout the Church. Although this prayer is no longer recited at the end of Mass, I ask everyone not to forget it and to recite it to obtain help in the battle against forces of darkness and against the spirit of this world.
> Pope John Paul II

Fallen Angels

> But they did not prevail, and a place for them was no longer found in heaven. And he was thrown out, that great dragon, that ancient serpent, who is called the devil and Satan, who seduces the whole world. And he was thrown down to the earth, and his angels were cast

down with him.
Revelation 12:8-9

The fallen angels are not to be part of your prayer community. Because of their malice and deceit toward humanity, it is worth speaking briefly of them.

God created all the angels as benevolent. Some freely chose to rebel and became malevolent, collectively they are known as the fallen angels. Satan is the chief of these fallen angels. The fallen angels retain the abilities associated with their nature, but because of their lack of right relationship with Christ they are not as powerful as the good angels. Likewise, the fallen angels are superior to man in their spiritual powers, yet lacking in God's grace they are, in a real sense, inferior to humans who remain in God's grace. Like the good angels, the fallen angels maintain a hierarchal structure; some fallen angels are more malevolent than others. They all desire to separate you from a life of grace; the very grace that provides you with all the protection you'll need. By God's grace, your humble submission of your will to His makes you greater than the fallen angels.

Thanks to Christ, the good angels are more powerful.
Saint Basil the Great

Though in the order of nature, angels rank above men, yet, by scale of justice, good men are of greater value than bad angels.
Saint Augustine

The Church Suffering

And, calling an assembly, he sent twelve thousand drachmas of silver to Jerusalem, to be offered for a sacrifice for the sins of the dead, thinking well and religiously about the resurrection, (for if he had not hoped that those who had fallen would be resurrected, it would have seemed superfluous and vain to pray for the dead), and because he considered that those who had fallen asleep with piety had great grace stored up for them. Therefore, it is a holy and beneficial thought

to pray on behalf of those who have passed away, so that they may be released from sins.
2 Maccabees 12:43-46

The Church Suffering is comprised of the souls in purgatory who are bound for glory in Heaven. Not yet experiencing the Beatific Vision, but no longer on earth, those who are part of the Church Suffering are at the same time hopeful and helpless. They are hopeful in that they are certain to enter Heaven upon completion of their purgation. They are helpless in that they are unable to pray on their own behalf. Your prayers and suffering for them can help get them to Heaven sooner.

Though unable to pray for themselves, the souls in purgatory can pray for you as you undergo trials. As they are purged from whatever final attachment they may have to sin, they are correspondingly growing in love and closer to God. As they do, their prayers for you become more powerful and more pure.

As a spiritual warrior, you should be aware of those who have gone before you and have been wounded in battle. The unfathomable joy they will experience as they cross the threshold of Heaven cannot help but translate into prayer for you and others. They are your comrades-in-Christ, soldiers who have fought the good fight. Never assume because one seemed saintly while on earth that they are in Heaven; pray for them anyway. Likewise, you should never assume any particular person is in Hell. What may have taken place between that person and God in their final breath is known only to God. Never presume, never despair; any prayers offered will not be wasted.   Prayer for these saints-in-waiting should be considered high priority.

When I am dead, people will say, "She saw Our Lady, she is a saint," But meanwhile I shall be roasting in purgatory.
Saint Bernadette Soubirous

If one knew what we may obtain from God by the intercession of the poor souls, [in purgatory] they would not be so much abandoned. Let us pray a great deal for

them, they will pray for us.
Saint John Vianney

Eternal Father, I offer You the most precious blood of Your Divine Son, Jesus, in union with the Masses said throughout the world today, for all the holy souls in purgatory, for sinners everywhere, for sinners in the universal church, those in my own home and within my family.
Our Lord to Saint Gertrude the Great

I would like to empty purgatory with one hand, and with the other fill it with souls snatched from the brink of Hell.
Blessed Mary of Providence

Earthly Support

The Church Militant

> For though we walk in the flesh, we do not battle according to the flesh. For the weapons of our battles are not carnal, yet still they are powerful with God, unto the destruction of fortifications: tearing down every counsel and height that extols itself contrary to the wisdom of God, and leading every intellect into the captivity of obedience to Christ, and standing ready to repudiate every disobedience, when your own obedience has been fulfilled.
> 2 Corinthians 10:3-6

The Church Militant is comprised of those baptized souls here on earth who are doing battle against the flesh, the world and Satan. The enemy is real, the battle is raging and the results are potentially deadly. Find support and comfort from those who are living here, but have their gaze and goals set upon eternal glory. Our God calls us to community, to bear witness to His love to one another, to encourage one another on the battlefield, to strive to enter Heaven together.

You must fight energetically, since you know very well

what great wounds the undefiled Spouse of Christ
Jesus has suffered, and how vigorous is the destructive
attack of Her enemies.
Venerable Pope Pius IX

If you go to God, take care not to go alone to Him.
Pope Saint Gregory the Great

Earthly Spiritual Director

And Philip, hurrying, heard him reading from the
prophet Isaiah, and he said, "Do you think that you
understand what you are reading?" And he said, "But
how can I, unless someone will have revealed it to me?"
And he asked Philip to climb up and sit with him.
Acts of the Apostles 8:30-31

The words of the Ethiopian eunuch from the verse
above were a humble admission of reality, a quality that is
often missing in today's culture. In these times, an earthly
spiritual director is not a luxury; it is a necessity. Equally, in
these times, an earthly spiritual director is not always easy to
find. The first step in finding a suitable spiritual director is
prayer. Pray to God that He will aid you in your discernment
and prepare the heart of your future spiritual director.

Ideally, your spiritually director will be a priest. This is
not always realistic. If a priest is not available, then a deacon,
religious brother or sister or, if necessary, a qualified lay
person would suffice. You should seek out a spiritual director
who is well known for being holy, virtuous and prudent. He
should be, by his actions, a witness to God's love, mercy and
truth. Perfection is not a virtue necessary for a spiritual
director, but humility and obedience to the Church are,
especially as it relates to the Church's teachings on sin and
evil. A devotion to the Blessed Mother should be considered
almost mandatory in a spiritual director.

It is better to have a spiritual director who is
challenging, rather than one who is comforting. Don't settle for
a spiritual director who will not confront you in the errors of
your ways. Nor should you settle for one who isn't committed to
helping you become a saint. Accountability is a Christian

necessity. Better that your spiritual director speaks the truth in love, than to speak love without truth. Listen to your spiritual director as if listening to your superior in the military.

Do you want to walk earnestly toward devotion? Then get a good spiritual director to guide you; that is the best of all advice.
Saint Francis de Sales

In desolation, darkness and various doubts, have recourse to Me and to your spiritual director. He will always answer you in My name.
Our Lord to Saint Faustina Kowalska

Earthly Prayer Partner

For wherever two or three are gathered in my name, there am I, in their midst.
Matthew 18:20

Christ promised that wherever two or more are gathered in His name, that He would be there as well. He also promised if you seek, you will find, ask and it will be given to you (cf. Matthew 7:7). So, the first step in choosing an earthly prayer partner is to pray to God for proper discernment. An earthly prayer partner can help make Christ present to you. He can provide you with a sense of love, comfort and support. Your earthly prayer partner should be mature, scripturally sound and loyal to the Church. He, in some sense, should provide a balance and a challenge to you in your spiritual life. A mutual devotion to the Blessed Mother should be part of your relationship.

Like a spiritual director, you should choose a prayer partner not because you are comfortable with him, but because he can help make you a better Christian and you, in turn, can help make him one. You should choose a prayer partner who can help you grow closer to life eternal with God. A prayer partner can be a spouse, a family member or a friend. He can be close by or far away. Whether it is the biological family or the spiritual family, prayer is the glue that holds these relationships together. As a spiritual warrior, prayer is your most effective protection and weapon. It is made even more so when two or more of you bear public witness.

> When people say the Rosary together it is far more formidable to the devil than one said privately, because in this public prayer it is an army that is attacking him.
> Saint Louis de Montfort

> The family that prays together stays together.
> Servant of God Patrick Peyton

Earthly Prayer Community

> Now they were persevering in the doctrine of the Apostles, and in the communion of the breaking of the bread, and in the prayers.
> Acts of the Apostles 2:42

An earthly prayer community, made up of members of the Church Militant, should provide a glimpse of the Church Triumphant. It should consist of souls who are united in their love of God. It should be an active, vital community of "prayers" who are led by the Holy Spirit. They are to be earthly only in the sense that they are presently living here with you, not earthly in the sense of worldly. Those who are worldly will not provide you the love and support you need.

Your prayer community should be Eucharistic, Spirit led, Marian and Magisterial. Its primary strength should be from the Eucharistic presence of Jesus. Its primary decision maker should be the Holy Spirit, speaking both through the leader and the group as a whole. Its primary devotion should be to the Blessed Mother. Its primary union should be with the Holy Father and the bishops in union with him. It should be characterized by a sense of humility, charity, order and obedience. If disorder or pride frequently manifest, then perhaps a different prayer group would be best, as chaos and pride are not of God.

> When we are linked by the power of prayer, we, as it were hold each other's hand as we walk side by side along a slippery path; and thus by bounteous

disposition of charity, it comes about that the harder each one leans on the other, the more firmly we are riveted together in brotherly love.
Pope Saint Gregory the Great

There is so much need today for mature Christian personalities, conscious of their baptismal identity, of their vocation and mission in the Church and in the world! There is great need for living Christian communities!
Pope John Paul II

An earthly prayer community provides a sense of protection, of belonging, of support and of rest. It also provides regularly scheduled time set aside to pray and offers support and an accountability structure. Further, it allows for an opportunity for communal discernment.

Communal discernment is an especially important source of protection for a spiritual warrior. In communal discernment it is harder to be fooled by the wiles of the evil one. It is a guard against deception and pride. It makes sense to seek out like-minded souls to develop an earthly prayer community corresponding to the heavenly one both for support and protection.

My chains, which I carry about on me for Jesus Christ, begging that I may happily make my way to God, exhort you: persevere in your concord and in your community prayers.
Saint Ignatius of Antioch

In the business world people have mentors, trainers and success coaches. In secular life, people have life coaches, accountability partners and physical trainers. Would it not make sense to have coaches and trainers and a team to sharpen your skills in the area of the spiritual where the focus is eternal and not earthly? Surround yourself with "saints-in-the-making" here on earth, with the saints in Heaven and with the soon to be saints in purgatory. Only pride seeks to go it alone. Cultivate community. Be your brothers' and your sisters' keeper. Pray for one another. Go to Heaven together.

Do not try to go to heaven alone. He will almost certainly ask you the embarrassing question: Where are your brothers and sisters?
Blessed Teresa of Calcutta

This self reliance was what destroyed me.
Saint Teresa of Avila

Death is not the end for those who believe in Jesus, only a new beginning. The Blessed Mother, all the holy angels and saints are just on the other side waiting to lend a hand. Their will for you is God's will for you. In union with other members of the Church Militant, invoke the intercession of Mary, the angels, the saints and all the members of the Church Triumphant as you pray for the members of the Church Suffering. They in turn will pray for you and your loved ones, even more so as your prayers help their souls to finish purgation and enter Heaven.

I ask Blessed Mary, ever virgin and all the angels and saints and you, my brothers and sisters, to pray for me to the Lord our God.
Confiteor

In your strife with the devil, you have for spectators the angels and the Lord of angels.
Saint Ephrem of Syria

When you are praying alone, and your spirit is dejected, and you are wearied and oppressed by your loneliness, remember then, as always, that God the Trinity looks upon you with eyes brighter than the sun; also all the angels, your own Guardian Angel, and all the Saints of God. Truly they do; for they are all one in God, and where God is, there are they also.
Saint John of Kronstadt

The good God will render us back the good we do for them [the souls in purgatory] a hundredfold.
Saint John Vianney

Chapter 20
Praise, Glory & Thanksgiving

Rejoice always. Pray without ceasing. Give thanks in everything. For this is the will of God in Christ Jesus for all of you.
1 Thessalonians 5:16-18

Giving thanks always for everything, in the name of our Lord Jesus Christ, to God the Father.
Ephesians 5:20

And we know that, for those who love God, all things work together unto good, for those who, in accordance with his purpose, are called to be saints.
Romans 8:28

Rejoice in the Lord always. Again, I say, rejoice. Be anxious about nothing, but in all things, with prayer and supplication, with acts of thanksgiving, let your petitions be made known to God. And so shall the peace of God, which exceeds all understanding, guard your hearts and minds in Christ Jesus.
Philippians 4:4, 6-7

When you give God praise, glory and thanksgiving you set in motion a whole series of events, with spiritual and physical manifestations. You invite and, really, release God's power upon you and everyone and everything you praise. Through your praise you can break down resistance to God's grace in your life and the life of others. Praise elevates you to the heavenly realm and allows you to love God with greater intensity.

> Why does God wish to be praised and glorified by us if not to make our love for Him more fervent?
> Saint John Chrysostom

Give God praise at all times and in all things. Give Him praise in the good; give Him praise in the bad. Give glory to God equally during moments of triumph and tragedy. Give Him glory through all you do and say. Give God thanks always and everywhere. Give Him thanks for the success and for the failures. God is due all praise, glory and thanksgiving because He is God; not for what He has done, but for who He is. Praise, glory and thanksgiving should be frequently upon the lips of every spiritual warrior.

One of the first benefits of giving God praise at all times, in all things, is a shift of focus off of you and onto God. Praise takes you from a selfish place to a selfless place. It recognizes that there is an entity outside of you who exists and who is greater than you are. It begins to put the relationship between you and God in right order. You acknowledge God as God of all things. You acknowledge the Word of God as truthful and relevant. You acknowledge God as everything and yourself as nothing. This is truth, this is humility. As a spiritual warrior, humility should be your foundation.

> Let us refer all good to the Lord, God Almighty and Most High, acknowledge that every good is His and thank Him.
> Saint Francis of Assisi

A second benefit of giving God praise at all times, in all things, is a sense of holy indifference that begins to grow. Holy indifference is distinct from being lukewarm. Being lukewarm means you don't care one way or the other. A holy indifference neither desires, nor doesn't desire. It only desires what God desires; it wills only what God wills. It does not judge, it does not have preferences, it does not seek its own end, it has no expectations; it surrenders to the will of God. To have expectations implies an attachment to an outcome and an attachment to an outcome is an expression of ego. It is better to offer a prayer of total surrender of all things to God. As a spiritual warrior, surrender is essential to victory.

Indifference loves nothing except for the will of God. The indifferent heart is a heart without choice, equally disposed to everything, without any other object of its will but the will of its God. It does not set its love on the things that God wills, but on the will of God that wills them.
Saint Francis de Sales

A third benefit of giving God praise at all times, in all things, is the flowering of unconditional love. If you only give God praise in the good, then your love for Him is conditional. "When things are going my way, I love you God. When they're not, I don't." That is not true love; that is conditional love. Unconditional love's response is the same whether things are good or whether things are bad. God loves you maximally at every moment, never more, never less. As God is love, it is His nature to love. You are called to love that same way and you can only do so by His grace. As a spiritual warrior, love for Him should be the impetus behind every action.

Grant, Lord, only that I may love you and then do with me as you will.
Saint Alphonsus Liguori

A fourth benefit of giving God praise at all times, in all things, is the realization that if you truly trust in God then there is no bad. Scripture states that when you love God all things work for good. The Crucifixion is the ultimate example of this. God is able to see above and beyond time and space. He is not stuck in a myopic world view. By giving praise to God, you began to place yourself in a position where you can trust God more and more for there is truly no bad if you trust in God. All is good, all can serve His will. If he permits it, He can redeem it. A lack of praise is really a lack of trust in God. As a

251

spiritual warrior, lack of trust in God is tantamount to trusting in the power of the evil one.

> Nothing can come but what God wills. And I am very sure that whatever that be, however bad it may seem, it shall indeed be the best.
> Saint Thomas More

A fifth benefit of giving God praise at all times, in all things, is the departure of Satan. If Satan is in any way involved in the current crisis facing you, and you stop and give God praise, Satan will have to flee. Praising God, then, can be like a mini-exorcism. Because of his pride, he cannot give God praise, not even indirectly. Praise God and Satan will flee, praise God and you foil Satan's plan. As a spiritual warrior, praising God in all things should flow naturally from your faith and trust in Him.

> Even if the sins of soul are as dark as night, when the sinner turns to My mercy he gives Me the greatest praise and is the glory of My Passion. When a soul praises My goodness, Satan trembles before it and flees to the very bottom of Hell.
> Our Lord to Saint Faustina Kowalska

A sixth benefit of giving God praise at all times, in all things, is the sense of peace and joy that you'll experience. It is the type of peace and joy that surpasses all understanding and that the world cannot give (cf. Philippians 4:6-7). This peace is what the world spends billions of dollars trying to achieve and yet God set it up so it would be free to receive. You were made to praise Him; that is what your very essence cries out for. When you are doing what you were created to do, your spirit, mind and body unite in heavenly peace and joy. As a spiritual warrior, your duty is to praise God.

> No duty is more important than that of returning thanks to Almighty God.
> Saint Ambrose

A seventh benefit of giving God praise at all times, in

all things, is turning your suffering into sanctification. When you praise God in your pain or suffering, you are able to elevate it above its earthly reality and transform it into a heavenly reality. Your suffering, united with Jesus' on the cross, can be sanctifying for yourself and others. As a spiritual warrior, you will suffer. Therefore, you might as well sanctify your suffering by praising God and giving Him glory.

> We should accept, as we would a favor, every moment of our lives and whatever it may bring, whether it is good or bad, but the crosses with even greater gratitude than the rest. Crosses release us from this world and by doing so bind up us to God.
> Blessed Charles de Foucauld

An eighth benefit of giving God praise at all times, in all things, is the increasing and intensifying of God's blessing. Giving God praise releases more blessings upon you, actually and perceptually. You both perceive more and receive more of God's blessings. He not only fills you to overflowing, He will also increase your capacity to receive His blessings when you pray and praise. As a spiritual warrior, anything that will increase your capacity and ability to receive and give blessings is beneficial. Correspondingly, a lack of praise can have the opposite effect.

> If we do not give thanks for the blessings given by God, it becomes necessary to withdraw these blessings in order to bring us to our senses. As the eyes fail to see what is too near, but need a suitable distance, so ungrateful souls, when deprived of blessings, often become aware of former mercies.
> Saint Basil the Great

A ninth benefit of giving God praise at all times, in all things, is a strengthening of the will. Giving God frequent praise does for the will what frequent exercise does for the body; it tones and toughens it. A will refined according to the fires of holy desire provides no entry points for the evil one. A will confirmed in grace and conformed to God's will is impervious to fear and adverse to sin. As a spiritual warrior, it is important to have a will that is strengthened in Him.

> Fear is cast out because of the strengthening of the will
> by which the soul knows it can no longer sin.
> Saint Bonaventure

A tenth benefit of giving God praise at all times, in all things, is the realization that doing so is a powerful demonstration of faith and trust in God. When you trust God enough to thank Him in advance you are putting your faith into action; you're giving life to your surrender. You are acknowledging that, despite appearances, God has a plan for you. Giving God praise in advance also softens up any resistance to the movement of the Holy Spirit in your life. As a spiritual warrior, it is important to be open to the movement of the Holy Spirit.

> Let us thank God ahead of time for whatever He
> foresees is pleasing to Him, leaving everything at His
> divine disposal.
> Venerable Solanus Casey

An eleventh benefit of giving God praise at all times, in all things, is a greater participation in the life of God. This participation in the life of God leads to our sanctification in God. As you praise God you become more aware of the beauty and truth and goodness that surround you. As you continue to praise God you, in a sense, heighten your receptivity to God and His majestic creation. As a spiritual warrior, it is important to recognize and appreciate the language of truth and beauty that creation speaks.

> This is the divine truth: we were created for the glory
> and praise of God's name and to participate in the
> eternal beauty of God and so be sanctified in God.
> Saint Catherine of Siena

A twelfth benefit of giving God praise at all times, in all things, is the hastening of the second coming of Christ. If the entire world abounded in praise of Him, Jesus Christ would return and the war would be over. The quality of your life can hasten the Second Coming of the Lord. As a spiritual warrior you should look forward to the day when there will be no battle to fight, only praise to give to God.

> Therefore, since all these things will be dissolved, what kind of people ought you to be? In behavior and in piety, be holy, waiting for, and hurrying toward, the advent of the day of the Lord, by which the burning heavens shall be dissolved, and the elements shall melt from the heat of the fire.
> 2 Peter 3:11-12

When you fail to give God praise at all times and in all things you are, in a sense, proclaiming your superiority to Him. Like Judas at the Last Supper, you become your own god, deciding what is good and what is bad. You seek to impose your beliefs about what is best for God as Peter did when he drew his weapon in the Garden of Gethsemane. Praise Him always, good, bad or otherwise for He remains God through it all.

When you fail to give God praise in the good and bad, you create a relationship of condition, one predicated on doing things your way. You also give Satan an angle to work you. He starts to multiply your doubts and fears. He starts to lay blame at God's doorstep. He starts to paint God as an uncaring, vindictive and unmerciful God. He whispers to you that God is holding something back from you, the same lie spoken in the Garden of Eden. When you fail to give God praise you wound your relationship with Him and others.

> Be sure if the enemy of our soul is pleased at anything in us, it is ingratitude of whatever kind. Why? Ingratitude leads to so many breaks with God and our neighbor.
> Venerable Solanus Casey

Praise God without exception. Praise God without expectations. For if you do not praise, do you really believe? For if you did believe, wouldn't you praise? Praise God in all things, at all times. Praise Him for the big events and the small ones. Praise Him in sickness and health, in riches or poverty, for better or worse. Praise Him in thought, word and deed.

Praise Him not because, but just because. Praise Him until it becomes second nature, because praising Him is really your first nature. It is only your sin nature, your fallen nature that prevents you from praising Him here and now. Once you are in Heaven, all you will be doing is praising Him. It is who you were created to be and what you were created to do.

> And all the Angels were standing around the throne, with the elders and the four living creatures. And they fell upon their faces in view of the throne, and they worshipped God, saying: "Amen. Blessing and glory and wisdom and thanksgiving, honor and power and strength to our God, forever and ever. Amen."
> Revelation 7:12-13

You are made to praise Him just as much as you are made to breathe. Praise Him when your cancer goes into remission and praise Him when it returns. Praise Him for your nasty neighbor and for your best friend. Praise Him for the accident you avoided and the one you didn't. Praise Him in your laughter and through your tears. Praise Him in the midst of miracles and in the midst of the mundane. Praise Him when you want to scream and when you want to sing. Praise Him for the rising sun and the setting sun. Praise Him for war and peace. Praise God when you resist temptation and when you fall into sin. Praise Him for faithful priests and bishops. Praise Him for those priests and bishops who have strayed. Praise Him for prayers answered, whether the answer was yes, no or not now.

Praise Him for your spouse who loves you or for the spouse who left you. Praise Him for your child who is on drugs. Praise Him for healing your friend. Praise God for your children remaining strong in their faith and passing it on to their children. Praise God for your family member who died too soon. Praise Him for losing your job. Praise Him for your family vacation. Praise Him for struggles in your marriage. Praise Him for His mercy and His judgment. Praise Him when natural disaster strikes. Praise Him where sin is abounding. Praise Him for your children. Praise Him in all and through all.

As a spiritual warrior, you need to know that all of your power and authority comes from God. All of your ability to fight, to hold your ground, to advance is a gift from God. He is the supplier of all the necessary equipment. One of the best ways to tap into His power is to praise Him. The spiritual warrior's primary stance is on bended knee in praise and worship of God.

> I ought to die of shame to think that I have not already died of gratitude to my good God.
> Saint Julia Billiart

> We should not accept in silence the benefactions of God, but return thanks for them.
> Saint Basil the Great

> In prosperity, give thanks to God with humility and fear lest by pride you abuse God's benefits and so offend him.
> Saint Louis IX

One of the simplest and best ways to give God praise, glory and thanksgiving is to participate in the Holy Sacrifice of the Mass. You cannot participate in Mass without praising God. Sacrifice and praise go together. The language of the Mass is the language of praise. Listen to some of the prayers recited during Mass.

- During the Gloria, the people pray, "Glory to God in the highest... we worship you, we give you thanks, we praise you for your glory... in the Glory of God the Father."

- In response to the first and second readings, the people say, "Thanks be to God."

- The Gospel Acclamation, depending on the season, is either, "Alleluia", which comes from combining the Hebrew words for "praise Jehovah" or if during Lent, "Praise and honor to you, Lord, Jesus Christ."

- Prior to the proclamation of the Gospel, the people say, "Glory to you, Lord." Upon its conclusion, the people respond, "<u>Praise to you, Lord Jesus Christ.</u>"

- During the Nicene Creed, these words are prayed, "...with the Father and Son he [the Holy Spirit] is <u>worshipped and glorified</u>..."

- During the Preparation of the Altar and Gifts, the people say, "May the Lord accept the sacrifice at your hands for the <u>praise and glory of his name</u>, for our good and the good of all his Church."

- In the Preface Dialogue to the Eucharistic Prayers, the priest says, "Let us <u>give thanks to the Lord, our God.</u>" The people's response is "<u>It right to give Him thank and praise.</u>"

- During the Sanctus, the people pray, "Heaven and earth are <u>full of your glory,</u> followed by <u>Hosanna in the highest.</u>" Hosanna is a shout of praise or adoration in recognition of Jesus as Messiah.

- In the preface to Eucharistic Prayer I, the priest prays, "<u>We come to you, Father, with praise and thanksgiving,</u> through Jesus Christ your Son."

- In the preface to Eucharistic Prayer II, the priest prays, "<u>Father, it is our duty and salvation, always and everywhere to give you thanks</u> through your beloved Son, Jesus Christ..."

- In the preface to Eucharistic Prayer III, the priest prays, "<u>Father, you are holy indeed and all creation rightly gives you praise...</u>"

- In the preface to Eucharistic Prayer IV, the priest prays, "<u>Father in Heaven, it is right that we should give you thanks and glory...</u>" and "<u>in the name of every creature under Heaven, we too praise your glory as we sing...</u>"

- In the preface to Eucharistic Prayer for Masses of

Reconciliation I, the priest prays, "<u>We do well always and everywhere to give you thanks and praise</u>..."

- In the preface to Eucharistic Prayer for Masses of Reconciliation II, the priest prays, "<u>We praise and thank you through Jesus Christ, our Lord</u>..."

- All three of the Eucharistic Prayers for Children begin with giving God thanks and praise.

- During the institution narrative of Eucharistic Prayer I, the priest prays, "...he took break in his sacred hands and looking up to Heaven, to you, his almighty Father, <u>he gave you thanks and praise</u>" and "When supper was ended, he took the cup. <u>Again he gave you thanks and praise</u>..."

- During the institution narrative of Eucharistic Prayer II, the priest prays, "Before he was given up to death, a death he freely accepted, <u>he took bread and gave you thanks</u>..." and "When the supper was ended, he took the cup. <u>Again he gave you thanks and praise</u>..."

- During the institution narrative of Eucharistic Prayer III, the priest prays, "On the night he was betrayed, he took bread and <u>gave you thanks and praise</u>" and "When supper was ended, he took the cup. <u>Again he gave you thanks and praise</u>..."

- During the institution narrative of Eucharistic Prayer IV, the priest prays, "In the same way, he took the cup, filled with wine. <u>He gave you thanks</u>..."

- Just prior to the conclusion of Eucharistic Prayer II, the priest prays, "<u>May we praise you in union with them and give you glory through your Son, Jesus Christ</u>."

- Just prior to the conclusion of Eucharistic Prayer IV, the priest prays, "...<u>we shall sing your glory with every creature through Christ our Lord</u>."

- In the Doxology concluding the Eucharistic prayers, the priest proclaims, "Through Him, with Him, in Him, in the unity of the Holy Spirit, <u>all glory and honor is yours almighty Father</u>, forever and ever."

- Just prior to the sign of peace, the people recite, "For the kingdom, power and <u>glory are yours, now and forever</u>."

From the Gloria, to the Gospel response, to the preparation of the gifts, from the beginning, middle and end of the Eucharistic prayers, the prayers of the Mass recognize the absolute need to give God praise, glory and thanksgiving at all times. As a spiritual warrior, giving God praise glory and thanksgiving during the celebration of the holy sacrifice of the Mass is the greatest prayer of all and receiving the Eucharist the greatest source of strength you could access.

Sincere praise, glory and thanksgiving can only flow from a humble, obedient heart. Sincere praise, glory and thanksgiving can only happen when you surrender to God and trust in Him. Sound familiar? Humility, obedience, surrender and trust are the words that make up the acronym HOST. Praise, glory and thanksgiving can help lead you to consume the HOST more frequently, more fervently and more effectively.

> We should spend as much time in thanking God for His benefits as we do in asking Him for them.
> Saint Vincent de Paul

> May God in His goodness unite us all in His holy abode to praise Him for all eternity.
> Saint Isaac Jogues

> Give thanks frequently to God for all the benefits He has conferred upon you, that you may be worthy to receive more.
> Saint Louis IX

> What a belch is to the satisfied stomach, that's what praise is to the satisfied heart.
> Saint Augustine

Part III
Advanced Warfare Training

⊕

Now as they were ministering for the Lord and fasting, the Holy Spirit said to them: "Separate Saul and Barnabas for me, for the work for which I have selected them."
Acts of the Apostles 13:2

All Christians are called to engage in spiritual warfare; it is part of the reality of the post Garden of Eden world. Not all Christians, however, are called to engage in all levels of spiritual warfare. Some are called by the Holy Spirit and set apart for deliverance ministry or what might be called extraordinary spiritual warfare. You should never engage in deliverance ministry unless you are called to do so by the Lord. The dangers are many, the potential harm severe.

Extraordinary spiritual warfare encompasses battling against any demonic activity beyond ordinary spiritual warfare, leading up to, but excluding, possession. That is, any demonic activity that is beyond what was previously discussed, but not properly the domain of an exorcist can be included in this category. Additionally, ordinary spiritual warfare performed on another person will typically fall into this category as well. There is no clear delineation between ordinary or extraordinary spiritual warfare; this can present problems for the under-prepared or the unprepared. Prudence, not pride, should be the determining factor.

A majority of Christ's life, thirty years, was spent in preparation for His ministry. During that time He was nurtured and formed. He grew in wisdom and maturity. He prayerfully, patiently awaited the anointing from above and only then did He begin His public ministry.

As a spiritual warrior, you should seek to imitate Christ in all you do. Before you engage in ministry, you should spend sufficient time in preparation, if not in the actual measure of time that Christ spent, then certainly in a proportionate manner. A bulk of your time should be spent in prayerful, patient preparation. Prayers for perseverance in the love of God, especially during spiritual warfare, are essential. Allow the Lord to mold you, to conform you to His will. Allow Him to impose His will for your salvation and His glory. Do not succumb to that most mortal of wounds, intellectual pride. Do not think for a moment that you can engage Satan without benefit of persevering in Christ Jesus. Wait for the call. Do not advance without permission.

In all things, I wait on our Lord.
Saint Joan of Arc

Only a general knows how and when to use one of his soldiers. Wait, your turn will come.
Saint Pio of Pietrelcina

Chapter 21
Authority, Ability, Acumen

☩

> I am writing these things to you, with the hope that I
> will come to you soon. But, if I am delayed, you should
> know the manner in which it is necessary to conduct
> yourself in the house of God, which is the Church of the
> living God, the pillar and the foundation of truth.
> 1 Timothy 3:14-15

Certain questions regarding deliverance ministry need
to be addressed. Is there a distinction between an exorcism and
deliverance ministry? Does the laity have permission to engage
in deliverance ministry?

Christ's church is authoritative, Christ's faithful need
to be obedient. A faithful Catholic must seek the mind of the
Church on all matters under Her authority or else he cannot be
considered faithful. Disobedience is from the devil and is
dangerous.

The manner in which you do battle as a spiritual
warrior must never come against the authority of the Church.
The Holy Spirit cannot contradict the Church, as it is the same
Spirit that leads the Church. As a spiritual warrior you must
submit to the wisdom and authority of the Church in all things.

Exorcism

Deliverance ministry, or "simple exorcism," is distinct
from exorcism, or "major exorcism." Major exorcism is properly

263

and exclusively the domain of the local bishop. The laity is not permitted, nor is able, to perform exorcisms. The ability to perform an exorcism in the Catholic Church is reserved to the bishop of the local diocese. At his discretion, the bishop may grant permission for a priest to act as an exorcist.

> 1673. Jesus performed exorcisms and from him the Church has received the power and office of exorcizing. In a simple form, exorcism is performed at the celebration of Baptism. The solemn exorcism, called "a major exorcism," can be performed only by a priest and with the permission of the bishop.
> *Catechism of the Catholic Church*

> 1172. No one may lawfully exorcise the possessed without the special and express permission of the local Ordinary. This permission is to be granted by the local Ordinary only to a priest who is endowed with piety, knowledge, prudence and integrity of life.
> *Code of Canon Law*

> 2. From these prescriptions it follows, therefore, that no member of the Christian faithful can use the formula of exorcism against Satan and fallen angels...

> 3. Finally, for the same reasons, bishops are asked to be vigilant that — for even cases in which true diabolical possession is excluded, diabolical influence nevertheless seems in some way to be revealed — those who do not have the required faculty not serve in the leading of meeting where, in order to gain freedom, prayers are used which dignify demons by directly questioning them and in searching to make known their identity.
> *Inde Ab Aliquot Annis, On The Current Norms Governing Exorcisms*

It is clear from the information presented from the *Catechism of the Catholic Church, Code of Canon Law* and *On the Current Norms Governing Exorcisms* that only those priests authorized by the local ordinary (bishop) may engage in major or solemn exorcisms. The question remains unanswered whether or not a deliverance ministry is a major or solemn exorcism, and therefore, off limits to the laity.

Deliverance Ministry

Deliverance ministry is prayer said in the name of Jesus, which seeks to neutralize any demonic influence being exerted over yourself or another person. It is simply an expression of your baptismal authority. It can be as simple as the recitation of the Saint Michael prayer, or as brief as a holy ejaculation of the name of Jesus. It can also be more complex, as in the binding up and casting out of demons or the breaking of curses, seals, etc. All deliverance ministry is predicated upon the name, power and authority of Jesus Christ.

Its purpose is both corrective and precautionary. It is corrective in that it either weakens or breaks the hold of the evil one; it is precautionary in that it both protects and defends against the efforts of the evil one. This is always done with respect for the free will of the person. Its end is the removal of any blockage to the free flow of sanctifying grace to the soul.

We block the wiles of the ancient and obstinate enemy with prayers to God and stern rebukes; you must stand up to him with your earnest prayers and contrition of heart, in order to be snatched from the power of darkness and transferred into the kingdom of glory. This is now your task and toil.
Saint Augustine

Deliverance Ministry Compared to Exorcism

There are important distinctions between a major or solemn exorcism and a deliverance ministry. In a major or solemn exorcism it is the power and authority of the Church that is exercised. This authority is proper to the local bishop only or to a priest whom he authorizes; it is done in the name of the Church. In deliverance ministry it is the power and authority of one's baptism that is exercised. This authority is proper to one who is baptized; it is done in the name of Jesus Christ. A major or solemn exorcism is a liturgical rite which requires the recitation of the Rite of Exorcism, an official Church prayer. A deliverance ministry is not a liturgical rite and the Rite of Exorcism is not recited. Additionally, part of a major or solemn exorcism is to directly confront and question the demon. It is never part of a deliverance ministry to confront or question the demon.

Deliverance ministry is substantially different than an exorcism. Deliverance ministry is not, therefore, a violation of any of the precepts of the *Catechism of the Catholic Church*, *Code of Canon Law* or *On The Current Norms Governing Exorcism*.

Assuming certain conditions, it appears that the laity has the authority to engage in spiritual warfare on themselves and on behalf of others. But, does Scripture and Tradition support this conclusion?

Scriptural Support

The Scriptural basis for this authority can be pieced together from the Gospels. One of the first authorities Jesus gave His apostles was the power to expel demons.

> And he acted so that the twelve would be with him, and so that he might send them out to preach. And he gave them authority to cure infirmities, and to cast out demons.
> Mark 3:14-15

After the authority to cast out demons was given to the apostles, it went next to the seventy-two disciples of Jesus.

> Then the seventy-two returned with gladness, saying, "Lord, even the demons are subject to us, in your name."
> Luke 10:17

In the middle of Mark's Gospel, the apostles came to Jesus with a concern. They were concerned that someone who was not following Jesus was casting out demons in Jesus' name. They even tried to prevent the person from doing so.

> John responded to him by saying, "Teacher, we saw someone casting out demons in your name; he does not follow us, and so we prohibited him." But Jesus said: "Do not prohibit him. For there is no one who can act

with virtue in my name and soon speak evil about me."
Mark 9:38

Here Jesus does not praise the apostles for their judgment against the person who was casting out demons. He, in fact, does that opposite when He corrects them. At the end of Mark's Gospel, just prior to ascending, Jesus is addressing the eleven Apostles and speaks to them of the great commission.

And he said to them: "Go forth to the whole world and preach the Gospel to every creature. Whoever will have believed and been baptized will be saved. Yet truly, whoever will not have believed will be condemned. Now these signs will accompany those who believe. In my name, they shall cast out demons. They will speak in new languages. They will take up serpents, and, if they drink anything deadly, it will not harm them. They shall lay their hands upon the sick, and they will be well."
Mark 16:15-18

The first sign that will accompany those who believe in Jesus is the driving out of demons. Notice it is the belief in Jesus that activates this charism. The progression of authority to cast out demons went from the Apostles, to disciples, to all believers. According to Sacred Scripture, it would seem all Christians possess the ability to bind up and cast out demons in the name of Jesus.

Patristic Evidence

The Patristic basis for this authority is limited, but telling. Saint Justin Martyr, writing between 155 A.D. and 165 A.D., in his *Apology 2*, says that "many" Christian men cast out demons.

And now you can learn this from what is under your own observation. For numberless demoniacs throughout the whole world and in your city, many of our Christian men exorcising them in the name of Jesus Christ, who was crucified under Pontius Pilate, have healed and do heal, rendering helpless and driving

267

the possessing devils out of the men, though they could not be cured by all the other exorcists and those who used incantations and drugs.
Saint Justin Martyr

Around the year 170 A.D., Saint Irenaeus, who was a disciple of Saint Polycarp, himself a disciple of Saint John the Evangelist, wrote *Against the Heretics.* In it he says that Christ's "disciples" are able to cast out demons.

Wherefore, also, those who are in truth His disciples, receiving grace from Him, do in His name perform [miracles], so as to promote the welfare of other men, according to the gift which each one has received from Him. For some do certainly and truly drive out devils, so that those who have thus been cleansed from evil spirits frequently both believe [in Christ] and join themselves to the Church.
Saint Irenaeus

Writing around the year 200 A.D., Tertullian wrote *On the Spectacles.* In it he states "Christian men" exorcise demons.

What nobler than to tread under foot the gods of the nations, to exorcise evil spirits, to perform cures, to seek divine revealings, to live to God? These are the pleasures, these, the spectacles that befit Christian men, holy, everlasting, free.
Tertullian

In his writing, *Against Celsus*, Origen, who was martyred in 258 A.D., notes that "many" and the "plainest" of Christians are able to cast out demons with "prayer and simple adjurations."

If, then, the Pythian priestess is beside herself when she prophesies, what spirit must that be which fills her mind and clouds her judgment with darkness, unless it be of the same order with those demons which many Christians cast out of persons possessed with them? And this, we may observe, they do without the use of

any curious arts of magic or incantations, but merely by prayer and simple adjurations which the plainest person can use. Because for the most part it is unlettered persons who perform this work; thus making manifest the grace which is in the word of Christ and the despicable weakness of demons, which, in order to be overcome and driven out of the bodies and souls of men, do not require the power and wisdom of those who are mighty in argument and most learned in matters of faith.
Origen

Though not extensive, Scripture and tradition demonstrate that casting out of evil spirits was a function not limited to the ordained. The evidence clearly supports the idea that the laity possessed the authority and the ability to engage in deliverance ministry – so long as it is down in the name of Jesus. Even the Angelic Doctor, Thomas Aquinas, writing in the Summa Theologica (II-II, 90 a. 2) agrees.

We are able to adjure the demons by the power of the name of Jesus, expelling them from ourselves as declared enemies, in order to avoid the spiritual and corporal damage that could come to us from them. This is a power which is given to us from Christ, Himself.
Saint Thomas Aquinas

If you must, tell the devil to depart. If you want the devil to go, tell him. But never engage him in conversation.
Servant of God John Hardon

The question now remains whether or not the laity possesses the acumen, or expertise, to engage in deliverance ministry. That is a question that each person will need to prayerfully consider, perhaps in the presence of a solid spiritual director or a trusted confessor. If the Holy Spirit is calling you to this ministry, He'll grace you with the skill set and knowledge you need. Should God grant you the grace necessary to do battle have no fear of engagement. Should He not grant you the grace to do so, for your own sake and the sake of those you would seek to minister to, please do not engage in this type of battle.

Deliverance ministry is a critical ministry with profound implications. The binding up and casting out of evil spirits should never be done frivolously.

Lastly, as a matter of obedience and faithfulness, should the Church issue authoritative documents that contradict the conclusion drawn herein, future editions of the book will be reflective of the Church's teaching. I fully submit to the authority of the Church as She is the pillar and foundation of truth (cf. 1 Timothy 3:15).

Rome has spoken; the case is closed.
Saint Augustine

Clearly the person who accepts the Church as an infallible guide will believe whatever the Church teaches.
Saint Thomas Aquinas

The Church has ever proved indestructible. Her persecutors have failed to destroy her; in fact, it was during times of persecution that the Church grew more and more; while the persecutors themselves, and those whom the Church would destroy, are the very ones who came to nothing. Again, errors have assailed her; but in fact, the greater the number of errors that have arisen, the more has the truth been made manifest. Nor has the Church failed before the assaults of demons: for she is like a tower of refuge to all who fight against the Devil.
Saint Thomas Aquinas

Chapter 22
Preparing for Deliverance Ministry

☩

Not all who say to me, "Lord, Lord," will enter into the
kingdom of Heaven. But whoever does the will of my
Father, who is in Heaven, the same shall enter into the
kingdom of Heaven. Many will say to me in that day,
"Lord, Lord, did we not prophesy in your name, and
cast out demons in your name, and perform many
powerful deeds in your name?" And then will I disclose
to them: "I have never known you. Depart from me, you
workers of iniquity."
Matthew 7:21-23

The authority to engage in deliverance ministry was
first given to the apostles (Matthew 10:1), later to the disciples
(Luke 10:17) and then to all who are baptized and believe
(Mark 16:15-18). Despite the scriptural and Patristic evidence,
deliverance ministry is the area of spiritual warfare that is the
most controversial.

It also tends to be the area of spiritual warfare that
people are drawn toward. The overzealous and unprepared
soldiers contribute to the dim view that some take of spiritual
warfare. Deliverance ministry is potentially dangerous as it
appeals to a sense of pride. Many want to engage in deliverance
ministry, but not all want to do what is necessary to prepare
their hearts and minds. They hear the call to arms, but ignore
the call to prayer and repentance.

Deliverance ministry is not the first option of spiritual warfare, very often it is the last option. It is important to remember that not all who drive out demons will be saved. It is not a measuring stick of sanctity or proof of holiness. It is merely a tool of the Kingdom. Used in accordance with and submission to God's will it is a very powerful tool. It, nonetheless, remains simply that, a tool. It is here toward the end of the book for a reason.

Be forewarned; prideful demonstrations may yield painful lessons. While God equips those whom He chooses to equip, generally speaking, those souls that respond to His call with humility are those whom He showers with His graces. If you are acting under His authority and are proceeding under His protection, have no fear. If you are acting against or away from His authority or have stepped out from under His protection, beware.

> It was pride that cause the fall of Lucifer and Adam. If you should ask me what are the ways of God, I would tell you that the first is humility, the second is humility and the third is still humility. Not that there are no other precepts to give, but if humility does not precede all that we do, our efforts are fruitless.
> Saint Augustine
>
> Pride never brings salvation, but humility does.
> Saint Jerome

Before you engage in deliverance ministry, especially for others, you should ensure you are properly prepared spiritually.

Be Baptized and Confirmed

An unbaptized spiritual warrior is an impotent spiritual warrior. An unconfirmed spiritual warrior is an under-powered spiritual warrior. Baptism initiates your life in God; confirmation strengthens and seals it. The gifts and graces received are invaluable to you as a spiritual warrior. They are the invisible sign and seal of your power and protection. Baptism destroys Satan's grips; confirmation bolsters you for the battle.

As Christ, after His baptism and the descent of the Holy Ghost upon Him, going forth overcame the Adversary, so you likewise after holy Baptism and the mysterious unction [of Confirmation,] clothed with the panoply of the Holy Ghost stand against the adverse power and subdue it saying, "I can do all things in Christ who strengthens me."
Saint Ambrose

The sacrament [of Confirmation] by which spiritual strength is conferred on one born again makes him in some sense a front line fighter for the faith of Christ.
Saint Thomas Aquinas

We cannot value too highly the importance of Confirmation in the supernatural life. It is a great source of strength in the warfare we must wage against the three great enemies of our salvation — the world, the flesh and the devil. The character of Confirmation remains on the soul forever, marking one who has been confirmed as a soldier of Christ, with the right and the duty of proclaiming and defending the Christian faith before the world.
Baltimore Catechism

In a State of Grace

Attempting to engage in spiritual warfare in a state of mortal sin is either the height of arrogance or the depth of ignorance. Either way, your efforts are futile unless and until you return to a state of grace through sacramental confession. Your humble confession is recognition of your own sinfulness. A soldier for Christ will make frequent use of the Sacrament of Penance.

Imagine the vanity of thinking that your enemy can do you more damage than your enmity.
Saint Augustine

We must exhibit a full and accurate confession of our sins. For, as the enemy knows that having confessed our sins and shown our wounds to the physician we

attain to abundant cure, he in a special manner opposes us.
Saint John Chrysostom

Committing sin makes us strangers to God and partners with the devil.
Saint Basil the Great

Partaking Frequently in Communion and Adoration

The Eucharist is and must be the primary nourishment of every soldier of Christ. It is both surety and sustenance. No power is greater. Frequent attendance at daily Mass and Holy Hour cannot be emphasized enough. To proceed into battle without benefit of Eucharistic grace is foolhardy.

In the Holy Eucharist we receive Jesus Christ Himself. This sacred flesh was sacrificed for our sins to destroy in our soul the empire of our mortal enemy.
Saint Elizabeth Ann Seton

My dear ones, the visit to the Blessed Sacrament is an extremely necessary way to conquer the devil. Therefore, go often to visit Jesus and the devil will not come out victorious against you.
Saint John Bosco

When you are before the altar where Christ reposes, you ought no longer to think that you are amongst men; but believe that there are troops of angels and archangels standing by you, and trembling with respect before the sovereign Master of Heaven and earth. Therefore, when you are in church, be there in silence, fear, and veneration.
Saint John Chrysostom

Led by the Holy Spirit

Jesus was obedient to the Spirit and was led into the desert (cf. Luke 4:1). Likewise, Ananias yielded to the Holy Spirit and was led to lay hands on Saul and help him regain his sight (cf. Acts of the Apostles 9:10-20). Paul was prevented by the Holy Spirit from preaching in Asia and entering Bithynia (cf. Acts of the Apostles 16:6-7). In humble obedience they all surrendered to the Holy Spirit's promptings and trusted in His decision. The simplest way to be in God's will is to yield to the Holy Spirit. Your docility allows His power to flow in and through you to help accomplish His will; it is your strength.

> In the presence of the Holy Spirit the devil lost his power.
> Saint Basil the Great

> And so it is the Holy Spirit who trains our hands for battle and our fingers for war.
> Saint Augustine

> Without the weapons of the Holy Spirit we cannot make headway in this battle.
> Saint Macarius

With an Ongoing, Active Life of Prayer

Engaging in spiritual warfare without an ongoing, active prayer life is akin to going into the middle of a raging battle with no protective gear and no weapons. It simply doesn't make sense. Prayer is the primary weapon to be wielded by you as a spiritual warrior. It should be engaged in frequently and fervently. It is fundamental to your relationship with God and the discharging of your spiritual duties.

> Prayer is our principal weapon. By it we obtain of God victory over our evil inclinations, and over all temptations of Hell.
> Saint Alphonsus Liguori

> Armed with prayer, the saints sustained a glorious warfare and vanquished all their enemies. By prayer, also, they appeased the wrath of God, and obtained from Him all they desired.
> Venerable Louis of Granada

> Arm yourself with prayer rather than a sword; wear humility rather than fine clothes.
> Saint Dominic

Steeped in Scripture

Contained in Scripture is the blueprint for battle and the promise of victory. It is the one manual for war and peace. It lists the weapons to be wielded and the virtues to be imitated. It contains valuable information about the enemy and his forces. More importantly, it contains the "Good News," that God has sent His Son to save us so that we might have eternal life. (cf. John 3:16). Knowledge of Scripture allows you access to the Word of God, Jesus. Trust and act upon His Word and you will, in God's time, celebrate victory.

Ignorance of Scripture is ignorance of Christ.
Saint Jerome

The cause of all evils is the failure to know the Scriptures well.
Saint John Chrysostom

Read unwearyingly the precepts of the Lord and, sufficiently instructed by them, you will know what to avoid and what to pursue.
Saint Bernard of Clairvaux

Clothed in the Armor of God

The metaphorical armor Paul speaks of in chapter six of Ephesians is every bit as critical as the armor of a soldier doing battle in the physical realm. All of it, the belt, the breastplate, the sandals, the shield, the helmet and the sword need to be properly fitted, fastened and worn. If you're missing one piece, in many ways, you're missing all of it.

But in the case of the evil one it is not possible ever to lay aside one's armor, it is not possible even to take sleep, for one who would remain always unscathed. For one of two things must be: either to fall and perish unarmed, or to stand equipped and ever watchful. For he ever stands with his own battle array, watching for our indolence, and laboring more zealously for our destruction, than we for our salvation.
Saint John Chrysostom

May your good angel be your breastplate to ward off the blows that the enemies of our salvation aim at you.
Saint Pio of Pietrelcina

Attend closely to the catechizing, and though we should prolong our discourse, let not your mind be wearied out. For you are receiving armor against the adverse power, armor against heresies, against Jews, and Samaritans, and Gentiles. You have many enemies; take to you many darts, for you have many to hurl them at: and you have need to learn how to strike down the Greek, how to contend against heretic, against Jew and Samaritan. And the armor is ready, and most ready the sword of the Spirit: but you also must stretch forth your right hand with good resolution, that you may war the Lord's warfare, and overcome adverse powers, and become invincible against every heretical attempt.
Saint Cyril of Jerusalem

Having Consumed the HOST

Along with the external armor, there is internal armor which needs to be donned. The virtues of humility, obedience, surrender and trust are essential for the spiritual warrior to cultivate and to continue to prayer for on a daily basis for together they combat the soul's enemy, pride.

The devil can imitate all the righteous acts that we appear to do, but he is defeated by love and humility.
Saint Melania the Younger

Perhaps it is not after all so difficult for a man to part with his possessions, but it is certainly most difficult for him to part with himself. To renounce what one has is a minor thing; but to renounce what one is, that is asking a lot.
Pope Saint Gregory the Great

My daughter, know that you give Me greater glory by a single act of obedience than by long prayers and mortifications.
Our Lord to Saint Faustina Kowalska

Go courageously to do whatever you are called to do. If you have any fears, say to your soul: "The Lord will provide for us." If your weakness troubles you, cast yourselves on God, and trust in him. The apostles were mostly unlearned fishermen, but God gave them learning enough for the work they had to do. Trust in him, depend on his providence; fear nothing.
Saint Francis de Sales

Having Fasted and Given Alms

Detachment from earthly goods, food and material goods alike, helps create an attachment to heavenly goods. A greedy, gluttonous soldier is focused on satisfying fleshy desires rather than God's desires. A lean, hungry sacrificing soldier is, ultimately, a stronger soldier. A soldier, detached from the world and worldly things, is able to lessen the grip of Satan, grow in attachment to God and help bring about lasting change.

> That which beats the devil is the curtailment of one's food, drink and sleep.
> Saint John Vianney

> If a man is earnest in fasting and making himself hungry, the enemies that trouble his soul will grow weak.
> Saint John the Dwarf

> Give me ten truly detached men and I will conquer the world with them.
> Saint Philip Neri

Being Attached to a Community

Imagine going into battle against a vast army by yourself; it would not be prudent. In order to best serve the Lord, it is advisable that you be under the protective prayers of a community and, if possible, a spiritual director. Even if it is as simple as gathering two or three in His name, it will serve you well to pray in community, whether you are praying for yourself or others.

Be eager for more frequent gatherings for thanksgiving to God and His glory, for when you meet thus, the forces of Satan are annulled and his destructive power is cancelled in the concord of your faith.
Saint Ignatius of Antioch

Remember me, you heirs of God, you brethren of Christ; supplicate the Savior earnestly for me, that I may be freed through Christ from him that fights against me day by day.
Saint Ephrem of Syria

Order your soul; reduce your wants; live in charity; associate in Christian community; obey the laws; trust in Providence.
Saint Augustine

Offering Prayers of Permission, Protection and Praise

Prayer is essential to the soldier of Christ. It must be woven in the fabric of all that you do as a spiritual warrior lest you lose your way on the battlefield. Three prayers specifically should precede engaging in any type of deliverance ministry, prayers of permission, protection and praise. This establishes right order with the Lord and allows you to work in concert with Him, not against Him.

God should be followed, not preceded. For whoever wishes to precede God, attempts what is not from the faith.
Saint Agobard of Lyons

The cruelty of the devil is such that he would devour us at any moment if the divine power did not protect us.
Saint Bonaventure

And remember that all assaults of dark and evil fortune contribute to the salvation of those who receive them with thankfulness, and are assuredly ambassadors of help.
Saint John Damascene

While the list above is not, strictly speaking, mandatory to follow, (cf. Mark 9:38-40), it is prudent to complete as many steps as possible. In many instances, especially after receiving absolution for your sins from a priest and praising God, the need to bind up and cast out no longer exists. (This is true more for a self-deliverance situation.)

For deliverance ministry involving someone else, it is preferable that you both complete the above steps. Obviously, that is not always possible or practical. Many times the deliverance ministry is required to free the other person so that they are then able to resume or establish a life in God. At times, you will need to intercede for others, to do what they cannot do own their own. That is why it is especially important that you ensure your observance of the above. Assuming proper preparation, it is now safe to proceed with the practice of binding up and casting out of evil spirits.

> It happened that a demon, whom many had been unable to bind, was overcome by the words of one man's prayer because of the Holy Spirit who dwelt in him.
> Saint Cyril of Jerusalem

> Today I have fought a battle with the spirits of darkness over one soul. How terribly Satan hates God's mercy! I see how he opposes this whole work.
> Saint Faustina Kowalska

> Doing little by little what we can, we will have hardly anything else to fight against; it is the Lord who in our defense takes up the battle against the demons and against the world.
> Saint Teresa of Avila

Chapter 23
Practice of Deliverance Ministry

✠

And having called together his twelve disciples, he gave
them authority over unclean spirits, to cast them out
and to cure every sickness and every infirmity.
Matthew 10:1

Deliverance ministry is not about controlling or
capturing another person's free will. Deliverance ministry is
about rescuing and releasing another's free will from the
bondage it has been subjected to by the enemy. In all matters
related to deliverance ministry, especially in regard to binding
up and casting out of evil spirits, the person's free will must be
respected. To the degree that the person's free will does not
give full consent, the deliverance ministry is compromised from
the start. This applies to self-deliverance and deliverance
ministry carried out on others.

The binding up of evil spirits is the spiritual equivalent
of tying up a hijacker on an airplane. In that situation, using
belts or a rope, you would bind the person to their seat so that
they can inflict no further damage. You would likely tape their
mouth closed, as well, to avoid any verbal attacks. Once
incapacitated, the hijacker would no longer pose an imminent
threat, though he still needs to be dealt with at some point.
When you bind up an evil spirit you are spiritually tying a rope
around that spirit and putting a gag in its mouth. This will
prevent the evil spirit from continuing its harassment or

temptation of you or others. It levels the playing fields so that the person being prayed for can catch his breath. It is only a temporary respite.

The casting out of evil spirits is the spiritual equivalent of tying up that hijacker and ejecting him from the airplane. Once ejected, the hijacker would land directly in the center of a jail where he'll remain. This is a permanent solution to the immediate problem at hand. It does not preclude other problems from popping up later, but it does take care of the immediate problem.

Said another way, if you were a company president, binding up would be suspending a person from your company for a period of time; casting out would be dismissing the person from your company. The suspension is a temporary solution to an ongoing problem. When the suspension is over, unless there has been some sort of change, the problem is likely to return. With the termination of the person's employment comes the termination of the problem. (Though, once again, terminating someone does not preclude hiring a new employee who turns out to be worse than the person that was terminated. Perhaps the screening and hiring process needs to be reviewed.)

Though there are obvious limits to the metaphors, they should give you a sense of what is meant by binding up and by casting out. When you bind up evil spirits, you temporarily inhibit their impact. When you cast out evil spirits you expel them and exempt them from having any further influence. That does not mean that binding up and casting out is a one-time event. Other spirits may attack; other doors may be opened through sin. The same spirits may even return if they are "invited" back. You may need to bind up and cast out often; frequently it is an ongoing process. In fact, it's not a bad idea to bind up and cast out regularly, either as a preventive measure or in response to temptations or harassment.

It is important to note that the mere presence of an evil spirit that needs to be bound up or cast out, does not equate with a life of sin. If the spirit of lust is attacking you, it does not necessarily mean you are a lustful person or that you have committed a sin of lust. It only signifies that is the spirit that is attempting to tempt or harass you at that moment. Likewise, if a spirit of suicide is manifesting itself, it does not mean you are suicidal. Do not be surprised at the type, frequency and intensity of the spirits that would seek to do you harm. A virtuous life often leads to greater attacks. A strong prayer life leads to strong attacks by Satan. But no matter the intensity or frequency of attacks, they cannot touch your free will when you surrender it to God.

> The tempter, ever on the watch, wages war most violently against those whom he sees most careful to avoid sin.
> Pope Saint Leo the Great

> Begone Satan, I belong to Jesus Christ. I have no will of my own. My will is that of my beloved spouse whose image is imprinted in my heart.
> Saint Rita of Cascia

> When the sly demon, after using many devices, fails to hinder the prayer of the diligent, he desists a little; but when the man has finished his prayer, he takes his revenge. He either fires his anger and thus destroys the fair state produced by prayer or excites an impulse toward some animal pleasure and thus mocks his mind.
> Saint Nilus of Sinai

God endowed you with free will; you can freely choose to accept Him or to reject Him. God does not violate your free will, God plays by the rules. Satan does all he can to intrude on your free will, he does not play by the rules. As God's spiritual warrior, as His intercessor, you must also play by the rules. God, because He wants you to choose to love Him freely, will not tip the scales; but He will balance them if need be. Binding up and casting out balances the scales where sin and Satan have created an imbalance.

> For it is the will which, although free, by consenting to sin became slave to sin: and it is the will which puts itself in subjection to sin by its willing servitude.
> Saint Bernard of Clairvaux

One last reminder, one last admonition is appropriate. Deliverance ministry is never your own; it is always and only

His. You are merely the implement He uses.

> If you could work wonders and drive out devils - all that would be extrinsic to you; it would not belong to you and you could not boast of it. But there is one thing of which we can boast; we can boast of our humiliations and in taking up daily the holy cross of our Lord Jesus Christ.
> Saint Francis of Assisi

There are limits to what may be done in terms of binding up and casting out, limits that need to be respected. These limits are related to free will, not of the evil spirit, but of the person being attacked. Someone who has freely chosen to invite evil spirits into their life, either by their words or deeds, (unconfessed mortal sin, unforgiveness, occult activities, etc.,) may not want to be set free. Casting out evil spirits from that person is likely to cause a more dangerous situation to manifest in his or her life. It would, therefore, not be advisable.

> How great is the stupidity of those who make themselves weak in spite of my strengthening, and put themselves into the devil's hands.
> Our Lord to Saint Catherine of Siena

> Thus, brethren, the venerable Antiochus teaches that when despair befalls us, we should not succumb to it but, strengthened and enveloped by Holy Faith, say with great bravery to the cunning spirit [the devil]: "What have you to do with us, O apostate from God, fugitive from Heaven and a slave of evil. You are unable to inspire us to do anything; for Christ, the Son of God, has authority over us and over all. And you, O murderer, depart from us. Strengthened by His Honorable Cross, we trample upon your serpent's head."
> Saint Seraphim of Sarov

Subject to the conditions previously mentioned, here are some simple guidelines to remember.

Binding Up of Evil Spirits

1. You have the authority to bind up evil spirits that are harassing or tempting you. You possess this authority by virtue of your baptism.
2. You can give someone else authority to bind up evil spirits affecting you. Someone else can give you authority to bind up evil spirits affecting them.
3. You have the authority to bind up evil spirits that are harassing or tempting others, even without their permission. You do not need their permission because the binding up of evil spirits does not interfere with a person's free will. Therefore, if the circumstances warrant it, and after prayerful discernment, you may bind up evil spirits without a person's permission.
4. When you bind up evil spirits on another person they do not need to be in your presence. Neither do you need to speak the commands out loud; you may do so silently.
5. When you bind up evil spirits on another person they need not be baptized; though, in many ways, it may prove futile to do so if they are not.

Here is a sample prayer for binding up of evil spirits.

Binding Up Prayer

By virtue of my baptism and in the name, power and authority of Jesus Christ, I bind up any and all spirits that are not of the Holy Spirit that are harassing or tempting _____ (person's name), especially the spirit(s) of _____ (name the spirit). Lord, I ask that these evil spirit(s) remain bound for as long as it serves Your most holy and perfect will.

By reciting this prayer you are exercising your baptismal authority. You are calling upon the name, power and authority of Jesus, the same name, power and authority that defeated Satan. You end the prayer with an acknowledgment and a submission to His divine will.

Should you need to do more than just bind up the evil spirits, the next step would be to cast them out. Adherence to certain guidelines will minimize your exposure to any retaliation.

Casting Out of Evil Spirits

1. You have the authority to cast out evil spirits that are harassing or tempting you. You possess this authority by virtue of your baptism.

2. If you are in a state of unconfessed mortal sin, the demons have a right to be there and casting them out will likely be ineffective and may even be injurious. In this instance, it would be better to bind the spirits, go to sacramental confession, and then, if necessary, cast out the evil spirits. You may find that the power of the sacrament has forced the spirits to flee.

3. You can give someone else permission to cast out evil spirits that are harassing or tempting you. This should be done only after prayerful, prudent discernment. It should be done by someone who has been called by the Lord to deliverance ministry, who you know to be prayerful and who is experienced. You don't want to complicate or aggravate matters by giving an inexperienced, or worse, an ill-intentioned person spiritual authority over you.

4. You may cast out evil spirits from those over whom you have spiritual authority. Typically, this would be your spouse, your children and your godchildren. It may extend to others in your charge, etc. You may also cast out evil spirits from those who have given you their permission to do so. This, too, should be done only after prayerful, prudent discernment.

5. You never cast out demons from someone without first getting a "green light" from the Lord. If you do cast out evil spirits from someone else, you do not need to be in their presence, nor do you need to speak the commands out loud.

6. Technically, you can cast out demons from someone else, whether or not you have their permission, though it is not prudent to do so. The reason for not doing so is made clear by Jesus in Matthew 12:43-45.

7. You have authority to bind up and cast out evil spirits that are dwelling in inanimate objects and animals. Since inanimate objects, animals and places have no free will, you are free to bind up and cast out evil spirits from them after seeking permission from the Lord. Evil spirits enjoy disturbing your peace by wreaking havoc with inanimate objects, especially electronics; computers, phones, speaker

systems, etc. Pets of all types are targets because they are loved and any harm done to them can create vulnerability in you and your loved ones.

Here is a sample deliverance prayer for binding up and casting out of evil spirits.

Casting Out Prayer
By virtue of my baptism and in the name, power and authority of Jesus Christ, I bind up any and all spirits that are not of the Holy Spirit that are harassing or tempting _____ (person's name), especially the spirit(s) of _____ (name the spirit). Lord, I ask that these evil spirit(s) remain bound for as long as it serves Your most holy and perfect will.

To the degree that I have Your permission Lord, I cast out these evil spirits now in the name, power and authority of Jesus Christ and send them immediately and directly to the foot of the cross to be washed in the most precious blood of Jesus, never to return here again. In their place Lord, I ask that You please send Your Holy Spirit, Your Spirit of love and truth, to fill those spaces to overflowing with Your graces.

A closer look at the deliverance prayer, with explanatory footnotes and scriptural references, follows.

Casting Out Prayer with Explanatory Footnotes
(1) By virtue of my baptism (2) and in the name, power and authority of Jesus Christ (3) I bind up (4) any and all spirits that are not of the Holy Spirit that are harassing or tempting me, (5) especially the spirit(s) of _____. (6) Lord, I ask that these evil spirits remain bound for as long as it serves Your most holy and perfect will. (7)

(8) To the degree that I have Your permission Lord, (9) I cast out these evil spirits now in the name, power and authority of Jesus Christ (10) and send them immediately and directly to the foot of the cross (11) to be washed in the most precious Blood of Jesus, (12) never to return here again. (13) In their place Lord, I ask that You please send Your Holy Spirit, Your Spirit of love and truth, to fill those spaces to overflowing with

Your grace, your peace, your mercy and your love. (13)

1. In deliverance ministry, you never proceed without permission of the Holy Spirit.
2. By virtue of your baptism, you have the right to call upon Christ's name.
3. Always and only do so in the name, power and authority of Jesus Christ.
4. First you bind up the evil spirits.
5. Here you can call out the spirits by name. For example, you could bind up the spirits of retaliation, mockery, blockage, division, fear, anger, etc. It is not mandatory to name the evil spirits.
6. This is an act of humble submission to the Lord and an admission that you desire His will be done, not your own.
7. If you are only binding up and not casting out, stop after this sentence.
8. This is a precautionary measure that protects your discernment.
9. Only cast out when you are certain you have the authority to do so.
10. Always send the spirits immediately and directly to the foot of the cross, lest on their way, they stop and harass others.
11. It is the blood of Jesus that defeated Satan.
12. Command the spirits to never return here again so that they don't try and return through an open door.
13. Make sure you complete the deliverance with a request for a fresh infilling of the Holy Spirit.

Casting Out Prayer with Scriptural References

By virtue of my baptism (1) and in the name, power and authority of Jesus Christ, (2) I bind up (3) any and all spirits that are not of the Holy Spirit that are harassing or tempting _____ (person's name), especially the spirit(s) of _____. (4) Lord, I ask that these evil spirits remain bound for as long as it serves Your most holy and perfect will.

To the degree that I have Your permission Lord, I cast out these evil spirits now in the name, power and authority of Jesus Christ (5) and send them immediately and directly to the foot of the cross (6) to be washed in the most precious Blood of

Jesus, never to return here again. (7) In their place Lord, I ask that You please send Your Holy Spirit, Your Spirit of love and truth, to fill those spaces to overflowing with Your grace, your peace, your mercy and your love. (8)

1. Mark 16:15-18
   And he said to them: "Go forth to the whole world and preach the Gospel to every creature. Whoever will have believed and been baptized will be saved. Yet truly, whoever will not have believed will be condemned. Now these signs will accompany those who believe. In my name, they shall cast out demons. They will speak in new languages. They will take up serpents, and, if they drink anything deadly, it will not harm them. They shall lay their hands upon the sick, and they will be well."

2. Luke 10:17-20
   Then the seventy-two returned with gladness, saying, "Lord, even the demons are subject to us, in your name." And he said to them: "I was watching as Satan fell like lightning from Heaven. Behold, I have given you authority to tread upon serpents and scorpions, and upon all the powers of the enemy, and nothing shall hurt you. Yet truly, do not choose to rejoice in this, that the spirits are subject to you; but rejoice that your names are written in Heaven."

3. Matthew 12:28-29
   But if I cast out demons by the Spirit of God, then the kingdom of God has arrived among you. Or how can anyone enter into the house of a strong man, and plunder his belongings, unless he first restrains the strong man? And then he will plunder his house.

4. Mark 9:25
   Jesus, on seeing a crowd rapidly gathering, rebuked the unclean spirit and said to it, "Mute and deaf spirit, I command you: come out of him and never enter him again!"

5. 1 John 5:16
   Anyone who realizes that his brother has sinned, with a sin that is not unto death, let him pray, and life shall be given to him who has sinned not unto death. There is a sin which is unto death. I am not saying that anyone should ask on behalf of that sin.

6. Matthew 12:43-45

   Now when an unclean spirit departs from a man, he walks through dry places, seeking rest, and he does not find it. Then he says, "I will return to my house, from which I departed." And arriving, he finds it vacant, swept clean, and decorated. Then he goes and takes with him seven other spirits more wicked than himself, and they enter in and live there. And in the end, the man becomes worse than he was at first. So, too, shall it be with this most wicked generation.

7. Mark 5:7-13

   And crying out with a loud voice, he said: "What am I to you, Jesus, the Son of the Most High God? I beseech you by God, that you not torment me." For he said to him, "Depart from the man, you unclean spirit." And he questioned him: "What is your name?" And he said to him, "My name is Legion, for we are many." And he entreated him greatly, so that he would not expel him from the region. And in that place, near the mountain, there was a great herd of swine, feeding. And the spirits entreated him, saying: "Send us into the swine, so that we may enter into them." And Jesus promptly gave them permission. And the unclean spirits, departing, entered into the swine. And the herd of about two thousand rushed down with great force into the sea, and they were drowned in the sea.

8. Luke 11:10, 13

   For everyone who asks, receives. And whoever seeks, finds. And whoever knocks, it shall be opened to him. Therefore, if you, being evil, know how to give good things to your sons, how much more will your Father give, from Heaven, a spirit of goodness to those who ask him?

These prayers are not a magic formula; the wording need not be verbatim. They do need to contain the essential elements: the name of Jesus, the commands and the infilling of the Holy Spirit. Over time, you will become comfortable with what to say and how say it. The best way to say it is with faith, hope and charity. Have faith in the name of Jesus, hope in His mercy and proceed in His charity. If you are uncertain, uncomfortable or in a state of mortal sin, it would be best to postpone the deliverance ministry rather than to proceed.

Curses, Spells, Hexes

Curses are a means of calling down evil upon someone, often those who are innocent. In effect, those who invoke a curse are asking Satan to focus his evil on a specific person at a specific time. Related, though somewhat distinct, are spells and hexes. When the will of the person invoking the curse is fully engaged, and the more malice with which it is announced, the more potentially injurious is the curse, spell or hex. It is the force of the evil intent within the person who speaks the curse that determines its efficacy. It is generally true that the greater the hate, the greater the impact of the curse. Despite that, curses, spells and hexes are often ineffective because they intrude on another's free will. Personal sin will make you more vulnerable to their harm. A life of grace is your best protection.

Seals and Soul Ties

Unlike curses, spells and hexes, seals and souls ties are not invoked by others against you. Seals and soul ties are generally self-invoked. A seal is any kind of pact or agreement or vow made with a demon. It is in mock imitation of the seal of the Holy Spirit in baptism. It can be said off handedly or with great intent. One way opens the door to evil slightly; the other throws it wide open. There can be generational or hereditary seals that are not self-invoked, but still need to be renounced. Soul ties are any sinful connections that your soul might have with other people, evil spirits or objects. Most often, soul ties are related to immoral sexual relationships and those relationships that are a near occasion of sin. Again, the degree to which the consent of the will is freely given is an important factor here as to the impact of the soul ties. As seals and souls ties are most often self-initiated, they must be renounced and repented from in order to be revoked.

Breaking curses, spells, hexes, seals and soul ties.

1. You have authority to break curses, spells, hexes, seals or soul ties that are affecting you. Curses, spells and hexes are placed on you by someone else. Seals and soul ties (usually) originate in your free will. They can all easily be broken in the name of Jesus Christ.
2. You have limited authority to break curses, spells, hexes, seals or soul ties connected to others, typically those over

whom you have spiritual authority. Curses, spells and hexes can be broken without the person's permission because they do not involve free will.

3. You must be given permission to break some one else's seals and soul ties, if they originated in that person's free will. They can easily be broken in the name of Jesus Christ.

Here is a sample deliverance prayer for breaking curses, spells, hexes, seals or soul ties. It is preferable that the person who is being affected speak the prayer if at all possible, as opposed to having somebody else speak it in their place.

Prayer to Break Curses, Spells, Hexes, Seals & Soul Ties
In the name of our Lord, Jesus Christ, I break all curses, spells, hexes, seals and soul ties attached to _____ (your name or the person's name if pronounced for someone else).

It is necessary to recite the single sentence three times to effectively break the hold. As Satan mocks what is true, binds like these are spoken three times to mock the Holy Trinity. To break them, repeat the sentence three times, once each in honor of the Father, Son and Holy Spirit. This supplants the evil with good.

Once you have successfully completed the initial steps of the deliverance ministry, whether it was binding up, casting out, breaking curses, spells, hexes, seals or soul ties or some combination of the above, more work may need to be done. The events after the deliverance ministry will have an impact on its long term success. In order to ensure the effectiveness of the ministry, it is important that there be a supportive structure in place. A new, fervent commitment to God and His will is the first step. Daily mass, daily scripture reading, acts of charity and service to others, weekly bible study, ongoing prayer group are all ways to help you in your daily walk toward God.

What if the deliverance ministry doesn't work? What if the situation gets worse? The first thing that needs to be done is to give God praise and thanksgiving. Remember, you are to praise Him in the good and the bad. There are many factors that come into play here, God's timing, physical or mental illness, free will, hidden roots, powerful strongholds and lack of spiritual preparation are some of the possible reasons. A balanced attitude of trust in God's mercy and submission to His will is the best way to approach deliverance ministry.

> You damned spirits! You can only do what the hand of God allows you to do. Therefore in the name of Almighty God I tell you to do whatever God allows you to do to my body. I will gladly endure it since I have no worse enemy than my body. If you take revenge on my enemy for me, you do me a great favor.
> Saint Francis of Assisi

While it is true that God wants to heal, He'll do so in the manner that best serves His will and therefore, best serves you. Sometimes God allows you to remain in a certain sin to prevent you from falling into deeper sin. Healing comes in His time and in His way. His timing and His remedy is always perfect, always effective.

> The Lord loves humility so much that, sometimes, He permits serious sins. Why? In order that those who committed these sins may, after repenting, remain humble.
> Pope John Paul I

> In order to overcome their pride, God punishes certain men by allowing them to fall into sins of the flesh.
> Saint Thomas Aquinas

Likewise, God may allow demons to continue to tempt and harass you (or others) in order to save your (or their) soul. You need to trust in Him. God's delays are not God's denials. What at first may seem like a block can actually be a blessing. Proceed in humility, not pride.

> It often happens that we pray to God to deliver us from some dangerous temptation and yet God does not hear us but permits the temptation to continue troubling us. In such a case, let us understand that God permits even this for our greater good.
> Saint Alphonsus Liguori

If your will (or the will of the person seeking prayer) is not congruent in his or her desire to be free from the influence of the evil one, the deliverance ministry will likely be ineffective despite your best intentions. Open doors such as unconfessed sin are impediments to a successful deliverance ministry. Deeply hidden roots, e.g. the occult or fear, severely diminish the likelihood of success. An intact root will hinder the deliverance ministry and may make matters worse when it grows back. A full, complete and thorough confessing and renouncing of past sins is like severing the taproot of Satan's influence. Repent and take an ax to the root of your sinful tree (cf. Matthew 3:10).

> It is in vain that we cut off the branches of evil if we leave intact the root, which continually produces new ones.
> Saint Alphonsus Liguori

> When you renounce Satan, trampling underfoot every covenant with him, then you annul that ancient "league with Hell," and God's paradise opens before you.
> Saint Cyril of Jerusalem

If curses, spells, hexes, seals or soul ties are present and are not broken the deliverance ministry will appear to fail. If you are coming up against a stronghold that is beyond your ability to handle, then success is unlikely. For example, a stronghold may exist over a person or city etc. or a person may be suffering from Satanic Ritual Abuse, SRA, which is beyond the scope of the average deliverance ministry (and this book.)

If the person being delivered is not leading a sacramental life, it may actually be more prudent to not cast out spirits from them, even if they give you permission to do so. Casting out evil spirits from a baptized Catholic who lacks the graces of a sacramental life is like sweeping the dirt out the back door while the front door is propped open and the wind is blowing fiercely carrying more dirt all throughout the house. Better to close the door first.

If you are going in unprepared, undermanned or without proper authority, you open yourself up to potential harm. If the deliverance team (if there is one) is operating without proper authority or is not in union and harmony with one another, then success is less likely. Harmony comes through humility and surrender. Prepare, discern and act according to His will and you shall not be harmed. Follow His plan down to every last detail. His every plan, while it may not always make sense to you, is perfect. His plan flows from His love; His plan will lead you to salvation.

> Oh what God must have ahead of us if we only leave all to His plan.
> Venerable Solanus Casey

> Whatever did not fit in with my plan did lie within the plan of God. I have an ever deeper and firmer belief that nothing is merely an accident when seen in the light of God, that my whole life down to the smallest details has been marked out for me in the plan of Divine Providence and has a completely coherent meaning in God's all-seeing eyes. And so I am beginning to rejoice in the light of glory wherein this meaning will be unveiled to me.
> Saint Teresa Benedicta of the Cross

> Everything comes from love, all is ordained for the salvation of man, God does nothing without this goal in mind.
> Saint Catherine of Siena

Lastly, your desired outcome of the deliverance ministry may not be consistent with God's timing or purpose. Though it can be stated with certainty that God desires your freedom from evil spirits, now might not be the time. God may allow the attack of the evil spirits to continue in order to bring about His plan and your salvation. Whether He is calling you to greater charity, greater humility or greater praise of His name, He will bring good from the bad, if you let Him. Don't despair and don't demand. Submit to His plan, His timing, His way.

> To practice humility it is absolutely necessary for us at times to suffer wounds in this spiritual warfare, but we are never vanquished unless we lose our life or our

courage.
Saint Frances de Sales

It constantly happens that the Lord permits a soul to fall so that it may grow humbler.
Saint Teresa of Avila

One act of thanksgiving when things go wrong with us is worth a thousand thanks when things are agreeable to our inclination.
Saint John of Avila

It may be the case that your very response of humility and charity and praise to the attacks of the evil spirits effects a deliverance and causes the demons to flee. This may give greater glory to God and a greater opportunity for you to grow in grace. Trust in His plan for you.

The act of humility I had just performed put the devil to flight since he had perhaps thought that I would not dare admit my temptation. My doubts left me completely as soon as I finished speaking.
Saint Therese of Lisieux

This is so terrifying to the evil spirit that as soon as he sees that his temptations urge us on to God's love he cease to tempt us.
Saint John of the Cross

The praise of God should know no limits. Let us strive, therefore, to praise Him to the greatest extent of our powers.
Saint Maximilian Kolbe

We ought to find all our delight in treating with our Lord, and be indifferent to his pleasure regarding us, whether he gives us solace and sweetness or rather distractions, troubles or toils. Provided his good pleasure be accomplished, that should be enough for us.
Saint Jane Frances de Chantal

Chapter 24
Deliverance Ministry in Action

But Paul, being grieved, turned and said to the spirit, "I command you, in the name of Jesus Christ, to go out from her." And it went away in that same hour.
Acts of the Apostles 16:18b

As a prayer team engaged in deliverance ministry, you will encounter a variety of evil spirits. As you are led deeper into deliverance ministry, and if the Lord graces you accordingly, you will have the ability to discern which spirits are operating in a particular situation. This is a great grace that will aid you in your ministry. Some of the more common spirits that you may encounter are:

Anger	Despair	Games	Mockery
Anxiety	Division	Guilt	Occult
Blockage	Doubt	Isolation	Overwhelm
Confusion	Envy	Jezebel	Pride
Death	Fatigue	Lust	Retaliation
Desolation	Fear	Malice	Shame

The following stories are stories of actual deliverance ministries. Collectively, they give you a sense of what the process might look like and what to expect. Individually, they offers an insight into how to best proceed and what to avoid.

Proceed Only in Accord with His Will

When it comes to deliverance ministry there is only one boss, and it's not me or you. It is the Holy Spirit. It is absolutely essential to follow His lead. Do not let pride propel you forward, do not let ignorance lead the way. Do not let your compassion become a tool of the evil one. Always obey the promptings of the Holy Spirit.

- A prayer team member seemed anxious about a certain prayer ministry. We lifted up a woman in need of prayer for a particular addiction. As we prayed we seemed to be getting further away from any sense of being able to know the Lord's will about how to pray for her. After a few minutes of unproductive prayer, we kept getting we were to cease praying for this woman until there was unity in the team. Suddenly the prayer team member who was anxious spoke up. He said that he was not spiritually prepared to engage in deliverance ministry as he was in need of availing himself of sacramental confession. He excused himself from prayer ministry that night. After checking back in with the Lord, we were able to proceed without him

- Our prayer team was interceding for the wife of a friend. The husband was present to the prayer team, but his wife was not. As we proceeded in prayer, we received a strong sense to stop what we were doing. Our first instinct was to bind up and cast out any false spirits that might be trying to prevent the prayer ministry. We did so and then proceeded to pray again for the wife. Again, we got a strong sense to stop. In obedience we did. We told the husband that we were being led by the Spirit to stop the deliverance ministry. He was disappointed. Months later we were led to pray for the wife and the deliverance ministry was fruitful. We never found out why we were called to stop praying the first time only to resume months later.

- Praying as a team is the ideal situation, though it is not always practical. Often I will come upon a situation that requires an immediate response. The first step is to always check with the Lord. There have been times where humanly I felt as if I should pray for a person, but after praying to the Lord about it I was told to leave things as they were. One time I proceeded without first praying for permission from the Lord. I will never do that again; it was as if all Hell broke loose right before my eyes. I was quickly in over my head backpedaling as fast as I could. The Lord was gracious, both in allowing me to learn a lesson and in bailing me out. Abide in His authority and you will not be lead into harm's way

- A woman came to a prayer ministry looking for deliverance for what she termed "evil spirits." She shared a vivid tale of how these spirits would manifest themselves and make her life miserable. We asked the Lord for His light on the situation and we got a clear signal to not proceed with the ministry and to excuse ourselves from her presence. We did as the Lord commanded. Within seconds, this sweet, middle-aged woman turned aggressive and foul-mouthed. We prayed prayers of protection for ourselves and she found herself being spiritually ushered toward the exit. It was as if there was a hedge of angelic protection around us that repelled the demons operating in and around her. Always check with the Lord and heed His commands.

> If you would keep yourself pure, shun dangerous occasions. Do not trust your own strength. In this matter we can not take too much precaution.
> Saint Alphonsus Liguori

> His wisdom is infinite and if I look to Him for counsel, I shall not be deceived.
> Pope Saint Pius X

Don't Expect to Go Unnoticed

As a spiritual warrior, expect retaliation. The more you surrender to God's will, the stronger you become in the Lord. The stronger you become in the Lord, the greater threat you pose to Satan. The greater threat you pose to Satan, the more demons he'll enlist to harass you. The more demons he enlists to harass you, the more he is admitting his inability to effectively battle against God's grace in your soul. Remember, whenever and wherever Satan escalates his efforts, God's grace is available in greater abundance.

- I can not tell you how many times Satan has attempted to disrupt and divide my family, ministries and prayer groups by his pre-emptive strikes. The days leading up to a talk I'm giving on spiritual warfare or a critical prayer meeting can be a nightmare. Seemingly out of nowhere chaos and conflict comes flying at us. Minor differences become major disagreements; simple challenges turn into grueling confrontations. Egos are bruised and feelings are hurt and suddenly you don't feel like praying anymore. Be aware of who is pushing the emotional buttons.

- Frequently when praying in intercession for someone, some or all of the prayer team will be harassed by a spirit of blockage. This manifests as a lack of words or images during prayer time; as if your spiritual antenna was knocked out of commission. The Evil spirits will do whatever they can to prevent intercessory prayers from being offered. If we sense a spirit of blockage, in the name of Jesus we simply take authority and recite the deliverance prayer. Often the spirits of blockage are accompanied by the spirits of games and retaliation and revenge and intimidation. The spirits are then bound up and cast out and the deliverance ministry is able to proceed. Without binding up and casting out of the evil spirits the deliverance ministry is much more difficult.

- When you pray as a team, one person may be called to act as a "lightning rod." They bear the brunt of the evil one's attacks so that the others may pray. In doing so, they become Christ-like; they willing offer themselves as a sacrifice so that the greater good can be accomplished. One young man on our prayer team was designated by the Holy Spirit as that week's target. While the rest of the team was able to pray easily, he was enduring aural and visual harassment. Though not easy, by God's grace, he was able to surrender, endure the onslaught and grow in virtue. The deliverance ministry was effective in large part because of his willingness to accept the role God desired him to play.

- I witnessed a prayer team praying over a couple. There seemed to be two members of the prayer team who were in competition with one another. There was a real sense of disunity. The tension only increased as the prayer ministry continued. Finally, the unspoken, but real tension overflowed in a verbal squabble. Obviously, the prayer ministry was discontinued. Make sure each team member understands and accepts their respective roles so that incidents such as this don't happen. Leave your ego at the door before you begin a deliverance ministry.

> If any of you [evil spirits] have any authority over me, only one would have been sufficient to fight me.
> Saint Antony of the Desert

> The people most tempted are those who are ready, with the grace of God, to sacrifice everything for the salvation of their poor souls, who renounce all those things which most people eagerly seek. It is not one devil only who tempts them, but millions seek to entrap them.
> Saint John Vianney

Bind Up When Appropriate

One of the primary functions of a spiritual warrior is to pray for those who are unable to do so for themselves. As the Holy Spirit leads, you are to intercede on behalf of the poor, the suffering, and the oppressed (cf. Luke 4:18-19). Bringing spiritual comfort to those who are in need is a true mission of mercy. Binding up and casting out of evil spirits is a tool of God's mercy.

- A young woman had run away from home and moved in with her boyfriend who lived in another state. Her parents requested prayer for her. As she was in her late teens and freely chose to leave, casting out of spirits was likely not to be an option. We prayed for guidance from the Holy Spirit and proceeded to bind up any and all evil spirits around her and her boyfriend. We bound up the spirits of lust and fornication and lies and Jezebel and suicide. Seven days later she arrived back home tired, but well. She later told her parents that one morning she woke up and seemingly out of nowhere said to herself, "What am I doing here? I don't want to be here anymore. I want to go home" Her parents asked her what day this "epiphany" had occurred. It was the morning after we had prayed for her.

- A toddler was acting aggressively and disrespectfully toward his mother one day at daily Mass. Her attempts to quiet and calm him were to no avail. You could see and sense that there was something more going on here than just a noisy toddler. After a few more minutes of his out of character and inappropriate behavior and after checking in with the Lord, I bound spirits on the little boy. I bound spirits of disobedience and defiance and anger and malice and retaliation. Within a few seconds after completing the prayer he stretched out on the kneeler and fell asleep. He remained that way until the final blessing and then woke up at peace.

- One day as I was walking through an airport, a boy was screaming at the top of his lungs. There wasn't any obvious cause for his actions that I could see; his parents were there with him trying to calm him down. As I continued to walk toward my destination, I felt a prompting. I prayed about whether or not the Lord wanted me to bind spirits on this boy; I got a strong sense to do so. I walked back toward where he was, and I bound spirits of fear and anger and infirmity and lies. Within moments he went from ear splitting screaming to soft moaning and sobbing.

- I was speaking at a local parish, where a man sitting in the front row was unusually restless. He kept shifting positions, making snide comments and causing distractions. His behavior was becoming increasingly disruptive, to the point where I needed to take a break. A member of the prayer team was with me and we were able to briefly pray together. We got a sense to proceed with the binding up prayer. Immediately after praying, the man came up to me. It was as if he was ready to pounce on me but was, somehow, prevented from doing so. He was like a bee that lost its stinger or a cat without its claws, harmless. The spirits afflicting him remained bound the rest of the evening.

He who truly loves his neighbor and can not efficaciously assist him, should strive at least to relieve and help him by his prayers.
Saint Teresa of Avila

We are only plotting to defeat the devil and to deprive him of the lordship that he has assumed over man by mortal sin, to take hate from man's heart and to pacify him with Christ crucified. These are the plots that we are weaving.
Saint Catherine of Siena

Cast Out When Necessary

Your sword of Spirit, the only offensive weapon that God has equipped you with, is the word of God. Satan has spun so many webs, and done so with a malevolent magnificence, that many people find themselves ensnared. Your sword of the Spirit will slice right through Satan's deceptions, giving others a chance to break free. Use you sword judiciously and in accord with the prompting of the Holy Spirit.

- After a *Saint Joseph Radio Presents* show, a listener related to me how his wife was suffering from fear attacks. Seemingly from nowhere, she would experience an intense fear sweep over her body. As the spiritual head of the household and with her full consent, he began to bind up and cast out a stronghold of fear whenever she had manifestations. Each time he did so the grip of fear seemed to lessen. After a few weeks of intense prayer and fasting by both of them, a sense of the woundedness that was behind the fears came to her heart. She brought this memory and all her fear to Jesus during adoration and was healed. She experienced the scriptural truth that perfect love casts out all fear (cf. 1 John 4:18).

- A young man was hearing voices that kept telling him to kill himself. The demons labeled him a "failure" and "worthless." He gave his permission to be prayed over. We bound up and cast out spirits of death, suicide, murder, lust and pornography. Immediately a sense of peace returned to his face and to his heart. We prayed with him to close any doors, to seal off any openings and to heal any wounds. He now has a renewed commitment to prayer and the attacks are diminishing in their frequency and intensity. He gives no ear to the lies and now focuses on the plans that Lord has for him, plans of peace, not of woe (cf. Jeremiah 29:11).

- A businessman was bothered by the means by which he was making a living. He felt like the endless quest he was on for more money and more power was leading him further and further away from God. He even wondered if it was too late for him. After binding up and casting the demons of greed, worldliness, power, pride, money, lust and lies, he said, "I feel like I have a heart again." After prayerful consideration he left his job and found another that provided him an opportunity to make money in a manner that was good for his soul.

- A grandmother had been keeping a secret for over sixty years. She said she felt too guilty to share it with anybody. Satan had frequently used this act of concealment against her, keeping her depressed and dispirited. We bound up and cast out the spirits of lies, molestation, concealment, false-guilt and deceit. After the deliverance prayer she revealed her secret for the first time. She said, "I feel like I'm taking my first breath in sixty years." It is interesting to note that the secret she kept was something for which she was not the least bit culpable. It was all a lie of the evil one. The truth set her free.

> Until the devil sees what to counterfeit, he does not begin anything and even does not know how to set to work. Therefore, when he has perceived that he can no longer carry off, or choke, or scorch that which has been sown and has taken root, he invents a different kind of deception, namely he sows his own seed.
> Saint John Chrysostom

> In catching birds, we employ decoys, that is, certain birds that are blinded, and tied in such a manner that they cannot fly away. It is thus the devil acts.
> Saint Alphonsus Liguori

With No Attachment to an Outcome

Not all deliverance ministries are successful. As a spiritual warrior you are not necessarily called to success, only obedience. God's ways are not necessarily your ways. God allows for free will, which means some people may choose evil. God will sometimes allow this, so that they might rise higher in Him. Again, His timing is perfect.

- A man came to us asking for prayers for his nephew, who was also his godchild. He asked for prayers to free his nephew from his homosexual lifestyle. We proceeded cautiously, only binding up any evil spirits, but not casting them out. We bound up the spirits of homosexuality, perversion, mockery, malice, suicide, death and Jezebel. The next morning, the young man called his uncle and asked if his uncle would pray for him. He told his uncle, "I want to get out of this lifestyle. I'm done with it." Within a couple of days he returned to his former ways. While effective short-term, binding up of spirits is not long lasting, especially when the will of the person has been compromised. The young man was not willing to consent to a full deliverance ministry even though he sensed it might be effective. He was not yet ready to receive God's healing.

- A wife asked for specific prayers of healing from an addiction for her husband. We lifted him up to the Lord and were given very clear instructions about how to pray and how not to pray for the man. We were not to pray for a healing for him as that was contrary to his will for himself. We were to pray that he might have a desire to be healed. To pray for him to have the desire to be healed seemed insufficient and inferior as compared to asking for a healing, yet it was the prayer that the Lord requested so we obliged. It was, of course, the perfect prayer.

- A friend was firmly entrenched in a freely chosen life of sin. Leaving his wife and children, he moved in with a co-worker with whom he had "fallen in love." Repeated conversations yielded no fruit. I began to pray for him daily, binding up spirits but not casting them out. I bound spirits of lies, lust, apathy, spiritual suicide, fear, retaliation and hopelessness. This occurred over a several month period. Every once in a while he would make contact with me, but nothing really changed. In his words, "I'm happy the way I am. Why would I want to go back?" His intonation belied his words. The binding up of evil spirits effected no lasting change in him because he desired none.

- A young woman asked for help. She felt like she was being attacked by the evil one. After asking her a few questions, she admitted that she had been seeing a psychic on a fairly regular basis. I told her that before we could go any further she would need to renounce and repent of her sin and to do so sacramentally. She replied, "Oh, I don't want to stop going to the psychic, I just don't want to be harassed by these spirits." When I told her that one was likely the cause of the other she wasn't too happy. I neither bound up nor cast out any spirits from her. As she consented to their presence through her actions, to bound up or cast out would have been to her detriment and possibly mine. I have not heard from her again.

> To sin is human, but to persist in sin is devilish.
> Saint Catherine of Siena

> Happy is he whose way is God's way; when he is used to it, it is as easy as any other way — nay, much easier, for God's service is perfect freedom, whereas Satan is a cruel taskmaster.
> Blessed John Henry Newman

Deliverance ministry is a grace. It is a joy. It is a privilege. It is the Lord's. You are only His chosen vessel. Deliverance ministry does not originate with you. Do not admire your gifts and graces as if they were your own; they are not. Do not be enamored with your success; do not be disappointed with your failures. You will be a far more effective spiritual warrior when you submit to His will, abide in His light and cooperate with His plan. When you engage in deliverance ministry have no attachment to a specific outcome. Do not act with a sense of vengeance or pride in your heart. Do not become malice to cast out malice, become charity so as to differentiate yourself from the evil spirits you are binding up and casting out. Be attached only to God's will and His peace will be your reward.

This then is the original evil; man regards himself as his own light and turns away from the light which would make himself light if he would set his heart on it.
Saint Augustine

In all your affairs rely wholly on God's providence through which you must look for success. Nevertheless, strive quietly on your part to cooperate with its designs.
Saint Francis de Sales

The enemy drive from us away, peace then give without delay; with you as guide to lead the way we avoid all cause of harm.
Veni Creator

Be on fire with the ardor of charity in order to differentiate yourself from demons.
Saint Augustine

Part IV
Ongoing Warfare Training

☩

And may the Lord direct your hearts, in the charity of God and with the patience of Christ.
2 Thessalonians 3:5

My brothers, when you have fallen into various trials, consider everything a joy, knowing that the proving of your faith exercises patience, and patience brings a work to perfection, so that you may be perfect and whole, deficient in nothing.
James 1:2-4

Every good soldier who desires to remain a good soldier needs ongoing training. Ongoing training of the body, mind and soul is necessary for all who desire to remain alive in the Lord. Ongoing training allows you to recognize and strengthen those areas that are weak, to add to your knowledge and wisdom of the enemy and of your cause. Ongoing training will help you refine what you do well so that you might do it better. It will also help you to rest and recuperate more quickly.

After Jesus' initial training in the desert, the Gospels relate how He frequently went off to be by Himself far away from the crowds. He did this so He could reconnect with His Father and His mission. He was not always on the front lines; He was not always "on call" to the people. He knew when He needed to recollect; He knew when He needed to regroup. He knew when He needed to be steeped in prayer and bathe His entire being in the Father's love. He did not prematurely proceed; He did not overextend His stay. He went where and when He was told to go, for as long as He was told to go. He listened to the promptings of the Holy Spirit with perfect humility and perfect obedience. His will is, was and always will be one with the Father's will.

No matter what your vocation may be, as a Christian you are called to ongoing formation, to grow in knowledge, love and service of God. You are to persevere in your faith, to be obedient to the Church and its teachings and to relentlessly strive to conform your will to the will of the Father in Heaven. As a spiritual warrior, difficulties await those who engage in battle without benefit of ongoing training, without humble submission of their will to the Father's will.

> Through obedience, discipline and training, man, who is created and contingent, grows into the image and likeness of the eternal God.
> Saint Irenaeus

> The virtue of obedience makes the will supple. It gives the power to conquer self, to overcome laziness, and to resist temptations. It inspires the courage with which to fulfill the most difficult tasks.
> Saint John Vianney

> Obedience is the sepulcher of the will and the resurrection of lowliness.
> Saint John Climacus

Chapter 25
Daily Reminders

☩

Consider, most beloved, this second epistle which I am
writing to you, in which I stir up, by admonition, your
sincere mind, so that you may be mindful of those
words, which I preached to you from the holy prophets,
and of the precepts of the Apostles of your Lord and
Savior.
2 Peter 3:1-2

While toiling on earth, the reality of concupiscence and
its wide ranging effects is obvious. Disordered emotions and a
diminished intellect flow from the stain of original sin. The
capacity to know what is right, to assent to it and then to act on
it, has been weakened since the fall of Adam and Eve. Equally,
the ability to retain knowledge, exercise the will properly and
persevere in goodness has been compromised.

The spiritual training you know you must do often does
not get done. Laziness, busyness, distractions and pride often
get in the way. To help combat the inherent weaknesses
present, it is beneficial to have some simple reminders to help
stay on God's path. As a soldier of Christ, it is a wise strategy
to daily recommit to follow in His footsteps, thereby avoiding
the minefields set by the world, the flesh and the devil. The
following list of reminders offers advice from Scripture and the
saints to help keep you on the right path.

Adore, don't ignore

> Therefore, everyone who acknowledges me before men, I also will acknowledge before my Father, who is in Heaven. But whoever will have denied me before men, I also will deny before my Father, who is in Heaven.
> Matthew 10:32-33

God is God. Because He is God, He deserves to be adored. He is Lord of all, creator of all, sustainer of all. He alone is worthy of worship, He alone is worthy of praise. To ignore God is to please Satan. Even in the midst of great trials of temptation or harassment, your primary focus should be on God and His grace and mercy. Only to the degree necessary are you to focus on Satan. Typically that would involve acknowledging that Satan exists and might be exerting an influence in a particular circumstance. Once that is acknowledged refocus your gaze upon God alone.

Adoration of Jesus is more than keeping your eyes on Him, though. It is seeing the Lord through the eyes of faith and worshipping Him in His Eucharistic Presence as if He stood before you in the flesh. For as Jesus, Himself, taught, He is right before you under the form of bread and wine. Even Satan knows and believes this. The demons flee from those who receive and adore the "hidden" Jesus in the consecrated Host.

> Do you realize that Jesus is there in the tabernacle expressly for you, for you alone? He burns with the desire to come into your heart. Don't listen to the demon, laugh at him, and go without fear to receive the Jesus of peace and love.
> Saint Therese of Lisieux

> In a world where there is so much noise, so much bewilderment, there is a need for silent adoration of Jesus concealed in the Host. Be assiduous in the prayer of adoration and teach it to the faithful. It is a source of comfort and light, particularly to those who are suffering.
> Pope Benedict XVI

What we need today is an army who is willing to fight, standing up and being counted for the cause of Christ in the Most Blessed Sacrament.
Saint Peter Julian Eymard

Pray, don't delay

Be vigilant and pray, so that you may not enter into temptation. Indeed, the spirit is willing, but the flesh is weak.
Matthew 26:41

Prayer is the means by which you keep in touch with God and He with you. Satan will seek to do whatever he can to interfere with this connection because he knows prayer is such a powerful weapon. He will annoy, harass and distract you to the point of frustration if you allow him. Do not panic, do not be anxious, do not grow weary; simply pray now, pray unceasingly. Do not give into the fear or frustration; rather, with the help of God's grace, continue in prayer. If you can't pray, stay in prayer until you can pray. Praise Him, thank Him, and then petition Him.

In the midst of triumph or tragedy, the extraordinary or the ordinary, pray. Check in with God early and often. Eve's mistake in the Garden of Eden was not checking in with God. Satan asked a simple question designed to create doubt in Adam and Eve's mind. Satan preyed on Adam and Eve's emotions. If only Adam and Eve had prayed on their knees in response.

Through fear, some souls grow slack in their prayer — which is what the devil wants — in order to struggle against these movements, and others give it up entirely, for they think these feelings come while they are engaged in prayer rather than at other times. This is true because the devil excites these feelings while souls are at prayer, instead of when they are engaged in other works, so that they might abandon prayer.
Saint John of the Cross

The devil attacks us at the time of prayer more

313

frequently than at other times. His object is to make us weary of prayer.
Blessed Henry Suso

To give up prayer because we are often distracted at it is to allow the devil to gain his cause.
Saint Alphonsus Liguori

The devil and his angels, these are the enemies against whom we pray. They envy us the kingdom of Heaven; they would not have us ascend to the place from which they were cast down. From these let us pray that our souls may be delivered.
Saint Augustine

Contemplate, don't instigate

Be still and confess that I am God.
Psalm 45:11

In the stillness God makes Himself known to you. In the stillness you hear His voice and feel His presence. In the stillness He speaks to your heart, moves your heart and expands your heart. It is in the stillness that He gives you your assignment as His soldier. It is in the stillness that you come to know God, you come to know His love. You are a soldier of His love. This stillness, contemplation, is absolutely essential for a soldier of Christ. In the battlefield, there are many voices, many temptations and many camouflages. The only way to know God's voice is to be still, to contemplate, even in the midst of battle — especially in the midst of battle.

Don't feel the need to always do something. Take the time to be present to Jesus, to absorb His words, to revel in His presence, to grow in His grace, to rest your head upon His breast. Contemplate. Meditate. Reflect. Don't waste any opportunity to just be with the Lord. Don't allow the world to distract or desensitize you. Ponder the depth and mystery of the cross, a true catechism of the faith. Sit with God and just be. Wait on Him; listen to Him. He'll tell you when to do and when not to do. Don't force the action; await your orders from on high and all shall be well. The devil is often the instigator of imprudent actions; he does not want you to contemplate God. For the more you contemplate God, the more you are able to recognize the actions of Satan.

> I don't say anything [to God in prayer]. I just listen. He doesn't say anything [to me in prayer]. He just listens.
> Blessed Teresa of Calcutta

> He, Christ, is the splendor of eternal glory, the brightness of eternal light, and the mirror without cloud. Look more deeply into the mirror and meditate on his humility. Behold the many labors and sufferings he endured to redeem the human race. Then, in the depths of this very mirror, ponder his unspeakable love which caused him to suffer on the wood of the cross and to endure the most shameful kind of death.
> Saint Clare of Assisi

> Shame upon you, wicked devil, for grudging us the sight of our Lord's likeness and our sanctification through it. You would not have us gaze at His saving sufferings nor wonder at His condescension, neither contemplate His miracles nor praise His almighty power. You grudge the saints the honor God gives to them. You would not have us see their glory put on record, nor allow us to become imitators of their fortitude and faith. We will not obey your suggestions, wicked and man-hating devil.
> Saint John Damascene

Acknowledge, don't overlook

> I am not praying that you would take them out of the world, but that you would preserve them from evil.
> John 17:15

It is important as a Christian and as a spiritual warrior that you recognize that Satan exists and that he desires to lure you away from God. Yet, you should not be anticipating or seeing the enemy at every turn in your life. Don't anticipate his antics, but courageously oppose him with all of God's might, for in this battle you will find your peace. This important maxim follows the need to adore God, pray to Him and meditate upon Him. Proper balance and order is necessary in order to serve in the Lord's army.

Soldiers of the Lord, that would be all who belong to the Church Militant, are seemingly paradoxically soldiers of peace. It is seemingly paradoxical because there is no contradiction between war and peace when properly understood. Jesus was and is at war against sin; yet, He is at peace with His Father. You are to be likewise at war against the devil by being in God's peace. In fact, the act of being in God's peace sets you in opposition to Satan. Acknowledge Satan and abound in God and you will not be harmed.

> Affirm Satan's existence. Admit his actuality.
> Servant of God John Hardon

> If we are at war with the devil, we are at peace with God.
> Saint John Chrysostom

> O dear Lord, teach us to suffer with You, and not be afraid of Satan's buffetings, when they come on us from resisting him.
> Blessed John Henry Newman

Reveal, don't conceal

> Whoever hides his crimes will not be guided. But whoever will have confessed and abandoned them shall overtake mercy.
> Proverbs 28:13

> For there is nothing secret, which will not be made clear, nor is there anything hidden, which will not be known and be brought into plain sight.
> Luke 8:17

Concealment is not of God. Satan knows Scripture well and knows it is the truth that will set you free. He also knows that your pride can be used as leverage against you. As long as actual sin remains concealed, you offer Satan an access point. Go to confession; give it over to God and Satan is powerless. More powerful than an exorcism is the Sacrament of Penance. An exorcism frees the body from the grip of the evil one; a sacramental confession frees the soul.

Do not let pride, shame or guilt prevent you from being cleansed under a shower of God's infinite mercy. Do not let Satan's whispers of your unworthiness prevent you from appealing to the infinite merits of Jesus Christ's salvific act on the cross. He shed His blood so that you might be saved, knowing of your unworthiness. If your sin didn't prevent God from extending the invitation, it should never prevent you from accepting it.

> Note well what the first condition the evil one makes with a soul he desires to seduce is for it to keep silence.
> Saint Francis de Sales

> When the enemy of human nature brings his wiles and persuasions to the just soul, he wants and desires that they be received and kept in secret; but when one reveals them to his good Confessor it is very grievous to him, because he gathers, from his manifest deceits being discovered, that he will not be able to succeed with his wickedness begun.
> Saint Ignatius of Loyola

> Do not fight against a temptation by yourself, but disclose it to the confessor at once, and then the temptation will lose all its force.
> Our Lord to Saint Faustina Kowalska

Petition, don't panic

> Be anxious about nothing, but in all things, with prayer and supplication, with acts of thanksgiving, let your petitions be made known to God. And so shall the peace of God, which exceeds all understanding, guard your hearts and minds in Christ Jesus.
> Philippians 4:6-7

Seek, ask, knock and be at peace. Your Father in Heaven knows your every need. Be not afraid to ask Him, He will provide. All that occurs is either part of God's perfect will or of His permissive will. Like the perfect Father that He is, He will provide for you in accordance with your needs to the degree that you allow Him to do so. Petition Him often, yielding to His will in the process. Plead your case before the Lord, then rest in His peace. His delays and His denials are an expression of His mercy and love.

Panic points to a lack of faith, a lack of trust, a lack of surrender to God. Panic is an expression of self-will. Panic produces opportunities for Satan to lace your mind with murmurs of "I told you so," "He doesn't care about you," or "You're not worthy of Him." He'll do anything he can to disturb your peace, to get you to give up on God. Recall Paul's words, have no anxiety, pray, petition, give thanks and be at peace.

> Whence all the disturbance of mind, if not from following one's own desires?
> Saint Bernard of Clairvaux

> Fear is the first temptation which the enemy presents to those who have resolved to serve God.
> Saint Francis de Sales

> The struggle with the enemy must not frighten you. The more God becomes intimate with your soul, the more the adversary fights in an interior manner. Have courage, therefore.
> Saint Pio of Pietrelcina

Bless, don't curse

> But I say to you who are listening: Love your enemies. Do good to those who hate you.
> Luke 6:27

> And finally, may you all be of one mind: compassionate, loving brotherhood, merciful, meek, humble, not repaying evil with evil, nor slander with slander, but, to the contrary, repaying with blessings. For to this you

have been called, so that you may possess the inheritance of a blessing.
1 Peter 3:9

Bless those who are persecuting you: bless, and do not curse.
Romans 12:14

A curse is Satan's version of a blessing. Satan would have you seek payback instead of prayer, revenge instead of reconciliation. By cursing your enemy you only serve to spread the disease of self that infected Satan and all the fallen angels. Your negative feelings toward someone can serve to keep that person (and yourself) bound. By blessing instead of cursing you confound your enemies, loose their binds and may even convert them. Regardless, you are called to respond at a higher level.

You have been given the grace necessary to bless those who curse you and to praise God in all things. If every time Satan attacked you, you took the time to praise God, It would not be long before Satan stopped attacking you. Bless those who curse you. Don't let their stinging barbs turns into festering wounds. Ward off their attacks with charity and humility. See and respond to the Jesus in them. Perhaps nobody else ever has. You might be the one person God can count on to reach out to this soul. Serve God with a zealous love and your reward will be eternal.

> True charity consists in doing good to those who do us evil, and in thus winning them over. Let us also pray for those who persecute us — this is the way the saints revenged themselves.
> Saint Alphonsus Liguori

Up till now you have not learned to love your neighbor. You answer men's dislike towards you by dislike on your part. But do the contrary; answer other's dislike by heartfelt goodwill and love; the more dislike you see towards you, the more you should love. Dislike is a malady, and a sick person should be more pitied, should be shown greater care and greater love, exactly because he is ill. Do you know that the bodiless enemy uses his

319

craftiness against all, infects all with the poison of his hatred? And you too, are not exempt from his craftiness. Do not serve him, then with the spirit of enmity, but serve the God of love with the utmost zeal.
Saint John of Kronstadt

Praise, don't grumble

And do everything without murmuring or hesitation. So may you be without blame, simple sons of God, without reproof, in the midst of a depraved and perverse nation, among whom you shine like lights in the world.
Philippians 2:14-15

To give God praise is to be humble. To give God praise is to acknowledge that God is God and you are not. The power of praise is profound. Grumbling is the anti-praise, it is the language of the prideful. When you praise God, you deflect all earthly glory and honor to God who is all good. Keep no glory for yourself. "Thank God," and "Praise God," should always be on your lips. When you engage in praise you tend toward humility allowing you to better accept God's will.

It is not enough to just accept God's will; He calls you to do so gracefully. Satan will attempt to goad you into grumbling. He'll push your buttons if you let him. He'll be glad to point out how things are unfair or inferior; he'll be happy to prod you into fault finding. His target is your wound, whatever it is.

Leave your grumbling behind and Satan will have once less point of entry and less leverage to get you to commit sin.

Thanksgiving is a special virtue. But ingratitude is opposed to thanksgiving. Therefore ingratitude is a special sin.
Saint Thomas Aquinas

If you begin to grieve at this, to judge your superior, to murmur in your heart, even though you outwardly fulfill what is commanded, this is not the virtue of obedience, but a cloak over your malice.
Saint Bernard of Clairvaux

The great enemy of the virtue of obedience is grumbling. Grumbling is the compensation self-love resorts to in its powerlessness in the face of authority.
Blessed Columba Marmion

Commend, don't condemn

And why do you see the straw that is in your brother's eye, while the log that is in your own eye, you do not consider? Or how can you say to your brother, "Brother, allow me to remove the straw from your eye," while you yourself do not see the log in your own eye? Hypocrite, first remove the log from your own eye, and then will you see clearly, so that you may lead out the straw from your brother's eye.
Luke 6:41-42

Grumbling inevitably leads to judgment; it is a simple, logical progression. Grumbling is a prideful expression of not getting your own way. Complaining leads to condemning, a toehold becomes a foothold then a stronghold. Criticism and condemnation is the bait that Satan uses to lure the holy into becoming holier-than-thou and hypocritical. When you criticize and condemn you act as judge and jury. Yet, it is the Lord, and only the Lord, who knows the heart, hurts and hopes of those whom you judge. It is He who searches souls. Do not attempt to ascribe to yourself what is properly the Lord's.

Commend to the Lord those you would criticize. Pray for them, love them and serve them — even your enemies, especially your enemies. Humble yourself; do not place yourself above others or apart from others. Seek out what is good in others and speak to that part of them. Commend, don't condemn: this will make Satan flee.

Nothing so despoils a man and leads so surely to perdition than fault finding, speaking evil and condemning one's neighbor.
Saint Dorotheus the Hermit

If something uncharitable is said in your presence, either speak in favor of the absent, or withdraw, or if

possible stop the conversation.
Saint John Vianney

The evil demons urge us to speak evil of one another,
or, speaking sweet words, to conceal bitterness in our
hearts, to criticize the outer aspect of our brother, while
we harbor a wild beast in ourselves, to quarrel among
ourselves and oppose one another, wishing to have our
own way and appear as the most upright.
Saint Antony of the Desert

Resist, don't succumb

Temptation should not take hold of you, except what is
human. For God is faithful, and he will not permit you
to be tempted beyond your ability. Instead, he will
effect his Providence, even during temptation, so that
you may be able to bear it.
1 Corinthians 10:13

The tempter will tempt, it is who he is and what he
does. Temptation is not sin, as long as there is no consent of the
will. An attack is not the same as a defeat. God, in His infinite
mercy, will always provide you with the grace necessary to
resist the temptations of the evil one. Simply beg for God's
grace. For Satan is nothing if not a coward who will back down
when faced with a soldier filled with God's grace.

Do not give up, do not give in, do not give over. When
you stumble, with God's grace, pick yourself up and continue to
do battle. When you sin, trust in His mercy. While you should
never presume upon God's mercy, you should not despair of it
either. Temptation will occur. Expect it, prepare for it and
resist it. Use the weapons of prayer, penance and good works.
Beg for God's infinite supply of grace and mercy to reach you so
you may resist.

In times of temptation continue the good you had begun
before temptation.
Saint Vincent Ferrer

Blessed are those who are tempted. It is when the devil

sees that a soul is tending toward union with God that he redoubles his efforts. The greatest of all evils is not to be tempted, because there are then grounds for believing the devil looks upon us as his property.
Saint John Vianney

If the devil, the world, and the flesh are making war upon you, he will give you the weapons with which to fight, to resist, and to win victory.
Saint John Vianney

Trust, don't doubt

Those who trust in him, will understand the truth, and those who are faithful in love will rest in him, because grace and peace is for his elect.
Wisdom 3:9

This is earth; it is not Heaven. Here on earth you will be subject to trials. You will have crosses to bear, sufferings to endure. Do not doubt, do not despair. Here on earth you are not necessarily given to know God's reasoning. Allow the trials to temper you. Allow the struggles to strengthen you. Realize that God is greater than any trial or temptation. Trust in His omnipotence and His omniscience. He knows what you need, how much you need and when you need it. All that comes your way is part of His plan for His glory and your salvation. He has a reason and a purpose for all He permits.

Trust in the Lord, not in the liar. Turn toward Him and trust Him. Do not doubt Him; do not turn to the evil one. The evil one is happy to instigate, exacerbate, exploit and isolate. He instigates by a cleverly worded question. He exploits your slight hesitancy, convincing you it is a doubt. He exacerbates your doubt into a crisis. Then he isolates you from community making you more vulnerable. Learn from Adam and Eve's errors. Allow the grace of God to help you overcome Satan's trickery. Trust in God; do not doubt, do not despair.

When we have once placed ourselves entirely in the hands of God, we need fear no evil. If adversity comes, He knows how to turn it to our advantage, by means

which will in time be made clear to us.
Saint Vincent de Paul

I understand that our enemies are strong, very strong, but when one fights alongside Jesus, how can one have any doubt about winning the battle?
Saint Pio of Pietrelcina

When boredom and discouragement beat against your heart, run away from yourself and hide in My heart. Do not fear struggle; courage itself often intimidates temptations, and they dare not attack us.
Our Lord to Saint Faustina Kowalska

Rejoice, don't sorrow

Blessed are you when they have slandered you, and persecuted you, and spoken all kinds of evil against you, falsely, for my sake: be glad and exult, for your reward in Heaven is plentiful.
Matthew 5:11-12a

Rejoice! Jesus Christ has risen. What a beautiful battle cry to proclaim from the mountaintops. What an indescribable joy to know that the victory over death has been achieved through the blood of the Lamb. Remain in the company of the Lamb and you shall not be harmed. You may have to suffer, much as the Lamb did, but you will not be harmed.

So, rejoice at all times. Know that the more Satan wages war against your soul, the more it speaks to the abundance of grace in your soul. To be tempted and harassed by the evil one is a cause for celebration. It means you are on a grace-filled path heading toward God. Stay on the path and praise and rejoice. Do not give into sorrow, sadness or sin for Jesus has come. He was born that He might die. He died that you might live. Rejoice and be glad.

For this day [Christmas] the ancient slavery is ended, the devil is confounded, the demons take to flight, the power of death is broken, paradise is unlocked, the curse is taken away, sin is removed from us, error

driven out, truth has been brought back.
Saint John Chrysostom

Rejoice and be glad always, for you shall not be put to shame.
Saint Boniface

The monks have no sadness. They wage war on the devil as though they were performing a dance.
Saint John Chrysostom

Accept, don't reject

May grace, mercy, and peace be with you from God the Father, and from Christ Jesus, the Son of the Father, in truth and in love.
2 John 1:3

God wants you to be free. He calls you to be His soldier of love, to be fully alive in Him. He wants you to accept His love, His grace, His peace, His mercy. He loves you too much to force you to accept His offering. You must freely choose to be with God. You are free to venture outside of His life of grace, but in doing so you become easy prey for Satan.

When you find yourself frightened, turn to Him who is love. When you find yourself in need, turn to Him who is grace. When you find yourself in turmoil, turn to Him who is peace. When you find yourself mired in sin, turn to Him who is mercy. When you find yourself frightened or anxious or uncertain or desperate or lonely or sad or wounded or naked or tired or cold or abandoned turn to Him who is your Creator, your "*Abba*," your Daddy, your Father. Accept His love, His grace, His peace, His mercy. You will be eternally grateful you did.

If I saw the gates of Hell open and I stood on the brink of the abyss, I should not despair; I should not lose hope of mercy, because I should trust in You, my God.
Saint Gemma Galgani

Oh, how beyond comprehension is God's mercy! But, horror, there are also souls who voluntarily and

consciously reject and scorn this grace!
Saint Faustina Kowalska

Allow these reminders to draw you deeper into Christ, to help you maintain proper perspective as a soldier of Christ. Spiritual warfare is a part of every Christian life, but only a part. Do not get caught up in the minutia; do not see demons lurking behind every temptation or harassment. Do not mistake earth for Heaven, this life for the next. You are not here to just live and die; you are not fighting battles just to fight battles. With every breath, every thought, every action you undertake, do it with your eternal reward in mind. Do everything you do for the glory of God and the salvation of souls. Never give up on yourself; never give up on others, never give up on God. God and His mercy can overcome all. Turn to Him, repent and watch Satan flee.

> We must often draw the comparison of time and eternity. That is the remedy for all troubles. How small will the present moment appear when we enter that great ocean! How much we will then wish we had doubled our penance and sufferings while that moment lasted.
> Saint Elizabeth Ann Seton

> Draw near to God, and Satan will flee from you.
> Saint Ephrem of Syria

> We have been called to heal wounds, to unite what has fallen apart, and to bring home those who have lost their way. Many who may seem to us to be children of the devil will still become Christ's disciples.
> Saint Francis of Assisi

> Your first task is to be dissatisfied with yourself, fight sin, and transform yourself into something better. Your second task is to put up with the trials and temptations of this world that will be brought on by the change in your life and to persevere to the very end in the midst of these things.
> Saint Augustine

Chapter 26
Promise, Perseverance & Peace

☩

Christ, as the first-fruits, and next, those who are of
Christ, who have believed in his advent. Afterwards is
the end, when he will have handed over the kingdom to
God the Father, when he will have emptied all
principality, and authority, and power. For it is
necessary for him to reign, until he has set all his
enemies under his feet.
1 Corinthians 15:23b-25

Jesus is Lord and God, eternally. He is Creator. He is
Victor. He has dominion over both the Kingdom of Light and
the Kingdom of Darkness. His dominion is absolute, eternal
and infinite.

Satan is creature; he is vanquished. His continued
existence is permitted only to the degree that it serves the
Father's will. He has no dominion over the infinite Kingdom of
Light, and only partial, fleeting and contingent dominion over
the finite Kingdom of Darkness.

Therefore, if you are baptized and in a state of
sanctifying grace, Satan has no dominion over you; although,
you can open the door to his influence through fear or sin. If
you persist in unrepentant serious sin, you do become
vulnerable to the powers of Satan. Repent and receive
sacramental confession and you are once again covered by
God's grace and Satan has no claim on you. Remember, do not

concentrate on the evil spirits; fix your eyes and your faith upon your Lord and Savior, Jesus Christ. Look to Him upon the cross for inspiration. As you take sight of the battle flag of victory, be emboldened, be encouraged, be grateful. He will not abandon you; He will not leave you to do battle alone. He has left you a treasury of graces and weaponry for you to utilize.

> The battle flag is always placed among warriors as a sign to which they look during the hardest fighting of the battle. We are continuously at war with the prince of darkness... If anyone is troubled, vanquished and overcome, let him look to the Lord hanging on the gibbet of the cross.
> Saint Thomas of Villanova

> With the name of Jesus we shall overthrow the demons
> Saint John Vianney

Within this treasury, you have the Scriptures, the sacraments and priests. What a powerful trinity that is! You have the Armor of God, the internal armor of humility, obedience, surrender and trust. You can pray, fast and give alms. You have the saints on your side, Mary, the Mother of God, her husband Joseph, who because of his humility and obedience to God is known as the Terror of Demons and all of the Church Triumphant. You have the angels, specifically Saint Michael and his holy angels. You have your Guardian Angel who never leaves your side. You have sacramentals galore: the rosary, scapulars, blessed medals, holy water, the sign of the cross, blessed salt, relics, icons, etc.

Lastly, you have one of the best tools possible against Satan and his evil spirits at your disposal; the grace, power and authority that reside in you by virtue of your baptism. You have been given authority over the evil one by virtue of your baptism. Your baptism claims for you the power and authority of Jesus Christ. So the next time you are tempted, use your power. The next time you are harassed, praise God. The next time you are retaliated against, offer a blessing in God's name. The next time you succumb to temptation, confess. The next time Satan tells you his lies, remember God's promise to you of eternal life.

Promise

> As for you, let what you have heard from the beginning remain in you. If what you have heard from the beginning remains in you, then you, too, shall abide in the Son and in the Father. And this is the Promise, which he himself has promised to us: Eternal Life.
> 1 John 2:24-25

It is a certainty that Jesus will triumph and Satan will be defeated. What hangs in the balance is the final destination of your immortal soul. If you persevere in Christ grace, Christ's triumph will be your own. You who have worked to expand the Kingdom of God, who have remained faithful until the end, will be happy with Him forever in Heaven.

Sin and suffering, trials and temptation are bound up with salvation. From Genesis through Revelation, the Holy Spirit has revealed the role of the evil one in salvation history. Much to Satan's consternation, as creature, all of his actions are ordered to God's will to help bring about your salvation and the salvation of others. Through sin and suffering, through trials and temptations, you have access to God's grace and mercy. No matter how ugly your sin, how severe your suffering, how intense your trials or how frequent your temptation, God's grace and mercy are sufficient.

> In spite of all opposition, His divine Heart will eventually triumph; Satan with all his adherents will be confounded. Happy will they be who have been the means of establishing His empire.
> Saint Margaret Mary Alacoque

> He said not: you shall not be troubled, you shall not be tempted, you shall not be distressed, but he said you shall not be overcome.
> Blessed Julian of Norwich

> Jesus permits the spiritual combat as purification, not as a punishment. The trial is not unto death but unto salvation.
> Saint Pio of Pietrelcina

Christianity is not just Christmas; Christianity is also Good Friday. To be baptized into Christ's life is to be baptized into His death. His victor's crown is made of thorns; His royal garments are red because of His spilt blood. Both crib and cross are made from the same wood. True Christianity is embracing equally the joy of both.

Your salvation was not achieved by means of a bloodless coup or without great suffering. It was achieved through the shedding of the precious blood of Jesus on the cross, accompanied by intense suffering. Likewise, expect your journey to the Kingdom of God to be fraught with suffering. When persecution and suffering inevitably come because you are on the path to God, count it as a joy, for at that moment you are nearer to Heaven than you think.

> You ask me whether I am in good spirits. How could I not be, so long as my trust in God gives me strength? The purpose for which we have been created shows us the path along which we should go, perhaps strewn with many thorns, but not a sad path. Even in the midst of intense suffering it is one of joy.
> Blessed Pier Giorgio Frassati

> Let us understand that God is a Physician and that suffering is a medicine for salvation, not a punishment for damnation.
> Saint Augustine

> Calvary is the spot on earth which is nearest to Heaven.
> Saint Madeleine Sophia Barat

Perseverance

> Blessed is the man who suffers temptation. For when he has been proven, he shall receive the crown of life which God has promised to those who love him.
> James 1:12

A victor's crown awaits, you need only remain in His love to claim it. Your trials are not without merit; your battles are not without benefit. God, who is so merciful and gracious, will not leave you without multiple channels to access His grace and mercy. He will provide you with grace sufficient to repel every trial or temptation of the evil one. As Satan increases the frequency and fervor of his attacks, God's grace and mercy will flow more abundantly.

It bears repeating that the primary battlefield is internal. The enemies of the soul are invisible, though very real. Satan's tactics are often imperceptible, except to those who have eyes to see (cf. Matthew 13:16). God's grace and mercy are the invisible means to defeat an invisible enemy. They are the invisible shields which deflect the invisible darts. They are the secret weapon of every successful spiritual warrior. His grace and mercy are your impenetrable armor. Pray His protection over your every action, your every thought, your every breath.

> The real conflict is the inner conflict. Beyond armies of occupation and the catacombs of extermination camps, there are two irreconcilable enemies in the depth of every soul: good and evil, sin and love. And what use are the victories on the battlefield if we ourselves are defeated in our innermost personal selves?
> Saint Maximilian Kolbe

> Inasmuch then as they are invisible enemies, by invisible means must they be subdued. A visible enemy indeed you may overcome by blows; your invisible enemy you conquer by belief. A man is a visible enemy; to strike a blow is visible also. The devil is an invisible enemy; to believe is invisible also. Against invisible enemies then there is an invisible fight.
> Saint Augustine

> Be vigilant, stand firm strong in faith. God is all-powerful and will prevail. Know your own weakness but be confident in God's power. Pray with hope and certainty that He will protect you.
> Servant of God John Hardon

> The evil one attacks most what he fears most. Humble,

sacrificial and prayerful soldiers are his frequent targets. Satan knows the power of prayer and expends considerable effort to dissuade you from praying and to distract you while you are praying. He launches both preemptive and retaliatory strikes. Let neither disturb your peace, for Satan's attacks are to be seen through God's eyes, as a source of grace and glory.

Perseverance in prayer is what binds you to God's promise and is the bridge to God's peace. Unless you continually renew and strengthen yourself through prayer, your spiritual zeal will dissipate. Prayer is restorative. It is the strength of saints and the scourge of sinners. A devout and disciplined prayer life is the common thread of the faithful. Prayer is the primary weapon for you as a spiritual warrior and is necessary for the salvation of your soul.

> The devil is afraid of us when we pray and make sacrifices. He is also afraid when we are humble and good. He is especially afraid when we love Jesus very much.
> Saint Antony of the Desert

> He who prays is certain to be saved; while he who prays not is certain to be damned. All the saints were saved, and came to be saints by praying; all the accursed souls in Hell were lost through neglect of prayer; if they had prayed, it is certain that they would not have been lost. And this will be one of the greatest occasions of their anguish in Hell, the thought that they might have saved themselves so easily; that they had only to beg God to help them, but that now the time is past when this could avail them.
> Saint Alphonsus Liguori

> I know that soldiers have a lot to endure, and to endure in silence. If upon rising they would only take the trouble to say to our Lord every morning this tiny phrase, "My God, I desire to do and to endure everything today for love of You," what glory they would heap up for eternity.
> Saint Bernadette Soubirous

Peace

My peace I leave you; my Peace I give to you. Not in the way that the world gives, do I give to you. Do not let your heart be troubled, and let it not fear.
John 14:27

May mercy, and peace, and love be fulfilled in you.
Jude 2

Be at peace in Christ. The battle and victory is the Lord's. Believe in Him and you will find peace and joy, though not necessarily rest and relaxation. There is still a battle and it is permitted to continue, for God's glory and your own salvation.

Peace in the midst of battle may sound contradictory, but it is not. Peace, true peace, God's peace is found on the crucifix. True peace flows from the unconditional surrender of your will to the Father's will. Dante, in his poem *Paradiso,* captures this feeling in a succinct and sublime manner, "In His will, our peace."

The will of God is my paradise.
Blessed Maria Maddalena Starace

My God, it is your will. I accept the cup which you have given me. Blessed be your holy name.
Saint Bernadette Soubirous

Satan will seek to disturb your peace whenever possible. He would be happy to have you see him everywhere, responsible for everything, so as to steal your attention away from Jesus. He is equally happy to have you ignore him and pretend he doesn't exist. Both make you more susceptible to Satan's temptations. Both rob you of your peace in Christ Jesus. As love of Christ is your motivation, peace in Christ is your goal. By His grace and your cooperation, this peace is achievable. This must be your constant prayer — to hold to the peace of God and to radiate the peace of Christ.

By the anxieties and worries of this life Satan tries to

dull man's heart and make a dwelling for himself there.
Saint Francis of Assisi

The Spirit of God is a spirit of peace. Even in the most serious faults He makes us feel a sorrow that is tranquil, humble, and confident. This is precisely because of His mercy. The spirit of the devil, instead, excites, exasperates, and makes us feel, in that very sorrow, anger against ourselves. We should, on the contrary, be charitable with ourselves first and foremost. Therefore if any thought agitates you, this agitation never comes from God, who gives you peace, being the Spirit of Peace, but from the devil.
Saint Pio of Pietrelcina

The peacemakers shall be called the sons of God, who came to make peace between God and man. What then shall the sowers of discord be called, but the children of the devil? And what must they look for but their father's portion?
Saint Bernard of Clairvaux

Your commission as a soldier of God and spiritual warrior is for life. Your rank may be elevated, your tour of duty may change, you may be offered a temporary respite, but a soldier you shall remain until death. Your enemy, the devil, will take no leave of his effort to claim victory over your soul for as long as you remain on earth.

This is the time when throughout the world the Christian battle line must combat the raging devil...now is the time to be equipped in spiritual arms and aroused by the heavenly trumpet, to enter the battle.
Pope Saint Leo the Great

I long to see you a true knight, strong in your fight against the devil's every trick as long as we are on this battlefield, surrounded by enemies who are constantly fighting against us.
Saint Catherine of Siena

Oh, how sweet it is to toil for God and souls! I want no respite in this battle, but I shall fight to the last breath for the glory of my King and Lord. I shall not lay the sword aside until He calls me before His throne.
Saint Faustina Kowalska

"Begone, Satan!" The Messiah's resolute attitude is an example and an invitation for us to follow him with courageous determination.
Pope John Paul II

Yet, despite Satan's best efforts, the promise of Christ's everlasting victory remains. Your time in the Church Militant will soon pass and your time in the Church Triumphant will soon begin. Stay focused; remain alert.

Now is the time. This is the place. The battle is before you. The devil is the enemy. The heavenly trumpet sounds. God is calling. Let nothing disturb you. You are His warrior. Be not afraid. Everything is a grace. Fight the good fight. All shall be well. Onward, Catholic soldier, onward!

> Let nothing disturb you. Let nothing frighten you. Though all things pass, God does not change. Patience wins all things, but he lacks nothing who possesses God; for God alone suffices.
> Saint Teresa of Avila

Everything is a grace because everything is God's gift. Whatever be the character of life or its unexpected events, to the heart that loves, all is well.
Saint Therese of Lisieux

All shall be well, all shall be well, and all manner of things shall be well.
Blessed Julian of Norwich

Appendix
Daily Spiritual Warfare Prayers

☩

Pursue prayer.
Colossians 4:2a

Daily prayer is an essential part of life as a Catholic and as a spiritual warrior. Whether you choose to pray aloud or silently, in community or on your own, contemplatively or charismatically, matters not. What does matter, what is imperative, is to pray daily. Simple, humble, heartfelt daily prayer will allow you to keep your gaze upon God.

On the next few pages are prayers that are particularly relevant for spiritual warriors. Allow these suggested daily prayers to serve as a gateway and not a destination. Go deeper as the Holy Spirit prompts you. Pray these prayers with your lips as well as your heart.

> Prayer is the best weapon we have; it is the key to God's heart. You must speak to Jesus not only with your lips, but with your hearts. In fact, on certain occasions you should speak to Him only with your heart.
> Saint Pio of Pietrelcina

> For me, prayer is a surge of the heart; it is a simple look turned toward heaven, it is a cry of recognition and of love, embracing both trial and joy.
> Saint Therese of Lisieux

Our Father

Our Father, who art in Heaven, hallowed be Thy name. Thy kingdom come, Thy will be done, on earth as it is in Heaven. Give us this day our daily bread and forgive us our trespasses as we forgive those who trespass against us. Lead us not into temptation, but deliver us from evil.

Hail Mary

Hail Mary, full of grace, the Lord is with thee. Blessed art thou among woman and blessed is the fruit of your womb, Jesus. Holy Mary, Mother of God, pray for us sinners, now, and at the hour of our death.

Glory Be

Glory be to the Father, and to the Son and to the Holy Spirit as it was in the beginning, is now, and ever shall be, world without end. Amen.

Memorare

Remember, O most gracious Virgin Mary, that never was it known that anyone who fled to thy protection, implored thy help, or sought thy intercession was left unaided. Inspired by this confidence, I fly unto thee, O Virgin of virgins, my mother; to thee do I come, before thee I stand, sinful and sorrowful. O Mother of the Word Incarnate, despise not my petitions, but in thy mercy hear and answer me. Amen.

Saint Michael Prayer

Saint Michael the Archangel Defend us in battle, be our safeguard against the wickedness and snares of the Devil. May God rebuke him, we humbly pray and do Thou, O Prince of the Heavenly Host, by the power of God, cast into Hell, Satan and all the evil spirits who prowl about the world seeking the ruin of souls.

Guardian Angel Prayer

Angel of God, my guardian dear, to whom God's love commits me here, ever this day be at my side to light and guard and rule and guide.

Prayer of Saint Gertrude

Eternal Father, I offer Thee the Most Precious Blood of Thy Divine Son, Jesus, in union with the masses said throughout the world today, for all the holy souls in purgatory, for sinners everywhere, for sinners in the universal church, those in my own home and within my family.

Ora Pro Nobis

Our Lady of Fatima, pray for us.
Our Lady of the Rosary, pray for us.
Our Lady of Guadalupe, pray for us.
Saint Joseph, Terror of demons, pray for us.
Saint Benedict, pray for us.
Saint Teresa of Avila, pray for us.
Saint John Marie Vianney, pray for us.
Saint Padre Pio, pray for us.
Saint Therese of Lisieux, pray for us.
Saint Gemma Galgani, pray for us.
Blessed Miguel Pro, pray for us.
Blessed Teresa of Calcutta, pray for us.
(insert the name of your patron or favorite saint.)

Anima Christi

Soul of Christ, sanctify me.
Body of Christ, save me.
Blood of Christ, inebriate me.
Water from Christ's side, wash me.
Passion of Christ, strengthen me.
O good Jesus, hear me.
Within Thy wounds hide me.
Suffer me not to be separated from Thee.
From the malicious enemy defend me.
In the hour of my death call me.
And bid me come unto Thee that I may praise Thee with Thy saints and with Thy angels forever and ever.

Sacred Heart of Jesus and the Immaculate Heart of Mary

Sacred Heart of Jesus, have mercy on us.
Sacred Heart of Jesus, have mercy on us.
Sacred Heart of Jesus, have mercy on us.
Immaculate Heart of Mary, pray for us.

Suscipe

Receive, O Lord, all my liberty. Take my memory, my understanding, and my entire will. Whatsoever I have or possess Thou hast bestowed upon me; I give it all back to Thee and surrender it wholly to be governed by Thy Will. Give me love for Thee alone along with Thy grace, and I am rich enough and ask for nothing more.

Morning Offering

O Jesus, through the Immaculate Heart of Mary, I offer you all my prayers, works, joys and suffering of this day: for all the intentions of Your Sacred heart, in union with the holy sacrifice of the Mass throughout the world, in reparation for all my sins, for the intentions of all our associates, and in particular, for the intention of our Holy Father.

Nighttime Prayer

O eternal God and Ruler of all creation, You have allowed me to reach this hour. Forgive the sins I have committed this day by word, deed or thought. Purify me, O Lord, from every spiritual and physical stain. Grant that I may rise from this sleep to glorify You by my deeds throughout my entire lifetime, and that I be victorious over every spiritual and physical enemy. Deliver me, O Lord, from all vain thoughts and from evil desires, for yours is the kingdom, and the power, and the glory, Father, Son, and Holy Spirit, now and ever, and forever.

Chaplet of Divine Mercy (Prayed on the Rosary)

First three beads: Our Father, Hail Mary, Apostles' Creed

On the large beads: Eternal Father, I offer Thee the Body and Blood, Soul and Divinity of Thy most beloved Son, our Lord, Jesus Christ, in atonement for our sins and the sins of the whole world.

On the small beads: For the sake of His sorrowful passion, have mercy on us and the whole world.

Concluding prayer: Holy God, Holy Mighty One, Holy Immortal one, have mercy on us and the whole world (Repeat three times.)

Prayer to Defeat the Work of Satan

O Divine Eternal Father, in union with Your Divine Son and the holy Spirit, and through the Immaculate Heart of Mary, I beg You to destroy the power of your greatest enemy – the evil spirits. Cast them into the deepest recesses of hell and chain them there forever. Take possession of Your Kingdom which You have created and which is rightfully Yours. Heavenly Father, give us the reign of the sacred Heart of Jesus and the Immaculate Heart of Mary. Amen.

Litany of Humility

O Jesus! Meek and humble of heart............. Hear me.

From the desire of being esteemed...............Deliver me Jesus.

From the desire of being loved.................... Deliver me Jesus.

From the desire of being extolled................ Deliver me Jesus.

From the desire of being honored................ Deliver me Jesus.

From the desire of being praised................. Deliver me Jesus.

From the desire of being preferred to others. Deliver me Jesus.

From the desire of being consulted............. Deliver me Jesus.

From the desire of being approved............. Deliver me Jesus.

From the fear of being humiliated ....Deliver me Jesus.

From the fear of being despised.................. Deliver me Jesus.

From the fear of suffering rebukes.............. Deliver me Jesus.

From the fear of being calumniated............Deliver me Jesus.

From the fear of being forgotten................ Deliver me Jesus.

From the fear of being ridiculed..................Deliver me Jesus.

From the fear of being wronged.................. Deliver me Jesus.

From the fear of being suspected................Deliver me Jesus.

That others may be loved more than I, Jesus grant me the grace to desire it. That others may be esteemed more than I, Jesus grant me the grace to desire it. That, in the opinion of the world, others may increase and I may decrease, Jesus grant me the grace to desire it. That others may be chosen and I set aside, Jesus grant me the grace to desire it. That others may be praised and I unnoticed, Jesus grant me the grace to desire it. That others may be preferred to me in everything, Jesus grant me the grace to desire it. That others may become holier than I, Provided that I may become as holy as I should, Jesus grant me the grace to desire it.

Saint Patrick's Breastplate

I arise today through a mighty strength, the invocation of the Trinity, through the belief in the Threeness, through the confession of the oneness of the Creator of Creation. I arise today through the strength of Christ's birth with his baptism, through the strength of his crucifixion with his burial, through the strength of his resurrection with his ascension, through the strength of his descent for the Judgment Day. I arise today through the strength of the love of Cherubim, in obedience of angels, in the service of archangels, in hope of resurrection to meet with reward, in prayers of patriarchs, in predictions of prophets, in preaching of apostles, in faith of confessors, in innocence of holy virgins, in deeds of righteous men. I arise today through the strength of heaven: light of sun, radiance of moon, splendor of fire, speed of lightning, swiftness of wind, depth of sea, stability of earth, firmness of rock. I arise today through God's strength to pilot me: God's might to uphold me, God's wisdom to guide me, God's eye to look before me, God's ear to hear me, God's word to speak for me, God's hand to guard me, God's way to lie before me, God's shield to protect me, God's host to save me from snares of demons, from temptations of vices, from everyone who shall wish me ill, afar and anear, alone and in multitude. I summon today all these powers between me and those evils, against every cruel merciless power that may oppose my body and soul, against incantations of false prophets, against black laws of pagandom against false laws of heretics, against craft of idolatry, against spells of witches and smiths and wizards, against every knowledge that corrupts man's body and soul. Christ to shield me today against poison, against burning, against drowning, against wounding, so that there may come to me abundance of reward. Christ with me, Christ before me, Christ behind me, Christ in me, Christ beneath me, Christ above me, Christ on my right, Christ on my left, Christ when I lie down, Christ when I sit down, Christ when I arise, Christ in the heart of every man who thinks of me, Christ in the mouth of everyone who speaks of me, Christ in every eye that sees me, Christ in every ear that hears me. I arise today through a mighty strength, the invocation of the Trinity, through belief in the Threeness, through confession of the oneness, of the Creator of Creation. Amen.

Pray (these prayers or others) the first moment you wake and the last moment before you go to sleep. Pray often throughout the day. Notice which prayers almost cry out for you to pray them, which ones move your heart. Pray these frequently, pray them fervently, pray them from the heart. Never stop praying. Prayer is the answer. Pray, pray, pray.

Let every faithful man and woman when they rise from sleep at dawn wash their hands and pray to God. Pray also before thy body rests upon thy bed.
Saint Hippolytus

Do not fail to apply yourself to whatever inspires the most devotion in you. The most beneficial prayer will be the one which moves your heart in the most beneficial way.
Blessed Jordan of Saxony

It is better to say one Pater Noster fervently and devoutly than a thousand with no devotion and full of distraction
Saint Edmund

Aspire to God with short but frequent outpourings of the heart.
Saint Francis de Sales

A prayer in which a person is not aware of Whom he is speaking to, what he is asking, who it is who is asking and of Whom, I don't call prayer, however much the lips may move.
Saint Teresa of Avila

Prayer unites us to God, sustains the world, renders souls beautiful, blots out sin, preserves us from temptation and defends us in the time of battle
Saint John Climacus

Prayer ought to be short and pure, unless it be prolonged by the inspiration of Divine grace.
Saint Benedict of Nursia

343

I psalmed down the devil.
Saint Antony of the Desert

We can begin to doubt that our prayer has been heard
only when we notice we have stopped praying.
Saint Claude de la Colombiere

Prayer serves the needs of the souls and draws down
the help they seek, delights the angels and infuriates
Hell and is to God a sacrifice that can not help but be
pleasing to Him.
Saint Augustine

If Saint Paul exhorts us to pray for one another, and we
gladly think it right to ask every poor man to pray for
us, should we think it evil to ask the holy saints in
heaven to do the same?
Saint Thomas More

I shall be able to do much more for you in heaven than I
can now while I am on earth.
Saint Pio of Pietrelcina

If we pray, we will believe; if we believe, we will love; if
we love, we will serve.
Blessed Teresa of Calcutta

After baptism, continual prayer is necessary to man, in
order that he may enter heaven; for though by baptism
our sins are remitted, there still remain concupiscence
to assail us from within, and the world and the devil to
assail us from without.
Saint Thomas Aquinas

Man by prayer merits to receive that which God had
from all eternity determined to give him.
Pope Saint Gregory the Great

Prayer is necessary for salvation.
Saint John Chrysostom

Afterword

Behold, I am the handmaid of the Lord. Let it be done
to me according to your word.
Luke 1:38

Do whatever he tells you.
John 2:5

In preparing for this second edition of *Onward Catholic
Soldier* I have been humbled by the overwhelmingly positive
response to the book. To date, over 10,000 copies have been
printed and sold, to God be the glory.

Your comments have been equally abundant. Whether
you have spoken to me at a parish talk, whether you saw me
discussing the book on EWTN or heard me on Saint Joseph
Radio, or whether we have communicated on the phone or via
e-mail, your comments have been gracious, uplifting and
inspiring. All glory to God!

> I ask that if you find anything edifying, anything
> consoling, anything well presented, that you give all
> praise, all glory and all honor to the Blessed Son of God
> Jesus Christ. If on the other hand, you find anything
> that is ill composed, uninteresting or not too well
> explained, you impute and attribute it to my weakness,
> blindness and lack of skill.
> Saint Anthony of Padua

To the degree that you found the book edifying, please do share it with others. The book and this ministry have grown primarily through word of mouth of good people like yourself. I am grateful to many people for their support. Specifically, I would like to acknowledge: Father Mark Bozada and Pam Meier of the Blessed Anne Catherine Emmerich Foundation, Warren Dazzio of Legatus, Mimi Kelly of the Mir Group, Kathie Caspary of Marytown, Michael and Lisa Brown of Spirit Daily, Father Edmund Sylvia C.S.C. and Johnette Benkovic of The Abundant Life, Dina Marie Hale of KBVM, Chuck Neff of Relevant Radio, Cookie Read of Focus Worldwide Television, local Catholic bookstores, the parishes and dioceses that have hosted me for retreats and missions and most of all, you the reader. I say thank you with a sincere and humble heart.

As a fellow soldier with you, I appreciate and need your support and prayers. Be assured of mine for you. We are on this road to heaven together. It is not an easy road, strewn as it is with rocks, thorns and debris, with many hills and valleys, subject to inclement weather and man made tolls, with an abundance of "attractive nuisances" and misleading signposts. Nonetheless, it is the road that will reunite us with our Lord and so we forge ahead recognizing that "eye has not seen, and the ear has not heard, nor has it entered into the heart of man, what things God has prepared for those who love him" (cf. 1 Corinthians 2:9).

May we do all things for the praise and glory of His name. May we always do whatever He tells us to do. May, in all things, His will be accomplished.

> Perhaps you and I will ourselves be soldiers of the same regiment, travelers on the same road, bound for the same destination. May His holy will, not ours, be done.
> Saint Theophane Venard

May our good and gracious God pour out His grace, mercy, peace and love upon you and all your loved ones. Mother Mary, pray for us.

John LaBriola
Feast of Saint Benedict 2009

Onward Catholic Soldier

To purchase additional copies of *Onward Catholic Soldier* or other products related to spiritual warfare such as books, cds and prayer aids, contact us at:

www.onwardcatholicsoldier.com

onwardcatholicsoldier@gmail.com

Also, use the above e-mail address to share your spiritual warfare stories with us for possible inclusion in a forthcoming book.

Now available

- Onward Catholic Soldier as an audio book.

- CDs and DVDs of John's talks

Visit www.onwardcatholicsoldier.com

Help Spread the Word

Please keep us in your prayers. If you have grown in faith because of this book, consider helping to spread the word. Perhaps you can purchase one or two or more books or cds or dvds for your friends and family. May God be praised!

What Other Are Saying About Onward Catholic Soldier

John LaBriola's book fills a very great need for knowledge that most Catholics don't have: how to fight spiritual battles. This knowledge is even more crucial at the present time, when evil has increased so much in the world. His book is especially useful and necessary for those of us who are in the pro-life movement, since we are much attacked by the enemy of souls. Thank you John for this valuable compendium!
Magaly Llaguno OCDS,
Executive Director, Vida Humana Internacional, Hispanic Division of Human Life International

Every once in a while I run across something that is written that reminds me why our journey to God is filled with resistance. I am thankful for people like John LaBriola who take the time to dive head first into the spiritual battle we all face and return from the depths to share new insights. This book will definitely help you see your journey through the eyes of faith!
Randy Raus
Life Teen President / CEO

Your book will offer a reliable and well-documented buffer and an assuring bulwark of protection for many who are facing the challenges of spiritual warfare. Your book will be of great help to many people, John. That will be my prayer. May God smile upon your work and bless you with an abundance of his grace. God bless you.
Fr. John H. Hampsch, C.M.F.
Claretian Teaching Ministry